NIGHT

LIGHT

NIGHT LIGHT

Evening Affirmations
for Renewing Your Mind.

Kenneth Boa

Wolgemuth & Hyatt, Publishers, Inc.
Brentwood, Tennessee

The mission of Wolgemuth & Hyatt, Publishers, Inc. is to publish and distribute books that lead individuals toward:

- A personal faith in the one true God: Father, Son, and Holy Spirit;

- A lifestyle of practical discipleship; and

- A worldview that is consistent with the historic, Christian faith.

- Moreover, the company endeavors to accomplish this mission at a reasonable profit and in a manner which glorifies God and serves His Kingdom.

© 1989 by Kenneth Boa
All rights reserved. Published June, 1989. First Edition.

Unless otherwise noted, all scripture quotations are the author's own.

Wolgemuth & Hyatt, Publishers, Inc.
P.O. Box 1941, Brentwood, Tennessee 37027.
Printed in the United States of America.

Library Of Congress Cataloging-in-Publication Data

Boa, Kenneth.
    Night light : Evening affirmations for renewing your mind /
    Kenneth Boa. — 1st ed.
        p.   cm.
    ISBN 0-943497-48-5
    1. Bible — Meditations.   I. Title.
BS491.5.B63   1989
242'.5 — dc20   89-9043
                                                        CIP

This collection of
Biblical affirmations
is dedicated with love
to my daughter Heather.

CONTENTS

ACKNOWLEDGMENTS

I would like to acknowledge the encouragement of my wife Karen and the Search Ministries team during the creation of *Night Light:*

Dan and Lucy Allison	Cal and Linda Laughlin
Don and Ann Barkley	Deborah and Tim Lubben
Priscilla and John Burton	Rod and Cindy MacIlvaine
Marco and Susan Ciavolino	Ken and Myrlane Mendenhall
David and Barbara Coldwell	Larry and Ruth Moody
Bill and Vera Deven	Dick and Susan Ostien
Ed and Gwen Diaz	Don and Marlene Prigel
Joe and Paula Ehrmann	John and Susan Rayls
Dave and Jean Fortune	Bob and Cindy Shelley
Sharon Gingrich	Jeff and Dawn Siemon
Bob and Aliece Hendricks	Al and Lorraine Van Horne
Clarice Kapraun	Dix and Cynthia Winston
Bill and Janet Kraftson	Debbie Zeigler
Mark and Carole Krieg	Dawn Zimmerman
Dave and Roxanne Krueger	

INTRODUCTION

The Purpose of *Night Light*

If I knew that I would never find a publisher for this book, I would still have created it, if only for use by my family and friends.

For years I have been frustrated by a hit and (usually) miss approach to catching a few thoughts from the Bible before going to sleep. In 1987, Max Anders and I created a guide to praying Scripture back to God called *Drawing Near*, and this significantly enhanced my morning devotional times. One of the eight forms of prayer in *Drawing Near* emphasizes affirmations of Biblical truth. It occurred to me that hundreds of affirmations could be derived from Scripture and compiled in a format that would act as a tool to enable people to renew their minds with Biblical truth on a daily basis. And what better time to use such a tool than just before going to sleep?

The thoughts we entertain after we turn out the light have a profound effect on the rest of the night, but few of us make good use of these strategic minutes. Instead, most people carry anxieties and other fleshly thought patterns to bed with them. Throughout the course of the day we are being bombarded by the temporal value system of the world through the things we see, hear, and read. Because of this, it is important that we renew our minds with the eternal value system of Scripture so that we regain a sense of focus on the crucial issues of who we are, where we came from, why we are here, and where we are going. No genuine life change will take place without a change in perspective.

Night Light is designed to assist you in this process of renewing your mind, and it is most effective when used just before going to sleep so that you set or "program" your conscious and subconscious mind for the rest of the night. This is consistent with David's practice: "When I remember You on my bed, I meditate on You in the night watches"

(Psalm 63:6). Rather than being conformed to this world, you will be transformed by the renewing of your mind (see Romans 12:2). This will assist you in "taking every thought captive to the obedience of Christ" (2 Corinthians 10:5), and setting your mind on the things of the Spirit rather than the things of the flesh (see Romans 8:5). *Night Light* will help you to "set your mind on the things above, not on the things on the earth" (Colossians 3:2), and to let your mind dwell on "whatever is true, whatever is noble, whatever is right, whatever is pure, whatever is lovely, whatever is of good report — if anything is excellent or praiseworthy" (Philippians 4:8).

The germ of truth in the growing body of "self-talk" literature is that people often need to be reminded of their identity and goals so that they have a clear sense of purpose and direction. The problem with this literature is that it often promotes an unbiblical value system and world view. Biblical affirmations are founded in truth; they are not like the self-talk that says, "Every day and in every way, I am getting better and better." The affirmations of Scripture encourage us to walk by faith, not by feelings, and tell us the way things really are regardless of our emotional, cultural, and theological filters. Our circumstances may threaten our commitment to the truths that God is in control of our affairs and has our best interests at heart, but Scripture affirms these foundational principles and tells us to cling to them even in the midst of life's pain.

These affirmations are not a matter of wishful thinking; they are true of every person who places his or her hope in Jesus Christ. They stress our identity in Christ, tell us that process is more important than product, and challenge us to value relationships more than objectives. They teach us that what we do does not determine who we are; rather, our being should shape our doing. They reinforce the realistic perspective that we are aliens and pilgrims, not citizens of this world, and tell us to walk in grace and live in the power of the Spirit of God instead of walking in obedience to a set of external rules and living in the power of the flesh. They counsel us to take the risks of applying Biblical precepts and principles and to place our hope in the character and promises of God, and not in the people, possessions, or prestige of this world.

Many of the affirmations in *Night Light* are expressed as desires; you will be affirming that these are the things you want to be true of your life. Using this book on a regular basis will be a faith-building exercise that will make these affirmations increasingly real in your life.

The Structure of *Night Light*

To create this collection of biblical affirmations, I consulted several translations as well as the original language of every passage. The result is essentially my own translation, though it shares much in common with existing translations. I then adapted the bulk of the passages into an affirmation format.

Some of the affirmations are directed to God, some are spoken about Him, some are statements of truth, and some are statements of what the reader should want to be true of his or her life. A number of these affirmations were derived from negative statements and evaluations in the Bible and then turned into positive statements. In other cases, principles have been derived from the lives of Biblical characters.

To assist you in personalizing these affirmations, I decided to put them in the singular whenever possible. However, some (e.g., 1 Corinthians 1:4-5, 7) could not be changed into the singular without excessive distortion. When you use *Night Light* with another person or with a group, turn the singulars into plurals.

Clearly, a large measure of subjectivity is unavoidable in the creation of a book like this. This relates to several issues, like the decision of selecting some passages and not using others, translation decisions, editorial choices involved in adapting passages into the form of affirmations, assignment of passages into categories, and arrangement of these categories. Inevitably, people will wonder why I overlooked some passages or categorized others in the way I did. These are all matters of judgment and interpretation, and I freely admit that there are many other ways in which these affirmations could have been expressed and arranged. In many cases, they overlapped my tidy categories, and I had to make choices on the basis of emphasis. Because of all this, I encourage you to make insertions and deletions whenever it will help make this a more effective tool for renewing your mind.

As you can see, there are two major sections in *Night Light*: "Evening Affirmations Guide" and the "Topical Affirmations Guide." All of the passages in the "Evening Affirmations Guide" are derived from the "Topical Affirmations Guide" and appear only once. In addition, the "Topical Affirmations Guide" includes a substantial number of affirmations that have not been used in the "Evening Affirmations Guide."

The "Evening Affirmations Guide" was created to expose you to a wide range of affirmations and to give you the opportunity to reaffirm them four times a year. These affirmations are so significant that they should be repeated on a regular basis. This evening guide adopts the five-part structure of the "Topical Affirmations Guide" for each of the 31 days in the First, Second, and Third Months:

1. The Attributes of God

2. The Works of God

3. My Relationship to God

4. The Character I Want to Cultivate

5. My Relationship to Others

There is a logical and progressive relationship in these five general categories that moves from God to self to others. The first two relate to loving God completely; the next two relate to loving self correctly; the last relates to loving others compassionately. The person, powers, and perfections of God are the bases for His works in creation, redemption, and consummation. The attributes and works of God are the foundation of my relationship to God, and growth in Christlikeness relates to the character I want to cultivate. When I find my security, significance, and sufficiency in Christ, I am free to be a giver rather than a grabber, and I can serve others in love as I have been called to do.

Each day includes all five parts for a well-balanced spiritual diet.

How to Use Night Light

This book was designed to be used in two ways: as a daily guide and as a topical guide.

The "Evening Affirmations Guide" realistically assumes that you are fatigued at the end of your day. For this reason, it was structured to be effective with only five minutes of use. Each of the five categories has a couplet of passages that are thematically related. Spend a full minute with the first couplet and go beyond reading the affirmations: think about them, make them your own, and pray them through. Then do the same for the other four. Obviously, you will increase your benefit by spending more than five minutes, but think of the five minutes as a workable minimum.

Try to make this the last activity of your day so that you can immediately review the five sets of affirmations in your mind after turning out the light as you go to sleep. This will initially require some discipline, since extraneous thoughts will clamor for your attention, but keep returning to the affirmations, and you will increase your skill with daily practice.

Use the "Topical Affirmations Guide" when you have more time, or when you want to develop in a particular area. This section is particularly helpful in guiding you during a retreat or when you schedule a large enough block of time to meditate and pray through one or more entire topics.

I also recommend using "Part One" and "Part Two" with another person and with groups. When you use the "Evening Affirmations Guide" with others, try pausing and praying together after each of the five couplets so that you can respond together.

Finally, be sure to use the "Personal Affirmations Pages" at the end of this book to write in the affirmations that are particularly meaningful to you as you use the "Evening Affirmations Guide" and the "Topical Affirmations Guide."

We ought always to thank God for other believers, and pray that their faith would grow more and more, and that the love each of them has toward one another would increase. (2 Thessalonians 1:3)

PART ONE

EVENING AFFIRMATIONS GUIDE

ONE

THE FIRST MONTH

DAY 1

1. The Attributes of God

You are my God, and I will give thanks to You; You are my God, and I will exalt You. I will give thanks to the LORD, for He is good; His loyal love endures forever. (Psalm 118:28-29)

God is the blessed and only Sovereign, the King of kings and Lord of lords, who alone has immortality and dwells in unapproachable light, whom no one has seen or can see. To Him be honor and eternal dominion. (1 Timothy 6:15-16)

2. The Works of God

When I consider Your heavens, the work of Your fingers, the moon and the stars, which You have set in place, what is man that You are mindful of him, and the son of man that You care for him? You made him a little lower than the heavenly beings and crowned him with glory and honor. You made him ruler over the works of Your hands, and You put everything under his feet. (Psalm 8:3-6)

O LORD of hosts, God of Israel, enthroned between the cherubim, You alone are God over all the kingdoms of the earth. You have made heaven and earth. (Isaiah 37:16)

3. My Relationship to God

You have blessed me and kept me; You have made Your face shine upon me and have been gracious to me; You have turned Your face toward me and given me peace. (Numbers 6:24-26)

I have been loved by God and called to be a saint; grace and peace have been given to me from God our Father and the Lord Jesus Christ. (Romans 1:7)

4. The Character I Want to Cultivate

LORD, who may dwell in Your tabernacle? Who may live on Your holy mountain? It is he who walks uprightly and works righteousness and speaks the truth in his heart; he does not slander with his tongue nor does evil to his neighbor nor takes up a reproach against his friend; he despises the reprobate but honors those who fear the LORD. He keeps his oath even when it hurts, lends his money without interest, and does not accept a bribe against the innocent. He who does these things will never be shaken. (Psalm 15:1-5)

I will let my eyes look straight ahead, and fix my gaze straight before me. I will ponder the path of my feet so that all my ways will be established. I will not turn to the right or to the left, but keep my foot from evil. (Proverbs 4:25-27)

5. My Relationship to Others

A friend loves at all times, and a brother is born for adversity. (Proverbs 17:17)

We must be devoted to one another in brotherly love, honoring one another above ourselves. (Romans 12:10)

DAY 2

1. The Attributes of God

God is not a man, that He should lie, nor a son of man, that He should change his mind. Has He spoken and not done it? Has He promised and not fulfilled it? (Numbers 23:19)

He who is the Glory of Israel does not lie or change His mind; for He is not a man, that He should change His mind. (1 Samuel 15:29)

2. The Works of God

One generation shall praise Your works to another, and shall declare Your mighty acts. I will meditate on the glorious splendor of Your majesty, and on Your wonderful works. Men shall speak of the might of Your awesome works, and I will proclaim Your great deeds. (Psalm 145:4-6)

Who is a God like You, who pardons iniquity and passes over the transgression of the remnant of His inheritance? You do not stay angry forever but delight to show mercy. You will have compassion on Your people; You will tread their iniquities underfoot and hurl all their sins into the depths of the sea. (Micah 7:18-19)

3. My Relationship to God

God lifted me out of the slimy pit, out of the mud and mire; He set my feet on a rock and gave me a firm place to stand. He put a new song in my mouth, a hymn of praise to our God. Many will see and fear and put their trust in the LORD. (Psalm 40:2-3)

I shall know the truth, and the truth shall set me free. Everyone who commits sin is a slave of sin. And a slave has no permanent place in the family, but a son belongs to it forever. So if the Son sets me free, I shall be free indeed. (John 8:32, 34-36)

4. The Character I Want to Cultivate

I will not let love and truth leave me; I will bind them around my neck and write them on the tablet of my heart. (Proverbs 3:3)

Love is patient, love is kind, it does not envy; love does not boast, it is not arrogant, it does not behave rudely; it does not seek its own, it is not provoked, it keeps no record of wrongs; it does not rejoice in unrighteousness but rejoices with the truth; it bears all things, believes all things, hopes all things, endures all things. Love never fails. (1 Corinthians 13:4-8)

5. My Relationship to Others

I will give generously to others without a grudging heart. (Deuteronomy 15:10)

I will not withhold good from those to whom it is due, when it is in my power to act. (Proverbs 3:27)

DAY 3

1. The Attributes of God

The Lord my God is God of gods and Lord of lords, the great God, mighty and awesome, who shows no partiality and accepts no bribes. He executes justice for the fatherless and the widow, and loves the alien, giving him food and clothing. (Deuteronomy 10:17-18)

As for God, His way is perfect; the word of the LORD is proven. He is a shield to all who take refuge in Him. For who is God besides the LORD? And who is the rock except our God? (Psalm 18:30-31)

2. The Works of God

To us a child is born, to us a son is given, and the government will be on His shoulders. And He will be called Wonderful Counselor, Mighty God, Everlasting Father, Prince of Peace. Of the increase of His government and peace there will be no end. He will reign on the throne of David and over His kingdom, establishing and upholding it with jus-tice and righteousness from that time on and forever. The zeal of the LORD of hosts will accomplish this. (Isaiah 9:6-7)

Jesus will be great and will be called the Son of the Most High. The Lord God will give Him the throne of His father David, and He will reign over the house of Jacob forever, and His kingdom will never end. (Luke 1:32-33)

3. My Relationship to God

The LORD is my rock and my fortress and my deliverer; my God is my rock, I will take refuge in Him; my shield and the horn of my salva-tion, my stronghold and my refuge; my Savior, You save me from vio-lence. I call on the LORD, who is worthy of praise, and I am saved from my enemies. (2 Samuel 22:2-4)

Who will bring a charge against those whom God has chosen? It is God who justifies. Who is he who condemns? It is Christ Jesus who died, who was furthermore raised to life, who is at the right hand of God, and is also interceding for me. (Romans 8:33-34)

4. The Character I Want to Cultivate

The fear of the Lord, that is wisdom, and to depart from evil is understanding. (Job 28:28)

The fear of the LORD is the beginning of wisdom; all who practice His commandments have a good understanding. His praise endures for-ever. (Psalm 111:10)

5. My Relationship to Others

I will stay away from a foolish man, for I will not find knowledge on his lips. (Proverbs 14:7)

I will not make friends with a hot-tempered man, or associate with one easily angered, lest I learn his ways and set a snare for my soul. (Proverbs 22:24-25)

DAY 4

1. The Attributes of God

You revealed Yourself to Moses as "I AM WHO I AM." (Exodus 3:14)
Jesus Christ is the same yesterday, today, and forever. (Hebrews 13:8)

2. The Works of God

Rejoice greatly, O daughter of Zion! Shout, O daughter of Jerusa-lem! Behold, Your King is coming to you; He is just and having salvation, humble and riding on a donkey, on a colt, the foal of a donkey. He will proclaim peace to the nations; His dominion will extend from sea to sea, and from the River to the ends of the earth. (Zechariah 9:9-10)

God sent His word to the children of Israel, telling the good news of peace through Jesus Christ, who is Lord of all. He commanded the apostles to preach to the people and to testify that He is the One whom God appointed as judge of the living and the dead. To Him all the prophets witness that through His name, everyone who believes in Him receives forgiveness of sins. (Acts 10:36, 42-43)

3. My Relationship to God

The LORD, my God, the LORD is one. I want to love the LORD, my God, with all my heart and with all my soul and with all my strength. (Deuteronomy 6:4-5)

He who loves his father or mother more than You is not worthy of You; he who loves his son or daughter more than You is not worthy of You. (Matthew 10:37)

4. The Character I Want to Cultivate

I will not follow the crowd in doing wrong. (Exodus 23:2)

There are six things the LORD hates, seven that are detestable to Him: haughty eyes, a lying tongue, hands that shed innocent blood, a heart that devises wicked plans, feet that run swiftly to evil, a false witness who breathes lies, and one who causes strife among brothers. (Proverbs 6:16-19)

5. My Relationship to Others

The LORD God said, "It is not good for the man to be alone; I will make a helper suitable for him." And the LORD God made a woman from the rib He had taken out of the man, and He brought her to the man. And the man said, "This is now bone of my bones and flesh of my flesh; she shall be called 'Woman,' because she was taken out of man." For this reason a man shall leave his father and mother, and shall cleave to his wife, and they shall become one flesh. (Genesis 2:18, 22-24)

From the beginning of creation God "made them male and female. For this reason a man shall leave his father and mother and shall cleave to his wife, and the two shall become one flesh." So they are no longer two, but one flesh. Therefore what God has joined together, let man not separate. (Matthew 19:4-6; Mark 10:6-9)

DAY 5

1. The Attributes of God

The LORD is great and greatly to be praised; He is to be feared above all gods. For all the gods of the nations are idols, but the LORD made the heavens. Splendor and majesty are before Him; strength and joy are in His place. I will ascribe to the LORD glory and strength. I will ascribe to the LORD the glory due His name and worship the LORD in the beauty of holiness. (1 Chronicles 16:25-29)

You are the high and lofty One who inhabits eternity, whose name is holy. You live in a high and holy place, but also with him who is contrite and lowly in spirit, to revive the spirit of the lowly and to revive the heart of the contrite. (Isaiah 57:15)

2. The Works of God

God completed the heavens and the earth in all their vast array. By the seventh day God finished the work which He had done, and He rested on the seventh day from all His creative work. And God blessed the seventh day and sanctified it, because on it He rested from all the work of creating that He (ad done. (Genesis 2:1-3)

O LORD, God of Israel, enthroned between the cherubim, You alone are God over all the kingdoms of the earth. You have made heaven and earth. (2 Kings 19:15)

3. My Relationship to God

Glory in the holy name of the LORD; let the hearts of those who seek the LORD rejoice. Seek the LORD and His strength; seek His face always. Remember the wonderful works He has done, His miracles, and the judgments He pronounced. (1 Chronicles 16:10-12)

Since I am receiving a kingdom that cannot be shaken, I will be thankful, and so worship God acceptably with reverence and awe; for my God is a consuming fire. (Hebrews 12:28-29)

4. The Character I Want to Cultivate

I will put away perversity from my mouth and keep corrupt talk far from my lips. (Proverbs 4:24)

I will not let any corrupt word come out of my mouth, but only what is helpful for building others up according to their needs, that it may impart grace to those who hear. (Ephesians 4:29)

5. My Relationship to Others

Like Abraham, I should direct my children and my household after me to keep the way of the LORD by doing what is right and just. (Genesis 18:19)

I will learn to fear You all the days I live on the earth and teach Your words to my children. (Deuteronomy 4:10)

DAY 6

1. The Attributes of God

Who is like You, O LORD? Who is like You—majestic in holiness, awesome in praises, working wonders? (Exodus 15:11)

"My thoughts are not your thoughts, neither are your ways My ways," declares the LORD. "As the heavens are higher than the earth, so are My ways higher than your ways and My thoughts than your thoughts." (Isaiah 55:8-9)

2. The Works of God

How great are Your works, O LORD! Your thoughts are very deep. The senseless man does not know; fools do not understand, that when the wicked spring up like grass and all the evildoers flourish, they will be destroyed forever. But You, O LORD, are exalted forever. (Psalm 92:5-7)

The LORD is near to all who call upon Him, to all who call upon Him in truth. He fulfills the desire of those who fear Him; He hears their cry and saves them. The LORD preserves all who love Him, but all the wicked He will destroy. (Psalm 145:18-20)

3. My Relationship to God

I am the salt of the earth; but if the salt loses its flavor, how can it be made salty again? It is no longer good for anything, except to be thrown out and trampled underfoot by men. I am the light of the world. A city set on a hill cannot be hidden. Neither do people light a lamp and put it under a basket, but on a lampstand, and it gives light to all who are in the house. In the same way, I must let my light shine before men, that they may see my good deeds and praise my Father in heaven. (Matthew 5:13-16)

We are the temple of God, and the Spirit of God lives in us. (1 Corinthians 3:16)

4. The Character I Want to Cultivate

When I am blessed with abundance, I will beware lest my heart becomes proud, and I forget the LORD, my God, who provided all good things, thinking that it was my power and the strength of my hand that brought this wealth. (Deuteronomy 8:11-14, 17)

Pride goes before destruction, and a haughty spirit before a fall. (Proverbs 16:18)

5. My Relationship to Others

How good and pleasant it is when brothers live together in unity! (Psalm 133:1)

The Lord Jesus prayed these words for the unity of all who would believe in Him: "[I ask] that all of them may be one, Father, just as You are in Me and I am in You, that they also may be in Us, that the world may believe that You sent Me. And the glory which You gave Me I have given to them, that they may be one, just as We are one: I in them, and You in Me, that they may be perfected in one, that the world may know that You have sent Me and have loved them, even as You have loved Me." (John 17:21-23)

DAY 7

1. The Attributes of God

I acknowledge this day and take it to my heart that the LORD is God in heaven above and on the earth below; there is no other. (Deuteronomy 4:39)

You are the LORD, and there is no other; apart from You there is no God. From the rising to the setting of the sun we know there is none besides You. You are the LORD, and there is no other. (Isaiah 45:5-6)

2. The Works of God

The wolf will dwell with the lamb, and the leopard will lie down with the goat, and the calf and the lion and the yearling together; and a little child will lead them. The cow will feed with the bear; their young will lie down together, and the lion will eat straw like the ox. The infant will play near the hole of the cobra, and the young child will put his hand into the viper's hole. They will neither harm nor destroy on all My holy mountain, for the earth will be full of the knowledge of the LORD as the waters cover the sea. (Isaiah 11:6-9)

The heavens will vanish like smoke; the earth will wear out like a garment, and its inhabitants will die in the same way. But Your salvation will last forever, and Your righteousness will never fail. (Isaiah 51:6)

3. My Relationship to God

The LORD is my strength and my shield; my heart trusts in Him, and I am helped. My heart greatly rejoices, and I will give thanks to Him in song. (Psalm 28:7)

I will not let my heart be troubled. I will trust in God, and trust also in Christ. (John 14:1)

4. The Character I Want to Cultivate

Instruct a wise man, and he will be wiser still; teach a righteous man, and he will increase in learning. (Proverbs 9:9)

He who heeds instruction is on the path of life, but he who refuses correction goes astray. (Proverbs 10:17)

5. My Relationship to Others

How beautiful on the mountains are the feet of those who bring good news, who proclaim peace, who bring good tidings, who proclaim salvation. (Isaiah 52:7)

As I follow You, You will make me a fisher of men. (Matthew 4:19; Mark 1:17)

DAY 8

1. The Attributes of God

You are the living God, and there is no god besides You. You put to death and You bring to life, You have wounded and You will heal, and no one can deliver from Your hand. (Deuteronomy 32:39)

O LORD, the God of our fathers, are You not the God who is in heaven? Are You not the ruler over all the kingdoms of the nations? Power and might are in Your hand, and no one is able to withstand You. (2 Chronicles 20:6)

2. The Works of God

God promised the gospel beforehand through His prophets in the Holy Scriptures, concerning His Son — who was a descendant of David according to the flesh, and who was declared with power to be the Son of God according to the Spirit of holiness, by His resurrection from the dead — Jesus Christ our Lord. (Romans 1:2-4)

God set forth Christ to be a propitiation through faith in His blood. He did this to demonstrate His righteousness, because in His forbearance He passed over the sins committed beforehand; He did it to demonstrate His righteousness at the present time, that He might be just and the justifier of those who have faith in Jesus. Where, then, is boasting? It is excluded. By what law? Of works? No, but by a law of faith. For we maintain that a man is justified by faith apart from works of the law. (Romans 3:25-28)

3. My Relationship to God

By God's grace, I will not despise my birthright for the things of this world. (Genesis 25:33-34)

I will fear the LORD and serve Him in truth with all my heart, for I consider what great things He has done for me. (1 Samuel 12:24)

4. The Character I Want to Cultivate

I will not wear myself out to get rich; I will have the understanding to cease. I will not set my desire on what flies away, for wealth surely sprouts wings and flies into the heavens like an eagle. (Proverbs 23:4-5)

I want to learn to be content in whatever circumstances I am. Whether I am abased or in abundance, whether I am filled or hungry, I want to learn the secret of being content in any and every situation. I can do all things through Him who strengthens me. (Philippians 4:11-13)

5. My Relationship to Others

I will not hate my brother in my heart. (Leviticus 19:17)

Hatred stirs up strife, but love covers all transgressions. (Proverbs 10:12)

DAY 9

1. The Attributes of God

The LORD, the LORD God, is compassionate and gracious, slow to anger, and abounding in lovingkindness and truth, maintaining love to thousands, and forgiving iniquity, transgression, and sin. (Exodus 34:6-7)

The LORD executes righteousness and justice for all who are oppressed. The LORD is compassionate and gracious, slow to anger, and abounding in lovingkindness. (Psalm 103:6, 8)

2. The Works of God

The LORD God formed man from the dust of the ground and breathed into his nostrils the breath of life; and man became a living being. And out of the ground the LORD God made every tree grow that is pleasing to the eye and good for food. In the middle of the garden were the tree of life and the tree of the knowledge of good and evil. Then the LORD God took the man and put him in the Garden of Eden to cultivate it and take care of it. (Genesis 2.7, 9, 15)

In the day that God created man, He made him in the likeness of God. (Genesis 5:1)

3. My Relationship to God

Has the LORD as much delight in burnt offerings and sacrifices as in obeying the voice of the LORD? To obey is better than sacrifice, and to heed is better than the fat of rams. For rebellion is like the sin of divination, and stubbornness is as iniquity and idolatry. (1 Samuel 15:22-23)

I desire not only to call You Lord, but to do what You say. By Your grace, I will come to You, hear Your words, and put them into practice. Then I will be like a man building a house, who dug down deep and laid the foundation on rock; and when a flood came, the torrent struck that house but could not shake it, because it was well built. (Luke 6:46-48)

4. The Character I Want to Cultivate

A fool shows his annoyance at once, but a prudent man overlooks an insult. (Proverbs 12:16)

I will not be quickly provoked in my spirit, for anger rests in the bosom of fools. (Ecclesiastes 7:9)

5. My Relationship to Others

I will learn to do good, seek justice, remove the oppressor, defend the orphan, and plead for the widow. (Isaiah 1:17)

When Christ comes to reign as king on His glorious throne, He will say to the sheep on His right hand, "Come, you who are blessed of My Father, inherit the kingdom prepared for you from the foundation of the world. For I was hungry, and you gave Me something to eat; I was thirsty, and you gave Me something to drink; I was a stranger, and you invited Me in; I was naked, and you clothed Me; I was sick, and you visited Me; I was in prison, and you came to Me." Then the righteous will answer Him, "Lord, when did we see You hungry, and feed You, or thirsty, and give You something to drink? And when did we see You a stranger, and invite You in, or naked, and clothe You? And when did we see You sick, or in prison, and come to You?" And the King will answer and say to them, "I tell you the truth, inasmuch as you did it to one of the least of these brothers of Mine, you did it to Me." (Matthew 25:31, 34-40)

DAY 10

1. The Attributes of God

Great is the LORD and most worthy of praise; He is to be feared above all gods. For all the gods of the nations are idols, but the LORD made the heavens. Splendor and majesty are before Him; strength and beauty are in His sanctuary. I will ascribe to the LORD glory and strength. I will ascribe to the LORD the glory due His name and worship the LORD in the beauty of holiness. (Psalm 96:4-9)

Holy, Holy, Holy is the LORD of hosts; the whole earth is full of His glory. (Isaiah 6:3)

2. The Works of God

The LORD upholds all who fall and lifts up all who are bowed down. The eyes of all look to You, and You give them their food at the proper time. You open Your hand and satisfy the desire of every living thing. (Psalm 145:14-16)

O LORD, You are my God; I will exalt You and praise Your name, for You have done wonderful things, planned long ago in perfect faithfulness. (Isaiah 25:1)

3. My Relationship to God

I know that my Redeemer lives, and that in the end He will stand upon the earth. And after my skin has been destroyed, yet in my flesh I will see God; whom I myself will see and behold with my own eyes, and not another. How my heart yearns within me! (Job 19:25-27)

I have hope in God, that there will be a resurrection of both the righteous and the wicked. In view of this, I strive always to keep my conscience blameless before God and men. (Acts 24:15-16)

4. The Character I Want to Cultivate

I will be strong and courageous; I will not be afraid or discouraged because of my adversaries, for there is a greater power with me than with them, for the LORD, my God, is with me to help me. (2 Chronicles 32:7-8)

I will not be afraid of my adversaries, but I will remember the Lord, who is great and awesome. (Nehemiah 4:14)

5. My Relationship to Others

Far be it from me that I should sin against the LORD by ceasing to pray for others. (1 Samuel 12:23)

I will do nothing out of selfish ambition or vain conceit, but in humility I will esteem others as more important than myself. I will look not only to my own interests, but also to the interests of others. (Philippians 2:3-4)

DAY 11

1. The Attributes of God

The LORD will guard the feet of His saints, but the wicked will be silenced in darkness. It is not by strength that one prevails; those who contend with the LORD will be shattered. He will thunder against them from heaven; the LORD will judge the ends of the earth. He will give strength to His king and exalt the horn of His anointed. (1 Samuel 2:9-10)

You have sworn by Yourself; the word has gone out of Your mouth in righteousness and will not return. Every knee will bow before You, and every tongue will acknowledge You. (Isaiah 45:23)

2. The Works of God

The Lord GOD will swallow up death forever, and He will wipe away the tears from all faces; He will remove the reproach of His people from all the earth. For the LORD has spoken. And it will be said in that day, "Behold, this is our God; we have waited for Him, and He will save us. This is the LORD, we have trusted in Him; let us rejoice and be glad in His salvation." (Isaiah 25:8-9)

You will create new heavens and a new earth. The former things will not be remembered, nor will they come to mind. (Isaiah 65:17)

3. My Relationship to God

How great is Your goodness, which You have stored up for those who fear You, which You have prepared for those who take refuge in You before the sons of men! (Psalm 31:19)

You know how I am formed; You remember that I am dust. As for man, his days are like grass; he flourishes like a flower of the field. The wind passes over it, and it is gone, and its place remembers it no more. But the lovingkindness of the LORD is from everlasting to everlasting on those who fear Him, and His righteousness with their children's children, to those who keep His covenant and remember to obey His precepts. (Psalm 103:14-18)

4. The Character I Want to Cultivate

The fear of man brings a snare, but he who trusts in the LORD is set on high. (Proverbs 29:25)

Cursed is the one who trusts in man, who depends on flesh for his strength, and whose heart turns away from the LORD. But blessed is the man who trusts in the LORD, whose confidence is in Him. (Jeremiah 17:5, 7)

5. My Relationship to Others

A virtuous wife is the crown of her husband, but she who causes shame is like decay in his bones. (Proverbs 12:4)

Who can find a virtuous wife? She is worth far more than jewels. (Proverbs 31:10)

DAY 12

1. The Attributes of God

Your lovingkindness, O LORD, reaches to the heavens, Your faithfulness to the skies. Your righteousness is like the mountains of God; Your judgments are like a great deep. O LORD, You preserve man and beast. How priceless is Your lovingkindness, O God! The children of men find refuge in the shadow of Your wings. For with You is the fountain of life; in Your light we see light. (Psalm 36:5-7, 9)

The LORD's lovingkindness is great toward us, and the truth of the LORD endures forever. Praise the LORD! (Psalm 117:2)

2. The Works of God

The foolishness of God is wiser than men, and the weakness of God is stronger than men. But God chose the foolish things of the world to shame the wise, and God chose the weak things of the world to shame the strong; and the lowly things of this world and the despised things God has chosen, and the things that are not, to nullify the things that are, so that no one may boast before Him. (1 Corinthians 1:25, 27-29)

The Lord said, "Behold, I stand at the door and knock. If anyone hears My voice and opens the door, I will come in to him and dine with him, and he with Me. To him who overcomes, I will give the right to sit with Me on My throne, just as I overcame and sat down with My Father on His throne." (Revelation 3:20-21)

3. My Relationship to God

Have mercy on me, O God, have mercy on me, for in You my soul takes refuge. I will take refuge in the shadow of Your wings until destruction passes by. I cry out to God Most High, to God who fulfills His purpose for me (Psalm 57:1-2)

This is what the Lord GOD, the Holy One of Israel, says: "In repentance and rest is your salvation, in quietness and trust is your strength." (Isaiah 30:15)

4. The Character I Want to Cultivate

You desire mercy, not sacrifice, and the knowledge of God more than burnt offerings. (Hosea 6:6)

Blessed are the merciful, for they shall obtain mercy. (Matthew 5:7)

5. My Relationship to Others

I will honor my father and my mother. (Exodus 20:12)

The father of the righteous will greatly rejoice, and he who begets a wise son will be glad in him. May my father and mother be glad; may she who gave me birth rejoice. (Proverbs 23:24-25)

DAY 13

1. The Attributes of God

O LORD, our Lord, how majestic is Your name in all the earth! You have set Your glory above the heavens! (Psalm 8:1)

Bless the LORD, O my soul. O LORD my God, You are very great; You are clothed with splendor and majesty. (Psalm 104:1)

2. The Works of God

In six days the LORD made the heavens and the earth, the sea, and all that is in them, and rested on the seventh day. Therefore the LORD blessed the Sabbath day and made it holy. (Exodus 20:11)

You alone are the LORD. You made the heavens, even the heaven of heavens, and all their starry host, the earth and all that is on it, the seas and all that is in them. You give life to all that is in them, and the host of heaven worships You. (Nehemiah 9:6)

3. My Relationship to God

The LORD is my shepherd, I shall not be in want. He makes me lie down in green pastures, He leads me beside quiet waters, He restores my soul. He guides me in the paths of righteousness for His name's sake. Even though I walk through the valley of the shadow of death, I will fear no evil, for You are with me; Your rod and Your staff, they comfort me. You prepare a table before me in the presence of my enemies. You anoint my head with oil; my cup overflows. Surely goodness and mercy will follow me all the days of my life, and I will dwell in the house of the LORD forever. (Psalm 23:1-6)

I know that all things work together for good to those who love God, to those who have been called according to His purpose. (Romans 8:28)

4. The Character I Want to Cultivate

LORD, make me to know my end, and what is the measure of my days; let me know how fleeting is my life. (Psalm 39:4)

Teach me to number my days that I may gain a heart of wisdom. (Psalm 90:12)

5. My Relationship to Others

Since we were called into fellowship with the Lord Jesus Christ, all of us should agree with one another so that there may be no divisions among us, and that we may be perfectly joined together in the same mind and in the same judgment. (1 Corinthians 1:9-10)

There is neither Jew nor Greek, there is neither slave nor free, there is neither male nor female, for we are all one in Christ Jesus. (Galatians 3:28)

DAY 14

1. The Attributes of God

The LORD does not see as man sees. Man looks at the outward appearance, but the LORD looks at the heart. (1 Samuel 16:7)

O LORD, You have searched me and You know me. You know when I sit down and when I rise up; You understand my thoughts from afar. You scrutinize my path and my lying down and are acquainted with all my ways. Before a word is on my tongue, O LORD, You know it completely. (Psalm 139:1-4)

2. The Works of God

A Shoot will come forth from the stump of Jesse; from his roots a Branch will bear fruit. The Spirit of the LORD will rest on Him — the Spirit of wisdom and of understanding, the Spirit of counsel and of power, the Spirit of knowledge and of the fear of the LORD — and He will delight in the fear of the LORD. He will not judge by what He sees with His eyes or decide by what He hears with His ears, but with righteousness He will judge the poor and decide with fairness for the meek of the earth. And He will strike the earth with the rod of His mouth; with the breath of His lips He will slay the wicked. Righteousness will be His belt, and faithfulness the sash around His waist. (Isaiah 11:1-5)

Behold, a virgin shall be with child and will give birth to a son, and they will call His name Immanuel, which means, "God with us " (Matthew 1:23)

3. My Relationship to God

The LORD, my God, wants me to fear Him, to walk in all His ways, to love Him, and to serve the LORD, my God, with all my heart and with all my soul. (Deuteronomy 10:12(

I want to know God and serve Him with a whole heart and with a willing mind; for the LORD searches all hearts and understands every motive behind the thoughts. (1 Chronicles 28:9)

4. The Character I Want to Cultivate

I know, my God, that you test the heart and are pleased with integrity. (1 Chronicles 29:17)

May those who hope in You not be ashamed because of me, O Lord GOD of hosts; may those who seek You not be dishonored because of me, O God of Israel. (Psalm 69:6)

5. My Relationship to Others

Whoever acknowledges You before men, You will also acknowledge him before Your Father in heaven. But whoever denies You before men, You will also deny him before Your Father in heaven. (Matthew 10:32-33)

I will not be ashamed to testify about our Lord, but I will join with others in suffering for the gospel according to the power of God. (2 Timothy 1:8)

DAY 15

1. The Attributes of God

God is the rock, His work is perfect, for all His ways are just. A God of faithfulness and without injustice, upright and just is He. (Deuteronomy 32:4)

The word of the LORD is upright, and all His work is done in faithfulness. He loves righteousness and justice; the earth is full of the lovingkindness of the LORD. (Psalm 33:4-5)

2. The Works of God

Multitudes who sleep in the dust of the earth will awake; some, to everlasting life; others, to shame and everlasting contempt. Those who are wise will shine like the brightness of the heavens, and those who lead many to righteousness, like the stars for ever and ever. (Daniel 12:2-3)

An hour is coming when all who are in the graves will hear the voice of the Son of Man, and will come out — those who have done good, to a resurrection of life, and those who have done evil, to a resurrection of judgment. (John 5:28-29)

3. My Relationship to God

I will praise You, O Lord my God, with all my heart, and I will glorify Your name forever. For great is Your love toward me, and You have delivered my soul from the depths of the grave. (Psalm 86:12-13)

I will exult in the LORD; I will rejoice in the God of my salvation. The Lord GOD is my strength; He makes my feet like the feet of a deer, and enables me to go on the heights. (Habakkuk 3:18-19)

4. The Character I Want to Cultivate

I will not spread false reports, nor will I help a wicked man by being a malicious witness. (Exodus 23:1)

Lying lips are hateful to the LORD, but He delights in those who deal faithfully. (Proverbs 12:22)

5. My Relationship to Others

I will not take vengeance or bear a grudge against others, but I will love my neighbor as myself. (Leviticus 19:18)

Whatever I want others to do to me, I will also do to them, for this is the law and the prophets. (Matthew 7:12)

DAY 16

1. The Attributes of God

There is no one holy like the LORD; there is no one besides You, nor is there any rock like our God. (1 Samuel 2:2)

There is but one God, the Father, from whom all things came and for whom I live, and there is but one Lord, Jesus Christ, through whom all things came and through whom I live. (1 Corinthians 8:6)

2. The Works of God

God so loved the world that He gave His only begotten Son, that whoever believes in Him should not perish but have eternal life. For God did not send His Son into the world to condemn the world, but to save the world through Him. (John 3:16-17)

The Lord said, "I have come as a light into the world that whoever believes in Me should not stay in darkness. And if anyone hears My words but does not keep them, I do not judge him; for I did not come to judge the world, but to save the world." (John 12:46-47)

3. My Relationship to God

Jesus is in His Father, and I am in Jesus, and He is in me. (John 14:20)

If I have been united with Christ in the likeness of His death, I will certainly also be united with Him in the likeness of His resurrection. (Romans 6:5)

4. The Character I Want to Cultivate

When pride comes, then comes dishonor, but with humility comes wisdom. (Proverbs 11:2)

The proud looks of man will be humbled, and the loftiness of men brought low; the LORD alone will be exalted. (Isaiah 2:11)

5. My Relationship to Others

Is this not the fast You have chosen: to loose the bonds of wickedness, to undo the cords of the yoke, and to let the oppressed go free and break every yoke? Is it not to share our food with the hungry and to provide the poor wanderer with shelter; when we see the naked, to clothe him, and not to turn away from our own flesh? Then our light will break forth like the dawn, and our healing will quickly appear, and our righteousness will go before us; the glory of the LORD will be our rear guard. Then we will call, and the LORD will answer; we will cry, and He will say, "Here I am." If we put away the yoke from our midst, the pointing of the finger and malicious talk, and if we extend our souls to the hungry and satisfy the afflicted soul, then our light will rise in the darkness, and our gloom will become like the noonday. (Isaiah 58:6-10)

I must help the weak and remember the words of the Lord Jesus that He said, "It is more blessed to give than to receive." (Acts 20:35)

DAY 17

1. The Attributes of God

The LORD will be gracious to whom He will be gracious, and He will have compassion on whom He will have compassion. (Exodus 33:19)

The Lord Jesus, who is holy and true, holds the key of David. What He opens no one can shut, and what He shuts no one can open. (Revelation 3:7)

2. The Works of God

God is the maker of the Bear and Orion, the Pleiades and the constellations of the south. He does great things that cannot be fathomed and wonderful works that cannot be counted. (Job 9:9)

The day is Yours; the night also is Yours; You established the sun and moon. It was You who set all the boundaries of the earth; You made both summer and winter. (Psalm 74:16-17)

3. My Relationship to God

I will not depend on human strength, but on the LORD, my God, for help and deliverance. (2 Chronicles 16:7-8, 12) .

I will trust in the LORD and do good; I will dwell in the land and feed on His faithfulness. I will delight myself in the LORD, and He will give me the desires of my heart. I will commit my way to the LORD and trust in Him, and He will bring it to pass. I will rest in the LORD and wait patiently for Him; I will not fret because of him who prospers in his way, with the man who practices evil schemes. (Psalm 37:3-5, 7)

4. The Character I Want to Cultivate

Before I was afflicted I went astray, but now I keep Your word. It was good for me to be afflicted so that I might learn Your statutes. (Psalm 119:67, 71)

I will not forget the exhortation that addresses me as a son: "My son, do not despise the Lord's discipline nor lose heart when you are rebuked by Him, for whom the LORD loves He disciplines, and He chastises every son whom He receives." (Hebrews 12:5-6)

5. My Relationship to Others

We who are strong ought to bear the weaknesses of those who are not strong, and not to please ourselves. Each of us should please his neighbor for his good, to build him up. (Romans 15:1-2)

No one should seek his own good, but the good of others. (1 Corinthians 10:24)

DAY 18

1. The Attributes of God

You must be treated as holy by those who come near You, and before all people, You will be honored. (Leviticus 10:3)

The LORD of hosts will be exalted in judgment, and the holy God will show Himself holy in righteousness. (Isaiah 5:16)

2. The Works of God

The eyes of the LORD move to and fro throughout the whole earth to strengthen those whose hearts are fully committed to Him. (2 Chronicles 16:9)

For those who revere Your name, the Sun of righteousness will rise with healing in His wings. And they will go out and leap like calves released from the stall. (Malachi 4:2)

3. My Relationship to God

I will not let Your word depart from my mouth, but I will meditate on it day and night so that I may be careful to do according to all that is written in it; for then I will make my way prosperous, and I will act wisely. (Joshua 1:8)

I am committed to God and to the word of His grace, which is able to build me up and give me an inheritance among all those who are sanctified. (Acts 20:32)

4. The Character I Want to Cultivate

I shall not covet my neighbor's house, my neighbor's wife, his manservant or maidservant, his ox or donkey, or anything that belongs to my neighbor. (Exodus 20:17)

I will beware and be on my guard against all covetousness, for my life does not consist in the abundance of my possessions. (Luke 12:15)

5. My Relationship to Others

Wives should submit to their own husbands as to the Lord. For the husband is the head of the wife, as Christ also is the head of the Church, and He is the Savior of the body. But as the Church is subject to Christ, so also wives should be to their husbands in everything. (Ephesians 5:22-24)

Husbands should love their wives, just as Christ also loved the Church and gave Himself up for her that He might sanctify and cleanse her by the washing with water through the word, that He might present her to Himself as a glorious Church, without spot or wrinkle or any other blemish, but holy and blameless. So husbands ought to love their own wives as their own bodies. He who loves his own wife loves himself; for no one ever hated his own flesh, but nourishes and cherishes it, just as Christ also does the Church, for we are members of His body. (Ephesians 5:25-30)

DAY 19

1. The Attributes of God

The LORD Most High is awesome, the great King over all the earth! God is the King of all the earth, and I will sing His praise. God reigns over the nations; God is seated on His holy throne. (Psalm 47:2, 7-8)

The Son is the radiance of God's glory and the exact representation of His being, upholding all things by His powerful word. After He cleansed our sins, He sat down at the right hand of the Majesty on high, having become as much superior to the angels as the name He has inherited is more excellent than theirs. (Hebrews 1:3-4)

2. The Works of God

Behold, the Lord GOD will come with power, and His arm will rule for Him. Behold, His reward is with Him, and His recompense accompanies Him. He will feed His flock like a shepherd; He will gather the lambs in His arms and carry them close to His heart; He will gently lead those that have young. (Isaiah 40:10-11)

When the Son of Man comes in His glory, and all the angels with Him, He will sit on His glorious throne. All the nations will be gathered before Him, and He will separate the people one from another as a shepherd separates the sheep from the goats. He will put the sheep on His right and the goats on His left. Then the King will say to those on His right, "Come, you who are blessed by My Father; inherit the kingdom prepared for you since the foundation of the world." (Matthew 25:31-34)

3. My Relationship to God

Like Josiah, I want to do what is right in the sight of the LORD and walk in all the ways of David, not turning aside to the right or to the left. (2 Kings 22:1-2)

I do not want to be like those rocky places on whom seed was thrown, who hear the word and at once receive it with joy, but since they have no root, last only a short time; when affliction or persecution comes because of the word, they quickly fall away. Nor do I want to be like those among the thorns on whom seed was sown, who hear the

word, but the worries of this world, the deceitfulness of riches and pleasures, and the desires for other things come in and choke the word,
making it immature and unfruitful. Instead, I want to be like the good
soil on whom seed was sown, who with a noble and good heart hear the
word, understand and accept it, and with perseverance bear fruit, yielding thirty, sixty, or a hundred times what was sown. (Matthew 13:20-23;
Mark 4:16-20; Luke 8:13-15)

4. The Character I Want to Cultivate

Blessed is the man who does not walk in the counsel of the wicked
or stand in the way of sinners or sit in the seat of scorners. But his
delight is in the law of the LORD, and in His law he meditates day and
night. And he shall be like a tree planted by streams of water, which
yields its fruit in its season and whose leaf does not wither, and whatever
he does will prosper. (Psalm 1:1-3)

I will be diligent to present myself approved to God, a workman who
does not need to be ashamed and who correctly handles the word of
truth. (2 Timothy 2:15)

5. My Relationship to Others

He who spares his rod hates his son, but he who loves him is careful
to discipline him. (Proverbs 13:24)

Foolishness is bound up in the heart of a child, but the rod of discipline will drive it far from him. (Proverbs 22:15)

DAY 20

1. The Attributes of God

Yours, O LORD, is the greatness and the power and the glory and
the victory and the majesty, for everything in heaven and earth is Yours.
Yours, O LORD, is the kingdom, and You are exalted as head over all.
Both riches and honor come from You, and You are the ruler of all
things. In Your hand is power and might to exalt and to give strength to
all. Therefore, my God, I give You thanks, and praise Your glorious
name. All things come from You, and I can only give You what comes
from Your hand. (1 Chronicles 29:11-14)

Your throne, O God, is forever and ever; a scepter of righteousness
is the scepter of Your kingdom. (Psalm 45:6)

2. The Works of God

Apart from law the righteousness of God has been made known, being witnessed by the law and the prophets, even the righteousness of God through faith in Jesus Christ to all who believe. For there is no difference, for all have sinned and fall short of the glory of God, being justified freely by His grace through the redemption that is in Christ Jesus. (Romans 3:21-24)

When we were helpless, at the right time, Christ died for the ungodly. For rarely will anyone die for a righteous man, though perhaps for a good man someone would even dare to die. But God demonstrates His own love for us in that while we were still sinners, Christ died for us. (Romans 5:6-8)

3. My Relationship to God

No one who waits for You will be ashamed, but those who are treacherous without cause will be ashamed. Show me Your ways, O LORD; teach me Your paths; lead me in Your truth and teach me, for You are the God of my salvation, and my hope is in You all day long. (Psalm 25:3-5)

"I know the plans I have for you," declares the LORD, "plans to prosper you and not to harm you, plans to give you a future and a hope." (Jeremiah 29:11)

4. The Character I Want to Cultivate

I will be strong and courageous, being careful to obey Your word; I will not turn from it to the right or to the left that I may act wisely wherever I go. (Joshua 1:7)

I will take courage and not be afraid, for the Lord Jesus is with me. (Mark 6:50)

5. My Relationship to Others

Just as we have many members in one body, but all the members do not have the same function, so we who are many are one body in Christ and individually members of one another. And we have different gifts, according to the grace given to us. (Romans 12:4-6)

There are different kinds of gifts, but the same Spirit. And there are different kinds of service, but the same Lord. And there are different kinds of working, but the same God works all of them in all people. But to each one the manifestation of the Spirit is given for the common good. (1 Corinthians 12:4-7)

DAY 21

1. The Attributes of God

As for God, His way is perfect; the word of the Lord is proven. He is a shield for all who take refuge in Him. For who is God besides the LORD? And who is the rock except our God? (2 Samuel 22:31-32)

The LORD longs to be gracious and rises to show compassion. For the LORD is a God of justice; blessed are all those who wait for Him! (Isaiah 30:18)

2. The Works of God

The heavens declare the glory of God, and the skies proclaim the work of His hands. Day after day they pour forth speech; night after night they reveal knowledge. (Psalm 19:1-2)

The LORD is the great God, the great King above all gods. In His hand are the depths of the earth, and the summits of the mountains are His also. The sea is His, for He made it, and His hands formed the dry land. He is our God, and we are the people of His pasture, and the sheep under His care. (Psalm 95:3-5, 7)

3. My Relationship to God

You have loved me with an everlasting love; You have drawn me with lovingkindness. (Jeremiah 31:3)

Who shall separate me from the love of Christ? Shall tribulation, or distress, or persecution, or famine, or nakedness, or danger, or sword? As it is written: "For Your sake we face death all day long; we are considered as sheep to be slaughtered." Yet in all these things I am more than a conqueror through Him who loved me. (Romans 8:35-37)

4. The Character I Want to Cultivate

I am not trying to win the approval of men, but of God. If I were still trying to please men, I would not be a servant of Christ. (Galatians 1:10)

Since I have been approved by God to be entrusted with the gospel, I speak not as pleasing men, but God who tests my heart. I will not seek glory from men. (1 Thessalonians 2:4, 6)

5. My Relationship to Others

You have called me to go and proclaim the Kingdom of God. (Luke 9:60)

Jesus said, "As the Father has sent Me, I also send you." (John 20:21)

DAY 22

1. The Attributes of God

I will arise and bless the LORD, my God, who is from everlasting to everlasting. Blessed be Your glorious name, which is exalted above all blessing and praise! (Nehemiah 9:5)

Glory to God in the highest, and on earth peace to those on whom His favor rests. (Luke 2:14)

2. The Works of God

I will remember the works of the LORD; surely, I will remember Your wonders of long ago. I will meditate on all Your works and consider all Your mighty deeds. Your way, O God, is holy. What god is so great as our God? You are the God who works wonders; You have revealed Your strength among the peoples. You redeemed your people with Your power, the descendants of Jacob and Joseph. (Psalm 77:11-15)

As the earth brings forth its sprouts and as a garden causes that which is sown to spring up, so the Lord GOD will make righteousness and praise spring up before all nations. (Isaiah 61:11)

3. My Relationship to God

Blessed be the Lord; day by day He bears our burdens, the God of our salvation. Our God is the God of salvation, and to GOD the Lord belong escapes from death. (Psalm 68:19-20)

Lord Jesus, all that the Father gives You will come to You, and whoever comes to You, You will never cast out. For You have come down from heaven not to do Your own will, but the will of Him who sent You. And this is the will of Him who sent You, that You will lose none of all that He has given You, but raise them up at the last day. For Your Father's will is that everyone who looks to the Son and believes in Him may have eternal life, and You will raise him up at the last day. (John 6:37-40)

4. The Character I Want to Cultivate

What is desired in a man is unfailing love. (Proverbs 19:22)

As one who has been chosen of God, holy and beloved, I will put on a heart of compassion, kindness, humility, gentleness, and patience, bearing with others and forgiving others even as the Lord forgave me; and above all these things, I will put on love, which is the bond of perfection. (Colossians 3:12-14)

5. *My Relationship to Others*

I will love my enemies and pray for those who persecute me. (Matthew 5:44)

I will love my enemies, do good to those who hate me, bless those who curse me, and pray for those who mistreat me. Just as I want others to do to me, I will do to them in the same way. (Luke 6:27-28, 31)

DAY 23

1. *The Attributes of God*

Will God indeed dwell on earth? Heaven and the highest heaven cannot contain You. (1 Kings 8:27)

God sits enthroned above the circle of the earth, and its inhabitants are like grasshoppers. He stretches out the heavens like a curtain and spreads them out like a tent to dwell in. He reduces rulers to nothing and makes the judges of this world meaningless. (Isaiah 40:22-23)

2. *The Works of God*

You will magnify Yourself and sanctify Yourself, and You will make Yourself known in the sight of many nations, and they will know that You are the LORD. (Ezekiel 38:23)

The earth will be filled with the knowledge of the glory of the LORD, as the waters cover the sea. (Habakkuk 2:14)

3. *My Relationship to God*

God is my refuge and strength, an ever-present help in trouble. Therefore I will not fear, though the earth changes and the mountains slip into the heart of the sea. (Psalm 46:1-2)

I will not fear, for You are with me; I will not be dismayed, for You are my God. You will strengthen me and help me; You will uphold me with Your righteous right hand. For You are the LORD, my God, who takes hold of my right hand and says to me, "Do not fear; I will help you." (Isaiah 41:10, 13)

4. *The Character I Want to Cultivate*

The fear of the LORD is the beginning of knowledge, but fools despise wisdom and discipline. (Proverbs 1:7)

The LORD gives wisdom; from His mouth come knowledge and understanding. He stores up sound wisdom for the upright; He is a shield to those who walk in integrity, guarding the paths of justice and protecting the way of His saints. Then I will understand righteousness and justice and honesty — every good path. For wisdom will enter my heart, and knowledge will be pleasant to my soul. Discretion will protect me, and understanding will guard me. (Proverbs 2:6-11)

5. My Relationship to Others

When I give, it will be given to me; good measure, pressed down, shaken together, running over, they will pour into my lap. For with the measure I use, it will be measured back to me. (Luke 6:38)

He who sows sparingly will also reap sparingly, and he who sows bountifully will also reap bountifully. Each one should give as he has decided in his heart, not reluctantly or under compulsion, for God loves a cheerful giver. And God is able to make all grace abound to us so that always having all sufficiency in everything, we may abound in every good work. As it is written: "He has scattered abroad His gifts to the poor; His righteousness endures forever." Now He who supplies seed to the sower and bread for food will also supply and increase our seed and will increase the fruits of our righteousness. (2 Corinthians 9:6-10)

DAY 24

1. The Attributes of God

Where does wisdom come from? Where does understanding dwell? It is hidden from the eyes of every living thing and concealed from the birds of the air. Destruction and Death say, "Only a rumor of it has reached our ears." God understands its way, and He knows its place. For He looks to the ends of the earth and sees everything under the heavens. (Job 28:20-24)

Oh, the depth of the riches both of the wisdom and knowledge of God! How unsearchable are His judgments, and His ways past finding out! For who has known the mind of the LORD? Or who has been His counselor? Or who has first given to Him that He should repay him? For from Him and through Him and to Him are all things. To Him be the glory forever! Amen. (Romans 11:33-36)

2. The Works of God

Christ was in the world, and the world was made through Him, and the world did not know Him. He came to His own, but His own did not receive Him. (John 1:10-11)

The light has come into the world, but men loved darkness rather than light because their deeds were evil. For everyone who does evil hates the light and will not come into the light for fear that his deeds will be exposed. But whoever practices the truth comes into the light so that his deeds may be clearly seen as having been done through God. (John 3:19-21)

3. My Relationship to God

I want to love the LORD, my God, obey His voice, and hold fast to Him. For the Lord is my life and the length of my days. (Deuteronomy 30:20)

I love You, O LORD, my strength. The LORD is my rock and my fortress and my deliverer; my God is my rock, in whom I take refuge. He is my shield and the horn of my salvation, my stronghold. I call upon the LORD who is worthy of praise, and I am saved from my enemies. (Psalm 18:1-3)

4. The Character I Want to Cultivate

I will not steal, nor deal falsely, nor deceive others. (Leviticus 19:11)

I will not pervert justice or show partiality. I will not accept a bribe, for a bribe blinds the eyes of the wise and perverts the words of the righteous. (Deuteronomy 16:19)

5. My Relationship to Others

Starting a quarrel is like breaching a dam, so I will stop a quarrel before it breaks out. (Proverbs 17:14)

If it is possible, as far as it depends on me, I will live at peace with all men. (Romans 12:18)

DAY 25

1. The Attributes of God

God is exalted beyond our understanding; the number of His years is unsearchable. (Job 36:26)

You are He; You are the first, and You are also the last. (Isaiah 48:12)

2. The Works of God

The earth is the LORD's, and everything in it; the world, and all who dwell in it. For He founded it upon the seas and established it upon the waters. (Psalm 24:1-2)

The LORD covers Himself in light as with a garment; He stretches out the heavens like a tent curtain and lays the beams of His upper chambers in the waters. He makes the clouds His chariot and walks on the wings of the wind. He makes the winds His messengers, flames of fire His servants. He set the earth on its foundations so that it can never be moved. You covered it with the deep as with a garment; the waters stood above the mountains. At Your rebuke, the waters fled; at the sound of Your thunder, they hurried away. They flowed over the mountains and went down into the valleys, to the place You assigned for them. You set a boundary they cannot cross, that they will not return to cover the earth. O Lord, how manifold are Your works! In wisdom You made them all; the earth is full of Your possessions. (Psalm 104:2-9, 24)

3. My Relationship to God
I will give thanks to the LORD, call upon His name, and make known to others what He has done. I will sing to Him, sing praises to Him, and tell of all His wonderful acts. (1 Chronicles 16:8-9)

I trust in Your loyal love; my heart rejoices in Your salvation. I will sing to the LORD, for He has dealt bountifully with me. (Psalm 13:5-6)

4. The Character I Want to Cultivate
In a multitude of words, transgression does not cease, but he who restrains his lips is wise. (Proverbs 10:19)

A fool has no delight in understanding, but only in airing his own opinions. (Proverbs 18:2)

5. My Relationship to Others
Love is as strong as death, and jealousy is as cruel as the grave; its flames are flames of fire, a flame of the LORD. Many waters cannot quench love, nor can rivers overflow it. If a man were to give all the wealth of his house for love, it would be utterly scorned. (Song of Solomon 8:6, 7)

Since she is a companion and a wife by covenant, a husband should not deal treacherously against the wife of his youth. The LORD God of hosts seeks a Godly offspring and hates divorce; therefore, we must take heed to our spirit and not deal treacherously. (Malachi 2:14-16)

DAY 26

1. The Attributes of God
Nothing is too difficult for the LORD. (Genesis 18:14)
All things are possible with God. (Matthew 19:26; Mark 10:27)

2. The Works of God
The Servant of God was despised and rejected by men, a man of sorrows, and acquainted with grief. And like one from whom men hide their faces, He was despised, and we esteemed Him not. Surely He has

borne our infirmities and carried our sorrows; yet we considered Him stricken, smitten by God, and afflicted. But He was pierced for our transgressions, He was crushed for our iniquities; the punishment that brought us peace was upon Him, and by His wounds we are healed. All of us like sheep have gone astray; each of us has turned to his own way, and the LORD has laid on Him the iniquity of us all. He was oppressed and afflicted, yet He did not open His mouth; He was led like a lamb to the slaughter, and as a sheep before her shearers is silent, so He did not open His mouth. By oppression and judgment He was taken away. And who can speak of His descendants? For He was cut off from the land of the living; He was stricken for the transgression of God's people. He was assigned a grave with the wicked, yet with a rich man in His death, though He had done no violence, nor was any deceit in His mouth. Yet it was the LORD's will to crush Him and cause Him to suffer. When He makes His soul a guilt offering, He will see His offspring and prolong His days, and the pleasure of the LORD will prosper in His hand. He will see the fruit of the travail of His soul and be satisfied; by His knowledge God's righteous Servant will justify many, and He will bear their iniquities. Therefore God will give Him a portion among the great, and He will divide the spoils with the strong, because He poured out His life unto death, and was numbered with the transgressors. For He bore the sin of many and made intercession for the transgressors. (Isaiah 53:3-12)

The Son of Man did not come to be served, but to serve and to give His life as a ransom for many. (Matthew 20:28)

3. My Relationship to God

I know that my old self was crucified with Christ so that the body of sin might be done away with, that I should no longer be a slave to sin, for the one who has died has been freed from sin. (Romans 6:6-7)

Through the law I died to the law so that I might live for God. I have been crucified with Christ, and it is no longer I who live, but Christ lives in me, and the life which I now live in the flesh, I live by faith in the Son of God who loved me and gave Himself for me. (Galatians 2:19-20)

4. The Character I Want to Cultivate

The fear of the LORD is the instruction for wisdom, and humility comes before honor. (Proverbs 15:33)

Thus says the LORD: "Let not the wise man boast of his wisdom, and let not the strong man boast of his strength, and let not the rich man boast of his riches, but let him who boasts boast about this: that he understands and knows Me, that I am the LORD, who exercises lovingkindness, justice, and righteousness on earth, for in these I delight," declares the LORD. (Jeremiah 9:23-24)

5. My Relationship to Others

Your commandments will be upon my heart, and I will teach them diligently to my children and talk about them when I sit in my house and when I walk along the way and when I lie down and when I rise up. (Deuteronomy 6:6-7)

A wise son heeds his father's instruction, but a scoffer does not listen to rebuke. (Proverbs 13:1)

DAY 27

1. The Attributes of God

The LORD, my God, is the faithful God who keeps His covenant and His lovingkindness to a thousand generations of those who love Him and keep His commands. (Deuteronomy 7:9)

I call this to mind and therefore I have hope: The LORD's mercies never cease, for His compassions never fail. They are new every morning; great is Your faithfulness. (Lamentations 3:21-23)

2. The Works of God

The Son of Man is going to come in the glory of His Father with His angels, and then He will reward each person according to his works. (Matthew 16:27)

As the lightning comes from the east and flashes to the west, so will be the coming of the on of Man. The sign of the Son of Man will appear in the sky, and all the nations of the earth will mourn, and they will see the Son of Man coming on the clouds of the sky with power and great glory. (Matthew 24:27, 30)

3. My Relationship to God

The LORD is my light and my salvation; whom shall I fear? The LORD is the strength of my life; of whom shall I be afraid? (Psalm 27:1)

When I am afraid, I will trust in You. In God whose word I praise, in God I have put my trust. I will not fear; what can mortal man do to me? (Psalm 56:3-4)

4. The Character I Want to Cultivate

He who listens to a life-giving rebuke will be at home among the wise. He who refuses instruction despises himself, but he who heeds correction gains understanding. (Proverbs 15:31-32)

A rebuke goes deeper into a wise man than a hundred lashes into a fool. (Proverbs 17:10)

5. My Relationship to Others

May the God who gives endurance and encouragement grant us to be of the same mind toward one another according to Christ Jesus so that with one accord and one mouth we may glorify the God and Father of our Lord Jesus Christ. (Romans 15:5-6)

There should be no division in the body, but its members should have the same concern for each other. If one member suffers, all the members suffer with it; if one member is honored, all the members rejoice with it. Now we are the body of Christ, and each one of us is a member of it. (1 Corinthians 12:25-27)

DAY 28

1. The Attributes of God

I will exalt You, my God and King; I will bless Your name for ever and ever. Every day I will bless You, and I will praise Your name for ever and ever. Great is the LORD and most worthy of praise; His greatness is unsearchable. (Psalm 145:1-3)

Every creature in heaven and on earth and under the earth and on the sea and all that is in them will sing: "To Him who sits on the throne and to the Lamb be blessing and honor and glory and power for ever and ever!" (Revelation 5:13)

2. The Works of God

We know the grace of our Lord Jesus Christ, that though He was rich, yet for our sakes He became poor, that we through His poverty might become rich. (2 Corinthians 8:9)

There is one God and one Mediator between God and men, the Man Christ Jesus who gave Himself as a ransom for all, the testimony given in its proper time. (1 Timothy 2:5-6)

3. My Relationship to God

Naked I came from my mother's womb, and naked I will depart. The LORD gives and the LORD takes away; blessed be the name of the LORD. (Job 1:21)

If anyone wishes to come after You, he must deny himself and take up his cross and follow You. For whoever wants to save his life will lose it, but whoever loses his life for Your sake and the gospel's will find it. For what is a man profited if he gains the whole world, yet forfeits his soul? Or what will a man give in exchange for his soul? (Matthew 16:24-26; Mark 8:34-37; Luke 9:23-25)

4. The Character I Want to Cultivate

He who loves money will not be satisfied with money, nor he who loves abundance with its increase. (Ecclesiastes 5:10)

Those who want to get rich fall into temptation and a snare, and into many foolish and harmful desires that plunge men into ruin and destruction. For the love of money is a root of all kinds of evil, and some by longing for it have wandered from the faith and pierced themselves with many sorrows. But I will flee from these things and pursue righteousness, godliness, faith, love, patience, and gentleness. (1 Timothy 6:9-11)

5. My Relationship to Others

The harvest is plentiful, but the workers are few. Therefore I will pray that the Lord of the harvest will send out workers into His harvest. (Matthew 9:37-38; Luke 10:2)

Do you not say, "Four months more and then comes the harvest"? Behold, I say to you, lift up your eyes and look at the fields, for they are white for harvest. Even now the reaper draws his wages and gathers fruit for eternal life, that he who sows and he who reaps may rejoice together. (John 4:35-36)

DAY 29

1. The Attributes of God

The LORD brings death and makes alive; He brings down to the grave and raises up. The LORD sends poverty and wealth; He humbles and He exalts. He raises the poor from the dust and lifts the needy from the ash heap to seat them with princes and make them inherit a throne of honor. For the foundations of the earth are the LORD's, and He has set the world upon them. (1 Samuel 2:6-8)

Whatever the LORD pleases He does, in the heavens and on the earth, in the seas and all their depths. (Psalm 135:6)

2. The Works of God

By the word of the LORD the heavens were made, and by the breath of His mouth their starry host. (Psalm 33:6)

"To whom will you compare Me? Or who is My equal?" says the Holy One. Lift your eyes to the heavens and see who has created them, He who brings out the starry host by number and calls them each by name. Because of His great might and the strength of His power, not one of them is missing. Do you not know? Have you not heard? The everlasting God, the LORD, the Creator of the ends of the earth, does not grow tired or weary. No one can fathom His understanding. (Isaiah 40:25-26, 28)

3. My Relationship to God

He who has Your commandments and obeys them, he is the one who loves You, and he who loves You will be loved by Your Father, and You will love him and manifest Yourself to him. (John 14:21)

I want to be a doer of the word and not merely a hearer who deceives himself. For if anyone is a hearer of the word and not a doer, he is like a man who looks at his natural face in a mirror, and after looking at himself, goes away and immediately forgets what kind of person he was. But the one who looks intently into the perfect law of freedom and continues in it and is not a forgetful hearer but a doer of the work, this one will be blessed in what he does. (James 1:22-25)

4. The Character I Want to Cultivate

He who is slow to anger is better than the mighty, and he who rules his spirit than he who takes a city. (Proverbs 16:32)

In my anger I will not sin; I will not let the sun go down while I am still angry, and I will not give the devil a foothold. (Ephesians 4:26-27)

5. My Relationship to Others

The foremost commandment is this: "Hear, O Israel! the LORD, our God, the LORD is one, and you shall love the LORD, your God, with all your heart and with all your soul and with all your mind and with all your strength." The second is this: "You shall love your neighbor as yourself." There is no commandment greater than these. To love God with all the heart and with all the understanding and with all the strength, and to love one's neighbor as himself are more important than all burnt offerings and sacrifices. (Mark 12:29-31, 33)

I will owe nothing to anyone except to love them, for he who loves his neighbor has fulfilled the law. For the commandments, "You shall not commit adultery," "You shall not murder," "You shall not steal," "You shall not covet," and if there is any other commandment, it is summed up in this saying: "You shall love your neighbor as yourself." Love does no harm to a neighbor; therefore, love is the fulfillment of the law. (Romans 13:8-10)

DAY 30

1. The Attributes of God

To God belong wisdom and power; counsel and understanding are His. (Job 12:13)

Hallelujah! Salvation and glory and power belong to our God because His judgments are true and righteous. (Revelation 19:1-2)

2. The Works of God

O LORD, what is man that You know him, or the son of man that You think of him? Man is like a breath; his days are like a passing shadow. (Psalm 144:3-4)

God gives strength to the weary and increases the power of the weak. Even youths grow tired and weary, and young men stumble and fall, but those who wait for the LORD will renew their strength; they will mount up with wings like eagles; they will run and not grow weary; they will walk and not be faint. (Isaiah 40:29-31)

3. My Relationship to God

Why are you downcast, O my soul? Why are you disturbed within me? Hope in God, for I will yet praise Him for the help of His presence. O my God, my soul is downcast within me; therefore, I will remember You. Why are you downcast, O my soul? Why are you disturbed within me? Hope in God, for I will yet praise Him, the help of my countenance and my God. (Psalm 42:5-6, 11)

I rejoice in my tribulations, knowing that tribulation produces perseverance, and perseverance character, and character hope. And hope does not disappoint because the love of God has been poured out into my heart through the Holy Spirit who was given to me. (Romans 5:3-5)

4. The Character I Want to Cultivate

I will be strong and courageous; I will not be afraid or discouraged, for the LORD, my God, will be with me wherever I go. (Joshua 1:9)

I will be strong and courageous, and act. I will not be afraid or discouraged, for the LORD God is with me. He will not fail me or forsake me. (1 Chronicles 28:20)

5. My Relationship to Others

A generous man will prosper, and he who waters will himself be refreshed. (Proverbs 11:25)

He who is generous will be blessed, for he shares his food with the poor. (Proverbs 22:9)

DAY 31

1. The Attributes of God

I will sing to the LORD, for He is highly exalted. The LORD is my strength and my song; He has become my salvation. He is my God, and I will praise him, my father's God; and I will exalt Him. (Exodus 15:1-2)

My Redeemer, the LORD of hosts is Your name; You are the Holy One of Israel. (Isaiah 47:4)

2. The Works of God

I must be ready, for the Son of Man will come at an hour when I do not expect Him. (Matthew 24:44; Luke 12:40)

Men will see the Son of Man coming in clouds with great power and glory. And He will send His angels and gather His elect from the four winds, from the ends of the earth to the ends of the heavens. We must take heed and be watchful, for we do not know when that time will come. (Mark 13:26-27, 33)

3. My Relationship to God

Having been justified by faith, I have peace with God through the Lord Jesus Christ, through whom I have gained access by faith into this grace in which I stand, and I rejoice in the hope of the glory of God. (Romans 5:1-2)

I am convinced that neither death nor life, nor angels nor principalities, nor things present nor things to come, nor powers, nor height nor depth, nor anything else in all creation, will be able to separate me from the love of God that is in Christ Jesus, my Lord. (Romans 8:38-39)

4. The Character I Want to Cultivate

Come, my children, listen to me; I will teach you the fear of the LORD. Who is the man who desires life and loves many days that he may see good? Keep your tongue from evil and your lips from speaking guile. Depart from evil and do good; seek peace and pursue it. The eyes of the LORD are on the righteous, and His ears are attentive to their cry. (Psalm 34:11-15)

I was once darkness, but now I am light in the Lord. I will walk as a child of light (for the fruit of the light consists in all goodness and righteousness and truth), learning what is pleasing to the Lord. (Ephesians 5:8-10)

5. My Relationship to Others

I will not defraud my neighbor or rob him. (Leviticus 19:13)

I will not mistreat my neighbor, but I will fear my God, for You are the LORD, my God. (Leviticus 25:17)

TWO

THE SECOND MONTH

DAY 1

1. The Attributes of God

God reveals deep things out of darkness and brings the shadow of death into the light. He makes nations great and destroys them; He enlarges nations and disperses them. (Job 12:22-23)

Blessed be the name of God for ever and ever, for wisdom and power belong to Him. He changes the times and the seasons; He raises up kings and deposes them. He gives wisdom to the wise and knowledge to those who have understanding. He reveals deep and hidden things; He knows what is in the darkness, and light dwells with Him. (Daniel 2:20-22)

2. The Works of God

The Son of Man did not come to be served, but to serve, and to give His life as a ransom for many. (Mark 10:45)

During His trials, some began to spit at Jesus and blindfold Him and strike Him with their fists and say to Him, "Prophesy!" And the guards received Him with slaps in the face. The soldiers put a purple robe on Him, then twisted together a crown of thorns and set it on Him. And they began to call out to Him, "Hail, king of the Jews!" Again and again they struck Him on the head with a staff and spit on Him, and bending their knees, they paid mock homage to Him. When they crucified Him, those who passed by hurled insults at Him, wagging their heads and saying, "Ha! You who are going to destroy the temple and build it in three days, save Yourself and come down from the cross!" And at the ninth hour Jesus cried out in a loud voice, "Eloi, Eloi, lama sabachthani?" which means, "My God, My God, why have You forsaken Me?" (Mark 14:65; 15:17-19, 29-30, 34)

3. My Relationship to God

Who is the man that fears the LORD? He will instruct him in the way he should choose. (Psalm 25:12)

You will instruct me and teach me in the way I should go; You will counsel me and watch over me. (Psalm 32:8)

4. The Character I Want to Cultivate

He who pursues righteousness and love finds life, righteousness, and honor. (Proverbs 21:21)

The goal of our instruction is love, which comes from a pure heart and a good conscience and a sincere faith. (1 Timothy 1:5)

5. My Relationship to Others

Houses and wealth are inherited from fathers, but a prudent wife is from the LORD. (Proverbs 19:14)

Charm is deceptive, and beauty is fleeting; but a woman who fears the LORD, she shall be praised. (Proverbs 31:30)

DAY 2

1. The Attributes of God

O LORD, God of Israel, there is no God like You in heaven above or on earth below; You keep Your covenant and mercy with Your servants who walk before You with all their heart. (1 Kings 8:23; 2 Chronicles 6:14)

I know that You are a gracious and compassionate God, slow to anger and abounding in lovingkindness; a God who relents from sending calamity. (Jonah 4:2)

2. The Works of God

Every animal of the forest is Yours, and the cattle on a thousand hills. You know every bird in the mountains, and everything that moves in the field is Yours. (Psalm 50:10-11)

The heavens are Yours; the earth also is Yours; You founded the world and all its fullness. (Psalm 89:11)

3. My Relationship to God

The joy of the Lord is my strength. (Nehemiah 8:10)

Better is one day in Your courts than a thousand elsewhere; I would rather be a doorkeeper in the house of my God than dwell in the tents of the wicked. For the LORD God is a sun and shield; the LORD will give grace and glory; no good thing does He withhold from those who walk in integrity. O LORD of hosts, blessed is the man who trusts in You! (Psalm 84:10-12)

4. The Character I Want to Cultivate

I will receive the words of wisdom and treasure her commands within me, turning my ear to wisdom and applying my heart to understanding. If I cry for discernment and lift up my voice for understanding, if I seek her as silver and search for her as for hidden treasures, then I will understand the fear of the LORD and find the knowledge of God. (Proverbs 2:1-5)

The fear of the LORD is the beginning of wisdom, and the knowledge of the Holy One is understanding. (Proverbs 9:10)

5. My Relationship to Others

I will discipline my child while there is hope and not be a willing party to his death. (Proverbs 19:18)

The rod and reproof impart wisdom, but a child left to himself brings shame to his mother. (Proverbs 29:15)

DAY 3

1. The Attributes of God

Great is the LORD, and most worthy of praise in the city of our God, His holy mountain. As is Your name, O God, so is Your praise to the ends of the earth; Your right hand is filled with righteousness. (Psalm 48:1, 10)

The Lord Jesus Christ received honor and glory from God the Father when the voice came to Him from the Majestic Glory who said, "This is My beloved Son, with whom I am well pleased." (2 Peter 1:17)

2. The Works of God

God's grace was given to us in Christ Jesus before the beginning of time and has now been revealed through the appearing of our Savior, Christ Jesus, who abolished death and brought life and immortality to light through the gospel. (2 Timothy 1:9-10)

We see Jesus, who was made a little lower than the angels, now crowned with glory and honor because He suffered death, that by the grace of God He might taste death for everyone. For it was fitting for Him, for whom are all things and through whom are all things, in bringing many sons to glory, to make the author of their salvation perfect through sufferings. (Hebrews 2:9-10)

3. My Relationship to God

I will praise You, O LORD, with all my heart; I will tell of all Your wonders. I will be glad and rejoice in You; I will sing praise to Your name, O Most High. (Psalm 9:1-2)

Rejoice in the Lord, O you righteous; praise is becoming to the upright. (Psalm 33:1)

4. The Character I Want to Cultivate

I will not be dishonest in judgment, in measurement of weight or quantity. I will be honest and just in my business affairs. (Leviticus 19:35-36)

The integrity of the upright guides them, but the unfaithful are destroyed by their duplicity. (Proverbs 11:3)

5. My Relationship to Others

I will pursue the things that lead to peace and to mutual edification. (Romans 14:19)

We should bear with one another in love and make every effort to keep the unity of the Spirit in the bond of peace. (Ephesians 4:2-3)

DAY 4

1. The Attributes of God

You are the great, the mighty, and the awesome God, who keeps His covenant of lovingkindness. (Nehemiah 9:32)

To whom can I liken You or count You equal? To whom can I compare You that You may be alike? (Isaiah 46:5)

2. The Works of God

An hour is coming and now is, when the dead will hear the voice of the Son of God, and those who hear will live. For as the Father has life in Himself, so He has granted the on to have life in Himself, and He has given Him authority to execute judgment, because He is the Son of Man. (John 5:25-27)

We will all stand before the judgment seat of God. For it is written, "As I live, says the LORD, every knee will bow before Me, and every tongue will confess to God." So then, each of us will give an account of himself to God. (Romans 14:10-12)

3. My Relationship to God

There is now no condemnation for those who are in Christ Jesus, because the law of the Spirit of life in Christ Jesus has set me free from the law of sin and death. (Romans 8:1-2)

I did not receive a spirit of slavery again to fear, but I received the Spirit of adoption by whom I cry, "Abba, Father." The Spirit Himself testifies with my spirit that I am a child of God. (Romans 8:15-16)

4. The Character I Want to Cultivate

A talebearer reveals secrets, but he who is trustworthy conceals a matter. (Proverbs 11:13)

These are the things I shall do: speak the truth to others, judge with truth and justice for peace, not plot evil against my neighbor, and not love a false oath; for all these things the LORD hates. (Zechariah 8:16-17)

5. My Relationship to Others

You have called us to go and make disciples of all nations, baptizing them in the name of the Father and of the Son and of the Holy Spirit, teaching them to observe everything You have commanded us. And surely You are with us always, even to the end of the age. (Matthew 28:19-20)

As the Father sent the Son into the world, He also has sent us into the world. And He has prayed for those who will believe in Him through our message. (John 17:18, 20)

DAY 5

1. The Attributes of God

I will give thanks to the LORD, for He is good; His love endures forever. (1 Chronicles 16:34)

Lovingkindness and truth have met together; righteousness and peace have kissed each other. Truth shall spring forth from the earth, and righteousness looks down from heaven. (Psalm 85:10-11)

2. The Works of God

Jesus fulfilled the words of the prophet Isaiah: "The Spirit of the LORD is upon Me, because He has anointed Me to preach good news to the poor. He has sent Me to proclaim freedom for the captives and recovery of sight to the blind, to set free those who are downtrodden, to proclaim the acceptable year of the LORD." (Luke 4:18-19)

The Son of Man came to seek and to save that which was lost. (Luke 19:10)

3. My Relationship to God

I will trust in the LORD with all my heart and lean not on my own understanding; in all my ways I will acknowledge Him, and He will make my paths straight. I will not be wise in my own eyes, but I will fear the LORD and depart from evil. (Proverbs 3:5-7)

"Not by might nor by power, but by My Spirit," says the LORD of hosts. (Zechariah 4:6)

4. The Character I Want to Cultivate

Before his downfall the heart of a man is haughty; but humility comes before honor. (Proverbs 18:12)

Blessed are the poor in spirit, for theirs is the kingdom of heaven. Blessed are those who mourn, for they will be comforted. Blessed are the meek, for they will inherit the earth. (Matthew 5:3-5)

5. My Relationship to Others

Peter came to Jesus and asked, "Lord, how often shall my brother sin against me and I forgive him? Up to seven times?" Jesus said to him, "I tell you, not seven times, but up to seventy times seven." (Matthew 18:21-22)

I will love my enemies, do good to them, and lend to them, expecting nothing in return. Then my reward will be great, and I will be a child of the Most High, for He is kind to the ungrateful and evil. I will be merciful, just as my Father is merciful. (Luke 6:35-36)

DAY 6

1. The Attributes of God

I will be still and know that You are God; You will be exalted among the nations; You will be exalted in the earth. (Psalm 46:10)

The God and Father of the Lord Jesus is blessed forever. (2 Corinthians 11:31)

2. The Works of God

You formed my inward parts; You wove me together in my mother's womb. I thank You because I am fearfully and wonderfully made; Your works are wonderful, and my soul knows it full well. My frame was not hidden from You when I was made in secret and skillfully wrought in the depths of the earth. Your eyes saw my embryo, and all the days ordained for me were written in Your book before one of them came to be. (Psalm 139:13-16)

Through Christ all things were made, and without Him nothing was made that has been made. In Him was life, and the life was the light of men. (John 1:3-4)

3. My Relationship to God

As for me and my household, we will serve the LORD. (Joshua 24:15)

By Your grace, I want to hear the words, "Well done, good and faithful servant; you have been faithful with a few things; I will put you in charge of many things. Enter into the joy of your lord." (Matthew 25:21)

4. The Character I Want to Cultivate

Whoever loves instruction loves knowledge, but he who hates correction is stupid. (Proverbs 12:1)

Pride breeds nothing but strife, but wisdom is found in those who take advice. (Proverbs 13:10)

5. My Relationship to Others

I will contribute to the needs of the saints and practice hospitality. (Romans 12:13)

I will not forget to do good and to share with others, for with such sacrifices God is well pleased. (Hebrews 13:16)

DAY 7

1. The Attributes of God

God is wise in heart and mighty in strength. Who has resisted Him without harm? (Job 9:4)

The eyes of the LORD are everywhere, keeping watch on the evil and the good. (Proverbs 15:3)

2. The Works of God

Christ has appeared once for all at the end of the ages to do away with sin by the sacrifice of Himself. And as it is appointed for man to die once, and after that to face judgment, so Christ was offered once to bear the sins of many, and He will appear a second time, not to bear sin, but to bring salvation to those who eagerly wait for Him. (Hebrews 9:26-28)

I have come to Mount Zion, to the heavenly Jerusalem, the city of the living God, to myriads of angels, and to the assembly and Church of the firstborn, who are enrolled in heaven. I have come to God, the Judge of all men, to the spirits of righteous men made perfect, to Jesus the mediator of a new covenant, and to the sprinkled blood that speaks better things than the blood of Abel. (Hebrews 12:22-24)

3. My Relationship to God

I want to follow Abraham's example of willingness to offer all that I have to You, holding nothing back and trusting in Your character and in Your promises. (Genesis 22:2-11)

Like Josiah, I want a tender and responsive heart so that I will humble myself before God when I hear His word. (2 Chronicles 34:27)

4. The Character I Want to Cultivate

I will not lay up for myself treasures on earth, where moth and rust destroy, and where thieves break in and steal. But I will lay up for myself treasures in heaven, where moth and rust do not destroy, and where thieves do not break in and steal. For where my treasure is, there my heart will be also. (Matthew 6:19-21; Luke 12:34)

I do not want to lay up treasure for myself without being rich toward God. (Luke 12:21)

5. My Relationship to Others

The sons of this world are more shrewd in dealing with their own kind than are the sons of light. I would be wise to use worldly wealth to make friends for myself so that when it is gone, they may welcome me into the eternal dwellings. (Luke 16:8-9)

What is my hope or joy or crown of rejoicing in the presence of the Lord Jesus at His coming? My glory and joy is the people in whose lives I have been privileged to have a ministry. (1 Thessalonians 2:19-20)

DAY 8

1. The Attributes of God

Let me fall into the hands of the LORD, for His mercies are very great, but do not let me fall into the hands of men. (1 Chronicles 21:13)

You, Lord, are good and ready to forgive and abundant in mercy to all who call upon You. (Psalm 86:5)

2. The Works of God

We should not be ignorant about those who fall asleep or grieve like the rest of men, who have no hope. For if we believe that Jesus died and rose again, even so God will bring with Him those who have fallen asleep in Jesus. According to the Lord's own word, we who are alive and remain until the coming of the Lord will not precede those who have fallen asleep. For the Lord Himself will come down from heaven with a loud command, with the voice of the archangel, and with the trumpet of God, and the dead in Christ will rise first. Then we who are alive and remain will be caught up together with them in the clouds to meet the Lord in the air. And so we will be with the Lord forever. (1 Thessalonians 4:13-17)

We are looking for the blessed hope and the glorious appearing of our great God and Savior, Christ Jesus, who gave Himself for us to redeem us from all iniquity and to purify for Himself a people for His own possession, zealous for good works. (Titus 2:13-14)

3. My Relationship to God

I would have lost heart unless I had believed that I would see the goodness of the LORD in the land of the living. I will hope in the LORD and be of good courage, and He will strengthen my heart; yes, I will hope in the LORD. (Psalm 27:13-14)

I wait for the LORD; my soul waits, and in His word I put my hope. I hope in the LORD, for with Him is unfailing love and abundant redemption. (Psalm 130:5, 7)

4. The Character I Want to Cultivate

I want to be above reproach, temperate, sensible, respectable, hospitable, able to teach, not given to drunkenness, not violent but gentle, not quarrelsome, not a lover of money, one who manages his own family well, and who keeps his children under control with proper respect. And I want a good reputation with outsiders so that I will not fall into disgrace and the snare of the devil. (1 Timothy 3:2-4, 7)

I want to be above reproach, blameless as a steward of God, not self-willed, not quick-tempered, not given to wine, not violent, not fond of dishonest gain, but hospitable, a lover of what is good, sensible, just, holy, and self-controlled. (Titus 1:6-8)

5. My Relationship to Others

The husband should fulfill his marital duty to his wife, and likewise the wife to her husband. The wife's body does not belong to her alone, but also to her husband. In the same way, the husband's body does not belong to him alone, but also to his wife. (1 Corinthians 7:3-4)

Each husband must love his own wife as he loves himself, and each wife must respect her husband. (Ephesians 5:33)

DAY 9

1. The Attributes of God

You have chosen me as Your witness and servant so that I may know and believe You and understand that You are the LORD. Before You no God was formed, nor will there be one after You. (Isaiah 43:10)

The Lord God is the Alpha and the Omega, who is, and who was, and who is to come, the Almighty. (Revelation 1:8)

2. The Works of God

Blessed be the Lord, the God of Israel, because He has visited us and has redeemed His people. He has raised up a horn of salvation for us in the house of His servant David (as He spoke by the mouth of His holy prophets of long ago), salvation from our enemies and from the hand of all who hate us — to show mercy to our fathers and to remember His holy covenant, the oath He swore to our father Abraham, to rescue us from the hand of our enemies, and to enable us to serve Him without fear in holiness and righteousness before Him all our days. (Luke 1:68-75)

The Scriptures predicted that the Christ should suffer and rise from the dead on the third day, and that repentance and forgiveness of sins should be preached in His name to all nations, beginning at Jerusalem. (Luke 24:46-47)

3. My Relationship to God

God will keep me strong to the end so that I will be blameless on the day of our Lord Jesus Christ. God is faithful, through whom I was called into fellowship with His Son Jesus Christ our Lord. (1 Corinthians 1:8-9)

Thanks be to God, who always leads us in triumph in Christ and through us spreads everywhere the fragrance of the knowledge of Him. (2 Corinthians 2:14)

4. The Character I Want to Cultivate

I will rejoice in hope, persevere in affliction, and continue steadfastly in prayer. (Romans 12:12)

I will fight the good fight of faith and lay hold of the eternal life to which I was called when I made the good confession in the presence of many witnesses. In the sight of God, who gives life to all things, and of Christ Jesus, who testified the good confession before Pontius Pilate, I want to keep this command without spot or blame until the appearing of our Lord Jesus Christ. (1 Timothy 6:12-14)

5. My Relationship to Others

Children should obey their parents in the Lord, for this is right. "Honor your father and mother" — which is the first commandment with a promise — "that it may go well with you, and that you may live long on the earth." (Ephesians 6:1-3)

Children should obey their parents in everything, for this is well-pleasing to the Lord. (Colossians 3:20)

DAY 10

1. The Attributes of God

LORD, You have been our dwelling place throughout all generations. Before the mountains were born or You brought forth the earth and the world, from everlasting to everlasting, You are God. You turn men back into dust and say, "Return, O children of men." For a thousand years in Your sight are like yesterday when it passes by or like a watch in the night. (Psalm 90:1-4)

My days are like a lengthened shadow, and I wither away like grass. But You, O LORD, will endure forever, and the remembrance of Your name to all generations. Of old You laid the foundations of the earth, and the heavens are the work of Your hands. They will perish, but You will endure; they will all wear out like a garment. Like clothing You will change them, and they will be discarded. But You are the same, and Your years will have no end. (Psalm 102:11-12, 25-27)

2. The Works of God

Christ has been raised from the dead, the firstfruits of those who have fallen asleep. For since death came through a man, the resurrection of the dead comes also through a man. For as in Adam all die, so in Christ all will be made alive. But each in his own order: Christ, the firstfruits; afterward, those who are Christ's at His coming. Then the end will come, when He delivers the kingdom to God the Father, when He has abolished all rule and all authority and power. For He must reign until He has put all his enemies under His feet. The last enemy that will be destroyed is death. (1 Corinthians 15:20-26)

We will not all sleep, but we will all be changed, in a moment, in the twinkling of an eye, at the last trumpet. For the trumpet will sound, and the dead will be raised imperishable, and we shall be changed. For this perishable must clothe itself with the imperishable, and this mortal with immortality. (1 Corinthians 15:51-53)

3. My Relationship to God

As many as received Christ, to them He gave the right to become children of God, to those who believe in His name, who were born not of blood, nor of the will of the flesh, nor of the will of man, but of God. (John 1:12-13)

Unless one is born again, he cannot see the Kingdom of God; unless one is born of water and the Spirit, he cannot enter into the Kingdom of God. That which is born of the flesh is flesh, and that which is born of the Spirit is spirit. The wind blows wherever it pleases, and we hear its sound, but we cannot tell where it comes from or where it is going. So it is with everyone born of the Spirit. (John 3:3, 5-6, 8)

4. The Character I Want to Cultivate

Who may ascend the hill of the LORD? Who may stand in His holy place? It is he who has clean hands and a pure heart; who has not lifted up his soul to an idol or sworn by what is false. (Psalm 24:3-4)

The path of the righteous is like the first gleam of dawn, shining ever brighter until the full light of day. But the way of the wicked is like darkness; they do not know what makes them stumble. (Proverbs 4:18-19)

5. My Relationship to Others

I want to speak words of encouragement to other believers. (Acts 20:2)

We should encourage one another and build each other up in Christ Jesus. (1 Thessalonians 5:11)

DAY 11

1. The Attributes of God

The Lord reigns forever; He has established His throne for judgment. He will judge the world in righteousness, and He will govern the peoples with justice. The LORD will also be a refuge for the oppressed, a stronghold in times of trouble. Those who know Your name will trust in You, for You, LORD, have never forsaken those who seek You. (Psalm 9:7-10)

The LORD is righteous in all His ways and gracious in all His works. (Psalm 145:17)

2. The Works of God

Christ died for our sins according to the Scriptures; He was buried, and He was raised on the third day according to the Scriptures. (1 Corinthians 15:3-4)

Our Lord Jesus Christ gave Himself for our sins to rescue us from the present evil age, according to the will of our God and Father, to whom be glory for ever and ever. (Galatians 1:3-5)

3. My Relationship to God

My Father knows what I need before I ask Him. (Matthew 6:8)

The Spirit helps me in my weakness, for I do not know what I ought to pray for, but the Spirit Himself intercedes for me with groans that words cannot express. And He who searches the hearts knows the mind of the Spirit, because the Spirit intercedes for the saints according to the will of God. (Romans 8:26-27)

4. The Character I Want to Cultivate

If I speak in the tongues of men and of angels but have not love, I am only a resounding gong or a clanging cymbal. And if I have the gift of prophecy and understand all mysteries and all knowledge, and if I have all faith so as to remove mountains but have not love, I am nothing. And if I give all my possessions to the poor and if I deliver my body to be burned but have not love, it profits me nothing. (1 Corinthians 13:1-3)

I want everything I do to be done in love. (1 Corinthians 16:14)

5. My Relationship to Others

Concerning the lost, Jesus said, "What man among you, if he has a hundred sheep and loses one of them, does not leave the ninety-nine in the open country and go after the one that is lost until he finds it? And when he finds it, he lays it on his shoulders, rejoicing. And when he comes into his house, (e calls his friends and neighbors together and says to them, 'Rejoice with me, for I have found my sheep which was lost!' I tell you that in the same way, there will be more joy in heaven over one sinner who repents than over ninety-nine righteous persons who need no repentance. There is joy in the presence of the angels of God over one sinner who repents." (Luke 15:4-7, 10)

From now on I will regard no one only according to the flesh. (2 Corinthians 5:16)

DAY 12

1. The Attributes of God

Your righteousness, O God, reaches to the heavens, You who have done great things. O God, who is like You? (Psalm 71:19)

You, the LORD, alone have declared what is to come from the distant past. There is no God apart from You, a righteous God and a Savior; there is none besides You. You are God, and there is no other. (Isaiah 45:21-22)

2. The Works of God

We must keep God's commandment without blemish or reproach until the appearing of our Lord Jesus Christ, which God will bring about in His own time. (1 Timothy 6:14-15)

The day of the Lord will come like a thief, in which the heavens will pass away with a roar, and the elements will be destroyed by intense heat, and the earth and its works will be laid bare. The day of God will bring about the destruction of the heavens by fire, and the elements will melt with intense heat. (2 Peter 3:10, 12)

3. My Relationship to God

Father in heaven, hallowed be Your name. Your kingdom come; Your will be done on earth as it is in heaven. (Matthew 6:9-10)

Though I have not seen Jesus, I love Him; and though I do not see Him now, but believe in Him, I rejoice with joy inexpressible and full of glory, for I am receiving the end of my faith, the salvation of my soul. (1 Peter 1:8-9)

4. The Character I Want to Cultivate

Wisdom is foremost; therefore I will get wisdom, and though it costs all I have, I will get understanding. I will esteem her, and she will exalt me; I will embrace her, and she will honor me. (Proverbs 4:7-8)

Blessed is the man who listens to wisdom, watching daily at her gates, waiting at her doorposts. For whoever finds wisdom finds life and obtains favor from the LORD. But he who sins against her injures his own soul; all who hate her love death. (Proverbs 8:34-36)

5. My Relationship to Others

You have given us a new commandment to love one another; even as You have loved us, so we must love one another. By this all men will know that we are Your disciples, if we have love for one another. (John 13:34)

This is Your commandment: that we love one another, as You have loved us. (John 15:12)

DAY 13

1. The Attributes of God

Where can I go from Your Spirit? Or where can I flee from Your presence? If I ascend to heaven, You are there; if I make my bed in Sheol, You are there. If I take the wings of the dawn, if I dwell in the furthest part of the sea, even there Your hand will lead me; Your right hand will lay hold of me. If I say, "Surely the darkness will cover me," even the night will be light around me. The darkness is not dark to You, and the night shines as the day; darkness and light are alike to You. (Psalm 139:7-12)

You know me, O LORD; You see me and test my thoughts about You. (Jeremiah 12:3)

2. The Works of God

Surely the LORD's hand is not too short to save, nor His ear too dull to hear. But our iniquities have separated us from our God; our sins have hidden His face from us, so that He will not hear. Yet the LORD saw that there was no one to intervene; so His own arm worked salvation for Him, and His righteousness sustained Him. He put on righteousness as His breastplate, and the helmet of salvation on His head; He put on the garments of vengeance and wrapped Himself in zeal as a cloak. From the west, men will fear the name of the LORD, and from the rising of the sun, they will revere His glory. For He will come like a flood that the breath of the LORD drives along. (Isaiah 59:1-2, 16-19)

You led Your people with cords of human kindness, with bands of love; You lifted the yoke from their neck and bent down to feed them. (Hosea 11:4)

3. My Relationship to God

I will sing of Your strength; yes, I will sing of Your mercy in the morning, for You have been my stronghold, my refuge in times of trouble. To You, O my Strength, I will sing praises, for God is my fortress, my loving God. (Psalm 59:16-17)

Bless the LORD, O my soul, and forget not all His benefits; who forgives all your iniquities and heals all your diseases; who redeems your life from the pit and crowns you with love and compassion; who satisfies your desires with good things, so that your youth is renewed like the eagle's. (Psalm 103:2-5)

4. The Character I Want to Cultivate

I will have accurate and honest standards in my business practices. (Deuteronomy 25:15)

He who walks in integrity walks securely, but he who perverts his way will be found out. (Proverbs 10:9)

5. My Relationship to Others

He who oppresses the poor reproaches his Maker, but whoever is kind to the needy honors Him. (Proverbs 14:31)

He who is kind to the poor lends to the LORD, and He will reward him for what he has done. (Proverbs 19:17)

DAY 14

1. The Attributes of God

The law of the LORD is perfect, restoring the soul. The testimony of the LORD is sure, making wise the simple. The precepts of the LORD are right, rejoicing the heart. The commandment of the LORD is pure, enlightening the eyes. The fear of the LORD is clean, enduring forever. The judgments of the LORD are true and altogether righteous. They are more desirable than gold, than much pure gold; they are sweeter than honey, than honey from the comb. Moreover, by them is Your servant warned; in keeping them, there is great reward. (Psalm 19:7-11)

The sum of Your words is truth, and all of Your righteous judgments are eternal. (Psalm 119:160)

2. The Works of God

The LORD, He is God. It is He who made us, and not we ourselves; we are His people and the sheep of His pasture. (Psalm 100:3)

God has made everything beautiful in its time. He has also set eternity in the hearts of men; yet they cannot fathom what God has done from beginning to end. (Ecclesiastes 3:11)

3. My Relationship to God

It is because of God that I am in Christ Jesus, who has become for me wisdom from God and righteousness and sanctification and redemption. (1 Corinthians 1:30)

God raised me up with Christ and seated me with Him in the heavenly realms in Christ Jesus, in order that in the coming ages He might show the surpassing riches of His grace in kindness toward me in Christ Jesus. (Ephesians 2:6-7)

4. The Character I Want to Cultivate

Reckless words pierce like a sword, but the tongue of the wise brings healing. (Proverbs 12:18)

Do you see a man who is hasty in his words? There is more hope for a fool than for him. (Proverbs 29:20)

5. My Relationship to Others

I will do no injustice in judgment, nor show partiality to the poor or favoritism to the great, but I will judge my neighbor fairly. (Leviticus 19:15)

In my faith in our glorious Lord Jesus Christ, I will not show partiality to some people above others. (James 2:1)

DAY 15

1. The Attributes of God

The LORD is the true God; He is the living God and the everlasting King. At His wrath, the earth trembles, and the nations cannot endure His indignation. (Jeremiah 10:10)

The Lord Jesus is the first and the last, and the Living One; He was dead, and behold He is alive forevermore and holds the keys of death and of Hades. (Revelation 1:17-18)

2. The Works of God

God's power toward us who believe is according to the working of His mighty strength, which He exerted in Christ when He raised Him from the dead and seated Him at His right hand in the heavenly realms, far above all rule and authority, power and dominion, and every title that can be given, not only in the present age but also in the one to come. (Ephesians 1:19-21)

By common confession, great is the mystery of godliness: He who was revealed in the flesh, vindicated in the Spirit, seen by angels, preached among the nations, believed on in the world, taken up in glory. (1 Timothy 3:16)

3. My Relationship to God

Peace You leave with me; Your peace You give to me. Not as the world gives, do You give to me. I will not let my heart be troubled, nor let it be fearful. (John 14:27)

It is in You, Lord Jesus, that I have peace. In this world I will have tribulation, but I will be of good cheer, because You have overcome the world. (John 16:33)

4. The Character I Want to Cultivate

I will not boast about tomorrow, for I do not know what a day may bring forth. (Proverbs 27:1)

I should not say, "Today or tomorrow I will go to this or that city, spend a year there, carry on business and make a profit." For I do not even know what my life will be tomorrow. I am a vapor that appears for a little while and then vanishes away. Instead, I ought to say, "If the Lord wills, I will live and do this or that." Otherwise, I boast in my arrogance, and all such boasting is evil. (James 4:13-16)

5. My Relationship to Others

Wives should be submissive to their own husbands, so that even if any of them disobey the word, they may be won without a word by the behavior of their wives, when they see their purity and reverence. (1 Peter 3:1-2)

Husbands should be considerate as they live with their wives and treat them with respect as the weaker vessel and as co-heirs of the grace of life. (1 Peter 3:7)

DAY 16

1. The Attributes of God

I know that You can do all things, and that no purpose of Yours can be thwarted. (Job 42:2)

From the rising of the sun to its setting, the name of the LORD is to be praised. The LORD is high above all nations; His glory, above the heavens. Who is like the LORD, our God, the One who is enthroned on high, who humbles Himself to behold the things that are in the heavens and in the earth? (Psalm 113:3-6)

2. The Works of God

In the resurrection of the dead, the body that is sown is perishable, but it is raised imperishable; it is sown in dishonor, but it is raised in glory; it is sown in weakness, but it is raised in power; it is sown a natural body, but it is raised a spiritual body. If there is a natural body, there is also a spiritual body. (1 Corinthians 15:42-44)

The first man is of the dust of the earth; the second man is from heaven. As was the earthly man, so are those who are of the earth, and as is the man from heaven, so also are those who are of heaven. And just as we have borne the image of the earthly man, so shall we bear the likeness of the heavenly man. (1 Corinthians 15:47-49)

3. My Relationship to God

He who does not take his cross and follow after You is not worthy of You. He who finds his life will lose it, and he who loses his life for Your sake will find it. (Matthew 10:38-39)

Whoever wishes to become great among others must become their servant, and whoever wishes to be first among them must be their slave. (Matthew 20:26-27; Mark 10:43-44)

4. The Character I Want to Cultivate

Your commandment is a lamp; Your teaching is a light; and Your reproofs of discipline are the way to life. (Proverbs 6:23)

All Scripture is God-breathed and is useful for teaching, for reproof, for correction, for training in righteousness, that the man of God may be thoroughly equipped for every good work. (2 Timothy 3:16-17)

5. My Relationship to Others

I will train up each child according to his way; even when he is old, he will not depart from it. (Proverbs 22:6)

Correct your son, and he will give you rest; he will bring delight to your soul. (Proverbs 29:17)

DAY 17

1. The Attributes of God

O LORD, God of heaven, You are the great and awesome God, keeping Your covenant of loyal love with those who love You and obey Your commands. (Nehemiah 1:5)

Great and marvelous are Your works, Lord God Almighty! Righteous and true are Your ways, King of the nations! Who will not fear you, O Lord, and glorify Your name? For You alone are holy. All nations will come and worship before You, for Your righteous acts have been revealed. (Revelation 15:3-4)

2. The Works of God

John was called a prophet of the Most High, for he went on before the Lord to prepare the way for Him and to give His people the knowledge of salvation through the forgiveness of their sins — because of the tender mercy of our God, with which the Sunrise from on high came from heaven to shine on those living in darkness and in the shadow of death — to guide their feet into the path of peace. (Luke 1:76-79)

Jesus is the Lamb of God who takes away the sin of the world. (John 1:29)

3. My Relationship to God

The grace of the Lord Jesus Christ and the love of God and the fellowship of the Holy Spirit are with me. (2 Corinthians 13:14)

In Christ I have obtained an inheritance, having been predestined according to the plan of Him who works all things according to the counsel of His will, that we who have trusted in Christ should be to the praise of His glory. (Ephesians 1:11-12)

4. The Character I Want to Cultivate

No one can serve two masters; for either he will hate the one and love the other, or he will be devoted to the one and despise the other. I cannot serve God and wealth. (Matthew 6:24; Luke 16:13)

I will not love the world or the things in the world. If anyone loves the world, the love of the Father is not in him. For all that is in the world — the lust of the flesh, the lust of the eyes, and the pride of life — is not of the Father but of the world. And the world and its lusts are passing away, but the one who does the will of God abides forever. (1 John 2:15-17)

5. My Relationship to Others

In Christ Jesus, God's whole building is joined together and growing into a holy temple in the Lord, in whom we also are being built together into a dwelling of God in the Spirit. (Ephesians 2:21-22)

Grace has been given to each one of us according to the measure of the gift of Christ. And He gave some to be apostles, some to be prophets, some to be evangelists, and some to be pastors and teachers, for the equipping of the saints for the work of ministry, for the building up of the body of Christ. (Ephesians 4:7, 11-12)

DAY 18

1. The Attributes of God

I will regard the LORD of hosts as holy; He shall be my fear, and He shall be my dread. (Isaiah 8:13)

The LORD is in His holy temple; let all the earth be silent before Him. (Habakkuk 2:20)

2. The Works of God

Who has measured the waters in the hollow of his hand or marked off the heavens with the breadth of his hand? Who has calculated the dust of the earth in a measure or weighed the mountains in the balance and the hills in scales? (Isaiah 40:12)

It is God the LORD who created the heavens and stretched them out, who spread out the earth and all that comes out of it, who gives breath to its people and spirit to those who walk on it. (Isaiah 42:5)

3. My Relationship to God

My soul waits in hope for the LORD; He is my help and my shield. My heart rejoices in Him, because I trust in His holy name. (Psalm 33:20-21)

Since I am a child of God, I am an heir of God and a joint heir with Christ, if indeed I share in His sufferings, in order that I may also share in His glory. For I consider that the sufferings of this present time are not worth comparing with the glory that will be revealed to me. (Romans 8:17-18)

4. The Character I Want to Cultivate

Since I belong to the day, I will be self-controlled, putting on the breastplate of faith and love, and the hope of salvation as a helmet. (1 Thessalonians 5:8)

I will prepare my mind for action and be self-controlled, setting my hope fully on the grace to be brought to me at the revelation of Jesus Christ. (1 Peter 1:13)

5. My Relationship to Others

I should walk in wisdom toward outsiders, making the most of every opportunity. My speech should always be with grace, seasoned with salt, so that I may know how to answer each person. (Colossians 4:5-6)

I will sanctify Christ as Lord in my heart, always being ready to make a defense to everyone who asks me to give the reason for the hope that is in me, but with gentleness and respect. (1 Peter 3:15)

DAY 19

1. The Attributes of God

I will ascribe to the LORD glory and strength. I will ascribe to the LORD the glory due His name and worship the Lord in the beauty of holiness. (Psalm 29:1-2)

The LORD reigns; He is clothed with majesty; the LORD is robed in majesty and is armed with strength. Indeed, the world is firmly established; it cannot be moved. Your throne is established from of old; You are from everlasting. Your testimonies stand firm; holiness adorns Your house, O LORD, forever. (Psalm 93:1-2, 5)

2. The Works of God

Jesus is the stone which was rejected by the builders, but which has become the chief cornerstone. Salvation is found in no one else, for there is no other name under heaven given to men by which we must be saved. (Acts 4:11-12)

In the past God overlooked the times of ignorance, but now He commands all people everywhere to repent. For He has set a day when He will judge the world with justice by the man He has appointed. He has given assurance of this to all men by raising Him from the dead. (Acts 17:30-31)

3. My Relationship to God

All of us have become like one who is unclean, and all our righteous acts are like filthy rags; we all shrivel up like a leaf, and our iniquities, like the wind, sweep us away. But now, O LORD, You are our Father. We are the clay; You are the potter; we are all the work of Your hand. (Isaiah 64:6, 8)

"Even now," declares the LORD, "return to Me with all your heart, with fasting and weeping and mourning." So rend your heart and not your garments. Return to the LORD, your God, for He is gracious and compassionate, slow to anger and abounding in lovingkindness, and He relents from sending calamity. (Joel 2:12-13)

4. The Character I Want to Cultivate

Thanks be to God, who gives us the victory through our Lord Jesus Christ. Therefore I will be steadfast, immovable, abounding in the work of the Lord, knowing that my labor in the Lord is not in vain. (1 Corinthians 15:57-58)

May our Lord Jesus Christ Himself and God our Father, who has loved us and has given us eternal consolation and good hope by grace, comfort our hearts and strengthen us in every good work and word. (2 Thessalonians 2:16-17)

5. My Relationship to Others

In obedience to the truth, I will purify my soul for a sincere love of the brethren, and I will love others fervently from the heart. (1 Peter 1:22)

This is the message we heard from the beginning, that we should love one another. We know that we have passed out of death into life, because we love the brethren. The one who does not love abides in death. By this we know love, that Christ laid down His life for us, and we ought to lay down our lives for the brethren. (1 John 3:11, 14, 16)

DAY 20

1. The Attributes of God

Once God has spoken; twice I have heard this: that power belongs to God, and that You, O Lord, are loving. For You reward each person according to what he has done. (Psalm 62:11-12)

The LORD is our judge; the LORD is our lawgiver; the LORD is our king; it is He who will save us. (Isaiah 33:22)

2. The Works of God

The Holy City, new Jerusalem, will come down out of heaven from God, prepared as a bride adorned for her husband. A loud voice from the throne will say, "Behold, the tabernacle of God is with men, and He will dwell with them, and they will be His people, and God Himself will be with them and be their God, and He will wipe every tear from their eyes. There will be no more death or mourning or crying or pain, for the first things have passed away." He who is seated on the throne will say, "Behold, I make all things new." (Revelation 21:2-5)

The Lord Jesus is coming quickly. His reward is with Him, and He will give to everyone according to what he has done. He is the Alpha and the Omega, the First and the Last, the Beginning and the End. Yes, He is coming quickly. Amen. Come, Lord Jesus. (Revelation 22:12-13, 20)

3. My Relationship to God

No temptation has overtaken me except what is common to man. And God is faithful, who will not let me be tempted beyond what I am able but with the temptation will also provide a way out, so that I may be able to endure it. (1 Corinthians 10:13)

The Lord is faithful, who will strengthen me and protect me from the evil one. (2 Thessalonians 3:3)

4. The Character I Want to Cultivate

Direct my footsteps according to Your word, and let no iniquity have dominion over me. (Psalm 119:133)

The hour has come for me to wake up from sleep, for my salvation is nearer now than when I first believed. The night is nearly over; the day is almost here. Therefore, I will cast off the works of darkness and put on the armor of light. (Romans 13:11-12)

5. My Relationship to Others

I will remember those in prison as though bound with them, and those who are mistreated, since I myself am also in the body. (Hebrews 13:3)

This is pure and undefiled religion before our God and Father: to visit orphans and widows in their affliction, and to keep oneself unspotted from the world. (James 1:27)

DAY 21

1. The Attributes of God

In the beginning was the Word, and the Word was with God, and the Word was God. He was in the beginning with God. (John 1:1-2)

The Word became flesh and dwelt among us. We have seen His glory, the glory of the only begotten of the Father, full of grace and truth. (John 1:14)

2. The Works of God

God will impute righteousness to us who believe in Him who raised Jesus our Lord from the dead, who was delivered over to death because of our sins and was raised because of our justification. (Romans 4:24-25)

If the many died by the trespass of the one man, how much more did the grace of God and the gift that came by the grace of the one man, Jesus Christ, abound to the many. And the gift of God is not like the result of the one man's sin, for the judgment followed one sin and brought condemnation, but the gift followed many trespasses and brought justification. (Romans 5:15-16)

3. My Relationship to God

As the deer pants for the water brooks, so my soul pants for You, O God. My soul thirsts for God, for the living God. When shall I come and appear before God? (Psalm 42:1-2)

O God, You are my God; earnestly I seek You; my soul thirsts for You; my body longs for You, in a dry and weary land where there is no water. (Psalm 63:1)

4. The Character I Want to Cultivate
I want to abound in faith, in speech, in knowledge, in all diligence, in love, and in the grace of giving. (2 Corinthians 8:7)

I want to abound in love and faith toward the Lord Jesus and to all the saints. (Philemon 5)

5. My Relationship to Others
I will trust in You enough to honor You as holy in the sight of others. (Numbers 20:12)

As iron sharpens iron, so one man sharpens another. (Proverbs 27:17)

DAY 22

1. The Attributes of God
All Your works will praise you, O LORD, and Your saints will bless You. They will speak of the glory of Your kingdom and talk of Your power, so that all men may know of Your mighty acts and the glorious majesty of Your kingdom. Your kingdom is an everlasting kingdom, and Your dominion endures through all generations. The LORD is righteous in all His ways and gracious in all His works. (Psalm 145:10-13, 17)

In Your majesty, You dwell in the likeness of a throne of sapphire, above the expanse that is over the cherubim. (Ezekiel 10:1)

2. The Works of God
The LORD by wisdom founded the earth; by understanding He established the heavens; by His knowledge the deeps were divided, and the clouds drop down the dew. (Proverbs 3:19-20)

You made the earth and created man upon it. Your own hands stretched out the heavens, and You ordered their starry hosts. (Isaiah 45:12)

3. My Relationship to God
We should not get drunk on wine, for that is dissipation. Instead, we should be filled with the Spirit, speaking to one another with psalms, hymns, and spiritual songs, singing and making music in our hearts to the Lord, always giving thanks to God the Father for everything in the name of our Lord Jesus Christ. (Ephesians 5:18-20)

I will rejoice always, pray without ceasing, and give thanks in all circumstances, for this is God's will for us in Christ Jesus. (1 Thessalonians 5:16-18)

4. The Character I Want to Cultivate

Blessed is the man who finds wisdom and the man who gains understanding, for its profit is greater than that of silver, and its gain than fine gold. She is more precious than jewels, and nothing I desire can compare with her. Long life is in her right hand; in her left hand are riches and honor. Her ways are pleasant ways, and all her paths are peace. She is a tree of life to those who embrace her, and happy are those who hold her fast. (Proverbs 3:13-18)

He who gets wisdom loves his own soul; he who keeps understanding will find good. (Proverbs 19:8)

5. My Relationship to Others

We must all attain to unity of the faith and of the knowledge of the Son of God to a mature man, to the measure of the stature of the fullness of Christ, so that we will no longer be infants, blown and carried around by every wind of doctrine, by the cunning and craftiness of men in their deceitful scheming; but speaking the truth in love, we must grow up in all things into Him who is the Head, that is, Christ. (Ephesians 4:13-15)

We must not forsake our meeting together, as some are in the habit of doing, but encourage one another, and all the more as we see the day approaching. (Hebrews 10:25)

DAY 23

1. The Attributes of God

You, O Lord, are a compassionate and gracious God, slow to anger, and abounding in lovingkindness and truth. (Psalm 86:15)

Great are the works of the LORD; they are pondered by all who delight in them. Splendid and majestic is His work, and His righteousness endures forever. He has caused His wonderful acts to be remembered; the LORD is gracious and compassionate. (Psalm 111:2-4)

2. The Works of God

My attitude should be the same as that of Christ Jesus, who, being in the form of God, did not consider equality with God something to be grasped, but emptied Himself, taking the form of a servant, being made in the likeness of men. And being found in appearance as a man, He humbled Himself and became obedient to death, even death on a cross. (Philippians 2:5-8)

Christ had to be made like His brothers in every way, in order that He might become a merciful and faithful high priest in things pertaining to God, to make propitiation for the sins of the people. Because He Himself suffered when He was tempted, He is able to help those who are being tempted. (Hebrews 2:17-18)

3. My Relationship to God

All of us who were baptized into Christ Jesus were baptized into His death. I was, therefore, buried with Him through baptism into death in order that, just as Christ was raised from the dead through the glory of the Father, so I too may walk in newness of life. (Romans 6:3-4)

If anyone is in Christ, he is a new creation; the old things passed away; behold, they have become new. (2 Corinthians 5:17)

4. The Character I Want to Cultivate

I will let the fear of the LORD be upon me, and I will be careful in what I do, for with the LORD, my God, there is no injustice or partiality or bribery. (2 Chronicles 19:7)

He who is faithful with very little is also faithful with much, and whoever is dishonest with very little will also be dishonest with much. If one is not faithful in handling worldly wealth, who will trust him with true riches? And if one is not faithful with someone else's property, who will give him property of his own? (Luke 16:10-12)

5. My Relationship to Others

We are the fragrance of Christ to God among those who are being saved and among those who are perishing; to the one an aroma from death to death; to the other, an aroma from life to life. And who is sufficient for these things? (2 Corinthians 2:15-16)

I pray that the sharing of my faith may become effective through the knowledge of every good thing which is in me for Christ. (Philemon 6)

DAY 24

1. The Attributes of God

Jesus is Your beloved Son in whom You are well pleased. (Matthew 3:17; Mark 1:11; Luke 3:22)

No one has ever seen God, but the only begotten God, who is in the bosom of the Father, has made Him known. (John 1:18)

2. The Works of God

God highly exalted Christ Jesus and gave Him the name that is above every name, that at the name of Jesus every knee should bow, in heaven and on earth and under the earth, and every tongue should confess that Jesus Christ is Lord, to the glory of God the Father. (Philippians 2:9-11)

Jesus Christ is coming with the clouds, and every eye will see Him, even those who pierced Him; and all the peoples of the earth will mourn because of Him. Even so, Amen. (Revelation 1:7)

3. My Relationship to God

You are the light of the world. He who follows You will not walk in the darkness but will have the light of life. (John 8:12)

You are the true vine, and Your Father is the vinedresser. He cuts off every branch in You that bears no fruit, while every branch that does bear fruit He prunes that it may bear more fruit. I will abide in You, and You will abide in me. As the branch cannot bear fruit of itself, unless it abides in the vine, neither can I, unless I abide in You. (John 15:1-2, 4)

4. The Character I Want to Cultivate

A simple man believes everything, but a prudent man considers his steps. (Proverbs 14:15)

A prudent man sees evil and hides himself, but the simple keep going and suffer for it. (Proverbs 22:3; 27:12)

5. My Relationship to Others

I will bless those who persecute me; I will bless and not curse. (Romans 12:14)

I will bear with others and forgive whatever complaints I have against them; I will forgive just as the Lord forgave me. (Colossians 3:13)

DAY 25

1. The Attributes of God

Who has directed the Spirit of the LORD or instructed Him as His counselor? Whom did the Lord consult to enlighten Him, and who taught Him the path of justice? Who taught Him knowledge or showed Him the way of understanding? Surely the nations are like a drop in a bucket and are regarded as dust on the scales; He weighs the islands as though they were fine dust. Before Him all the nations are as nothing; they are regarded by Him as less than nothing and worthless. To whom, then, will I compare God? Or what likeness will I compare with Him? (Isaiah 40:13-15, 17-18)

You are the LORD, the God of all mankind. Nothing is too difficult for You. (Jeremiah 32:27)

2. The Works of God

Through Jesus the forgiveness of sins is proclaimed, 4hat through Him everyone who believes is justified from all things from which they could not be justified by the law of Moses. (Acts 13:38-39)

What the law was powerless to do in that it was weakened through the flesh, God did by sending His own Son in the likeness of sinful flesh, on account of sin; He condemned sin in the flesh, in order that the requirement of the law might be fully met in us, who do not walk according to the flesh, but according to the Spirit. (Romans 8:3-4)

3. My Relationship to God

Christ must increase; I must decrease. (John 3:30)

Unless a grain of wheat falls to the ground and dies, it remains alone. But if it dies, it bears much fruit. The one who loves his life will lose it, and the one who hates his life in this world will keep it for eternal life. (John 12:24-25)

4. The Character I Want to Cultivate

Should I seek great things for myself? I will seek them not. (Jeremiah 45:5)

Whoever exalts himself will be humbled, and whoever humbles himself will be exalted. (Matthew 23:12; Luke 14:11; 18:14)

5. My Relationship to Others

I will submit myself to the governing authorities. For there is no authority except from God, and the authorities that exist have been established by God. Consequently, he who resists authority has opposed the ordinance of God, and those who do so will bring judgment on themselves. (Romans 13:1-2)

I will submit myself for the Lord's sake to every human authority, whether to a king as being supreme, or to governors as sent by him to punish evildoers and to praise those who do right; for it is the will of God that by doing good I may silence the ignorance of foolish men. (1 Peter 2:13-15)

DAY 26

1. The Attributes of God

Be exalted, O God, above the heavens; let Your glory be over all the earth. For Your mercy reaches to the heavens, and Your faithfulness reaches to the skies. (Psalm 57:5, 10)

Your word is settled in heaven forever, O LORD. Your faithfulness continues through all generations; You established the earth, and it stands. They continue to this day according to Your ordinances, for all things serve You. (Psalm 119:89-91)

2. The Works of God

The Lord who created the heavens, He is God. He fashioned and made the earth and established it; He did not create it to be empty but formed it to be inhabited. He is the LORD, and there is no other. (Isaiah 45:18)

God made the earth by His power; He established the world by His wisdom and stretched out the heavens by His understanding. (Jeremiah 10:12; 51:15)

3. My Relationship to God

By this is Your Father glorified, that I bear much fruit, showing myself to be Your disciple. (John 15:8)

Just as I presented the members of my body as slaves to impurity and to ever-increasing lawlessness, so I now present my members as slaves to righteousness, leading to holiness. (Romans 6:19)

4. The Character I Want to Cultivate

The way of a fool is right in his own eyes, but a wise man listens to counsel. (Proverbs 12:15)

I will listen to counsel and accept instruction, that I may be wise in my latter days. (Proverbs 19:20)

5. My Relationship to Others

We should always thank God for other believers, mentioning them in our prayers. (1 Thessalonians 1:2)

We should ask for one another's prayers. (1 Thessalonians 5:25)

DAY 27

1. The Attributes of God

O Sovereign Lord, You are God! Your words are true, and You have promised good things to Your servant. (2 Samuel 7:28)

The Lord is the Spirit, and where the Spirit of the Lord is, there is freedom. (2 Corinthians 3:17)

2. The Works of God

When You promised to make a new covenant with the house of Israel, You said, "I will put My law within them and write it on their hearts. I will be their God, and they will be My people. No longer will each one teach his neighbor, or each one his brother, saying, 'Know the LORD,' because they shall all know Me, from the least of them to the greatest of them. For I will forgive their iniquity and will remember their sins no more." (Jeremiah 31:33-34)

Jesus took bread, gave thanks, and broke it, and gave it to His disciples, saying, "Take and eat; this is My body." Then He took the cup, gave thanks, and offered it to them, saying, "Drink from it, all of you. This is My blood of the new covenant, which is poured out for many for the forgiveness of sins." (Matthew 26:26-28)

3. My Relationship to God

Having the firstfruits of the Spirit, I groan inwardly as I wait eagerly for my adoption, the redemption of my body. For in hope I have been saved, but hope that is seen is not hope; for who hopes for what he sees? But if I hope for what I do not yet see, I eagerly wait for it with perseverance. (Romans 8:23-25)

The God of hope will fill me with all joy and peace as I trust in Him, so that I may overflow with hope by the power of the Holy Spirit. (Romans 15:13)

4. The Character I Want to Cultivate

I will not worry about my life, what I will eat or what I will drink; or about my body, what I will wear. Life is more than food, and the body more than clothes. The birds of the air do not sow or reap or gather into barns, and yet my heavenly Father feeds them. Am I not much more valuable than they? Who by worrying can add a single hour to his life? And why do I worry about clothes? I will consider how the lilies of the field grow; they neither labor nor spin, yet not even Solomon in all his splendor was dressed like one of these. But if God so clothes the grass of the field, which is here today and tomorrow is thrown into the fire, will

He not much more clothe me? So I will not worry, saying, "What shall I eat?" or "What shall I drink?" or "What shall I wear?" For the pagans run after all these things, and my heavenly Father knows that I need them. But I will seek first His kingdom and His righteousness, and all these things will be added to me. (Matthew 6:25-33; Luke 12:22-31)

I will keep my life free from the love of money and be content with what I have, for You have said, "I will never leave you, nor will I forsake you." (Hebrews 13:5)

5. My Relationship to Others

I pray that words may be given to me, that I may open my mouth boldly to make known the mystery of the gospel. (Ephesians 6:19)

I pray that God may open to me a door for the word, so that I may speak the mystery of Christ and proclaim it clearly, as I ought to speak. (Colossians 4:3-4)

DAY 28

1. The Attributes of God

You are the righteous God, who searches the hearts and secret thoughts. (Psalm 7:9)

All a man's ways are right in his own eyes, but the LORD weighs the hearts. (Proverbs 21:2)

2. The Works of God

Like the roar of rushing waters and like loud peals of thunder, a great multitude will shout, "Hallelujah! For the Lord God Almighty reigns. Let us rejoice and be glad and give Him glory! For the marriage of the Lamb has come, and His bride has made herself ready." Blessed are those who are invited to the marriage supper of the Lamb. (Revelation 19:6-7, 9)

John saw heaven opened, and there before him was a white horse, whose rider is called Faithful and True; and in righteousness He judges and makes war. His eyes are like a flame of fire, and on His head are many crowns. He has a name written on Him that no one knows except Himself. He is clothed in a robe dipped in blood, and His name is the Word of God. And the armies of heaven, riding on white horses and dressed in fine linen, white and clean, were following Him. And out of His mouth goes a sharp sword with which He will strike down the nations; and He will rule them with a rod of iron. He treads the winepress of the fury of the wrath of God Almighty. And on His robe and on His thigh He has a name written: KING OF KINGS AND LORD OF LORDS. (Revelation 19:11-16)

3. My *Relationship to God*

Many, O LORD my God, are the wonders You have done, and Your thoughts toward us no one can recount to You; were I to speak and tell of them, they would be too many to declare. (Psalm 40:5)

God chose me in Christ, before the foundation of the world, to be holy and blameless in His sight. In love He predestined me to be adopted as His son through Jesus Christ, according to the good pleasure of His will, to the praise of the glory of His grace, which He bestowed upon me in the One He loves. (Ephesians 1:4-6)

4. The Character I Want to Cultivate

I want to be worthy of respect, not double-tongued, not addicted to wine, not fond of dishonest gain, but holding the mystery of the faith with a clear conscience. (1 Timothy 3:8-9)

The grace of God has appeared, bringing salvation to all men, teaching us to deny ungodliness and worldly passions, and to live sensibly, righteously, and godly in the present age. (Titus 2:11-12)

5. My Relationship to Others

Above all, I will have a fervent love for others, because love covers a multitude of sins. (1 Peter 4:8)

In this is love, not that we loved God, but that He loved us and sent His Son to be the propitiation for our sins. Since God so loved us, we also ought to love one another. No one has ever seen God; but if we love one another, God abides in us, and His love is perfected in us. (1 John 4:10-12)

DAY 29

1. The Attributes of God

The LORD is righteous; He loves righteousness; the upright will see His face. (Psalm 11:7)

Your eyes are too pure to look at evil; You cannot look on wickedness. (Habakkuk 1:13)

2. The Works of God

The Lord said, "In My Father's house are many dwellings; if it were not so, I would have told you. I am going there to prepare a place for you. And if I go and prepare a place for you, I will come again and receive you to Myself, that you also may be where I am." (John 14:2-3)

John looked and heard the voice of many angels encircling the throne and the living creatures and the elders; and their number was myriads of myriads, and thousands of thousands, saying with a loud voice, "Worthy is the Lamb, who was slain, to receive power and riches and wisdom and strength and honor and glory and blessing!" (Revelation 5:11-12)

3. My Relationship to God

God will not always strive with us, nor will He harbor His anger forever; He does not treat us as our sins deserve or repay us according to our iniquities. For as high as the heavens are above the earth, so great is His love for those who fear Him; as far as the east is from the west, so far has He removed our transgressions from us. As a father has compassion on His children, so the LORD has compassion on those who fear Him. (Psalm 103:9-13)

"Come now, let us reason together," says the LORD. "Though your sins are like scarlet, they shall be as white as snow; though they are red as crimson, they shall be like wool." (Isaiah 1:18)

4. The Character I Want to Cultivate

I will be on my guard, stand firm in the faith, act with courage, and be strong. (1 Corinthians 16:13)

I will be self-controlled in all things, endure hardship, do the work of an evangelist, and fulfill my ministry. (2 Timothy 4:5)

5. My Relationship to Others

I will obey those who are in authority over me with fear and trembling, and with sincerity of heart, as to Christ; not with external service, as a pleaser of men, but as a slave of Christ, doing the will of God from my heart. With good will I will serve as to the Lord and not to men, knowing that I will receive back from the Lord whatever good I do. (Ephesians 6:5-8)

I will treat subordinates with respect, not threatening them, knowing that both their Master and mine is in heaven, and there is no partiality with Him. (Ephesians 6:9)

DAY 30

1. The Attributes of God
I will proclaim the name of the LORD and praise the greatness of my God. (Deuteronomy 32:3)

I know that You alone, whose name is the LORD, are the Most High over all the earth. (Psalm 83:18)

2. The Works of God
The Lord GOD of hosts — He who touches the earth and it melts, and all who live in it mourn; He who builds His staircase in the heavens and founded the expanse over the earth; He who calls for the waters of the sea and pours them out over the face of the earth — the LORD is His name. (Amos 9:5-6)

God, who made the world and everything in it, since He is Lord of heaven and earth, does not dwell in temples built by hands. And He is not served by human hands, as though He needed anything, since He Himself gives all men life and breath and everything else. (Acts 17:24-25)

3. My Relationship to God
I will both lie down in peace and sleep, for You alone, O LORD, make me dwell in safety. (Psalm 4:8)

May the God of peace, who through the blood of the eternal covenant brought back from the dead our Lord Jesus, that great Shepherd of the sheep, equip me in every good thing to do His will, working in me what is pleasing in His sight, through Jesus Christ, to whom be glory forever and ever. (Hebrews 13:20-21)

4. The Character I Want to Cultivate
You have shown me what is good; and what does the LORD require of me but to act justly, and to love mercy, and to walk humbly with my God? (Micah 6:8)

I will not seek my own interests but those of Christ Jesus. (Philippians 2:21)

5. My Relationship to Others
Just as the body is one but has many members, and all the members of the body, being many, are one body, so also is Christ. (1 Corinthians 12:12)

From Christ the whole body is being joined and held together by every supporting ligament, according to the effective working of each individual part, and this causes the growth of the body for the edifying of itself in love. (Ephesians 4:16)

DAY 31

1. The Attributes of God

All men are like grass, and all their glory is like the flower of the field. The grass withers, and the flower fades, because the breath of the LORD blows on it. Surely the people are grass. The grass withers, and the flower fades, but the word of our God stands forever. (Isaiah 40:6-8)

How great are God's signs, and how mighty are His wonders! His kingdom is an eternal kingdom; His dominion endures from generation to generation. (Daniel 4:3)

2. The Works of God

He who enters by the door is the shepherd of his sheep. To him the doorkeeper opens, and the sheep listen to his voice; and he calls his own sheep by name and leads them out. When he brings out his own, he goes before them, and his sheep follow him, because they know his voice. And they will never follow a stranger, but will run away from him, because they do not recognize the voice of strangers. Jesus used this figure of speech, but His hearers did not understand what He was telling them. Therefore Jesus said again, "I tell you the truth; I am the door of the sheep. All who came before Me were thieves and robbers, but the sheep did not listen to them. I am the good Shepherd; the good Shepherd lays down His life for the sheep. I am the good Shepherd; I know My sheep and My sheep know Me — just as the Father knows Me, and I know the Father — and I lay down My life for the sheep." (John 10:2-8, 11, 14-15)

Greater love has no one than this, that he lay down his life for his friends. (John 15:13)

3. My Relationship to God

Whom have I in heaven but You? And there is nothing on earth I desire besides You. My flesh and my heart may fail, but God is the strength of my heart and my portion forever. Those who are far from You will perish; You have cut off all who are unfaithful to You. But as for me, the nearness of God is my good. I have made the Lord GOD my refuge, that I may tell of all Your works. (Psalm 73:25-28)

I will give You my heart and let my eyes delight in Your ways. (Proverbs 23:26)

4. The Character I Want to Cultivate

I will be an imitator of God as a beloved child, and I will walk in love, just as Christ loved me and gave Himself up for me as a fragrant offering and sacrifice to God. (Ephesians 5:1-2)

This is love: that I walk in obedience to God's commandments. And this is the commandment: that as I have heard from the beginning, I should walk in love. (2 John 6)

5. My Relationship to Others

Knowing the fear of the Lord, I seek to persuade men. (2 Corinthians 5:11)

All things are from God, who reconciled us to Himself through Christ and gave us the ministry of reconciliation: namely, that God was reconciling the world to Himself in Christ, not counting their trespasses against them. And He has committed to us the message of reconciliation. Therefore, we are ambassadors for Christ, as though God were appealing through us, as we implore others on Christ's behalf to be reconciled to God. (2 Corinthians 5:18-20)

THREE

THE THIRD MONTH

DAY 1

1. The Attributes of God

I will sing of the mercies of the LORD forever; with my mouth I will make Your faithfulness known through all generations. I will declare that Your lovingkindness will be built up forever, that you will establish Your faithfulness in the heavens. And the heavens will praise Your wonders, O LORD, Your faithfulness also in the assembly of the holy ones. For who in the heavens can be compared with the LORD? Who is like the LORD among the sons of the mighty? God is greatly feared in the council of the holy ones and more awesome than all who surround Him. O LORD God of hosts, who is like You, O mighty LORD? Your faithfulness also surrounds You. (Psalm 89:1-2, 5-8)

I will sing of Your lovingkindness and justice; to you, O LORD, I will sing praises. (Psalm 101:1)

2. The Works of God

Nothing is hidden that will not be revealed, and nothing is secret that will not be known and come out into the open. (Luke 8:17)

Whoever is ashamed of Jesus and His words, the Son of Man will be ashamed of him when He comes in His glory and in the glory of the Father and of the holy angels. (Luke 9:26)

3. My Relationship to God

Blessed are those who have learned to acclaim You, who walk in the light of Your presence, O LORD. They rejoice in Your name all day long, and they are exalted in Your righteousness. (Psalm 89:15-16)

Through Jesus, I will continually offer to God a sacrifice of praise, that is, the fruit of lips that give thanks to His name. (Hebrews 13:15)

4. The Character I Want to Cultivate

Wisdom is better than jewels, and all desirable things cannot be compared with her. Wisdom dwells together with prudence and finds knowledge and discretion. (Proverbs 8:11-12)

The wisdom that comes from above is first pure, then peaceable, gentle, submissive, full of mercy and good fruits, without partiality and hypocrisy. And the fruit of righteousness is sown in peace by those who make peace. (James 3:17-18)

5. My Relationship to Others

I will not judge my brother or regard him with contempt. Instead of judging him, I will resolve not to put a stumbling block or obstacle in my brother's way. (Romans 14:10, 13)

I will accept others, just as Christ accepted me to the glory of God. (Romans 15:7)

DAY 2

1. The Attributes of God

The LORD lives! Blessed be my rock! Exalted be God, the rock of my salvation! (2 Samuel 22:47)

I will trust in the LORD forever, for in Yahweh, the LORD, I have an everlasting rock. (Isaiah 26:4)

2. The Works of God

The wages of sin is death, but the gift of God is eternal life in Christ Jesus our Lord. (Romans 6:23)

Since God's children have partaken of flesh and blood, He too shared in their humanity so that by His death He might destroy him who holds the power of death, that is, the devil, and free those who, all their lives, were held in slavery by their fear of death. (Hebrews 2:14-15)

3. My Relationship to God

If I died with Christ, I believe that I will also live with Him, knowing that Christ, having been raised from the dead, cannot die again; death no longer has dominion over Him. For the death that He died, He died to sin once for all; but the life that He lives, He lives to God. In the same way, I must consider myself to be dead to sin, but alive to God in Christ Jesus. (Romans 6:8-11)

With regard to my former way of life, I am to put off my old self, which is being corrupted by its deceitful desires, and be renewed in the spirit of my mind; and I am to put on the new self, which was created according to God in righteousness and true holiness. (Ephesians 4:22-24)

4. The Character I Want to Cultivate

The fear of the LORD is to hate evil; wisdom hates pride, and arrogance, and the evil way, and the perverse mouth. (Proverbs 8:13)

I will walk properly, as in the daytime, not in revelings and drunkenness, not in promiscuity and debauchery, not in strife and jealousy. Rather, I will put on the Lord Jesus Christ and make no provision to gratify the lusts of the flesh. (Romans 13:13-14)

5. My Relationship to Others

I will not become conceited, provoking others and envying others. (Galatians 5:26)

I will do all things without complaining or arguing, so that I may become blameless and pure, a child of God without fault in the midst of a crooked and perverse generation, among whom I shine as a light in the world, holding fast the word of life. (Philippians 2:14-16)

DAY 3

1. The Attributes of God

The Almighty is beyond our reach; He is exalted in power; and in His justice and great righteousness, He does not oppress. (Job 37:23)

Great is our Lord, and mighty in power; His understanding is infinite. (Psalm 147:5)

2. The Works of God

The LORD appoints the number of the stars and calls them each by name. (Psalm 147:4)

The LORD gives the sun for light by day and decrees the moon and stars for light by night; He stirs up the sea so that its waves roar — the LORD of hosts is His name. (Jeremiah 31:35)

3. My Relationship to God

I am always of good courage and know that as long as I am at home in the body I am away from the Lord. For I live by faith, not by sight. I am of good courage and would prefer to be absent from the body and to be at home with the Lord. (2 Corinthians 5:6-8)

Faith is the reality of things hoped for and the conviction of things not seen. (Hebrews 11:1)

4. The Character I Want to Cultivate

A gentle answer turns away wrath, but a harsh word stirs up anger. The tongue of the wise uses knowledge rightly, but the mouth of the fool pours out folly. (Proverbs 15:1-2)

I will put away all of these things: anger, wrath, malice, slander, and abusive language from my mouth. (Colossians 3:8)

5. My Relationship to Others

We should bear one another's burdens and so fulfill the law of Christ. (Galatians 6:2)

We should submit to one another out of reverence for Christ. (Ephesians 5:21)

DAY 4

1. The Attributes of God

It is good to give thanks to the LORD and to sing praises to Your name, O Most High, to declare Your lovingkindness in the morning and Your faithfulness at night. (Psalm 92:1-2)

How precious are Your thoughts to me, O God! How vast is the sum of them! If I should count them, they would outnumber the grains of sand. When I awake, I am still with You. (Psalm 139:17-18)

2. The Works of God

The Son of Man went up to Jerusalem where He was delivered to the chief priests and to the scribes. They condemned Him to death and handed Him over to the Gentiles, who mocked Him, and spat upon Him, and scourged Him, and killed Him. But on the third day He rose again. (Mark 10:33-34)

After His resurrection, Jesus said to the two disciples on the road to Emmaus, "Did not the Christ have to suffer these things and then enter His glory?" And beginning with Moses and all the Prophets, He explained to them what was said in all the Scriptures concerning Himself. Later, He appeared to His disciples and said to them, "These are the words I spoke to you while I was still with you, that everything must be fulfilled that is written about Me in the law of Moses, the Prophets, and the Psalms." (Luke 24:26-27, 44)

3. My Relationship to God

I will not let sin reign in my mortal body, that I should obey its lusts. Nor will I present the members of my body to sin, as instruments of wickedness, but I will present myself to God, as one who is alive from the dead, and my members, as instruments of righteousness, to God. (Romans 6:12-13)

In view of God's mercy, I present my body as a living sacrifice, holy and pleasing to God, which is my reasonable worship. (Romans 12:1)

4. The Character I Want to Cultivate

This is the one You esteem: he who is humble and contrite of spirit, and who trembles at Your word. (Isaiah 66:2)

Who makes me different from anyone else? And what do I have that I did not receive? And if I did receive it, why should I boast as though I had not received it? (1 Corinthians 4:7)

5. My Relationship to Others

My love must be sincere. I will hate what is evil and cling to what is good. (Romans 12:9)

I will rejoice with those who rejoice and weep with those who weep. (Romans 12:15)

DAY 5

1. The Attributes of God

Jesus is the Christ, the Son of the living God. (Matthew 16:16)

Jesus is the way and the truth and the life. No one comes to the Father except through Him. (John 14:6)

2. The Works of God

The kingdom of the world has become the kingdom of our Lord and of His Christ, and He will reign for ever and ever. (Revelation 11:15)

You are the Alpha and the Omega, the Beginning and the End. To him who is thirsty You will give to drink without cost from the spring of the water of life. He who overcomes will inherit all this, and You will be his God, and he will be Your son. (Revelation 21:6-7)

3. My Relationship to God

I will incline my ear and come to You; I will hear You, that my soul may live. (Isaiah 55:3)

Everyone who hears Your words and does them is like a wise man who built his house on the rock. (Matthew 7:24)

4. The Character I Want to Cultivate

I will endure discipline, for God is treating me as a son. For what son is not disciplined by his father? If I am without discipline, of which all have become partakers, then I am an illegitimate child and not a true son. Moreover, we have all had human fathers who disciplined us, and we respected them; how much more should I be subjected to the Father of spirits and live? (Hebrews 12:7-9)

Our fathers disciplined us for a little while as they thought best; but God disciplines us for our good, that we may share in His holiness. No discipline seems pleasant at the time, but painful; later on, however, it produces the peaceable fruit of righteousness for those who have been trained by it. (Hebrews 12:10-11)

5. My Relationship to Others

I will not repay anyone evil for evil, but I will seek to do what is right in the sight of all men. (Romans 12:17)

I will not repay evil for evil to anyone, but I will pursue what is good for others. (1 Thessalonians 5:15)

DAY 6

1. The Attributes of God

The LORD is in His holy temple; the LORD is on His heavenly throne. He observes the sons of men; His eyes examine them. (Psalm 11:4)

The heart is deceitful above all things and incurably sick. Who can understand it? You, the LORD, search the heart and test the mind to reward a man according to his ways, according to the fruit of his deeds. (Jeremiah 17:9-10)

2. The Works of God

There is one body and one Spirit, just as we were called in one hope of our calling; one Lord, one faith, one baptism; one God and Father of all, who is over all and through all and in all. (Ephesians 4:4-6)

Christ is the head of the body, the Church; He is the beginning and the firstborn from among the dead, so that in everything He might have the supremacy. (Colossians 1:18)

3. My Relationship to God

Eye has not seen, ear has not heard, nor have entered the heart of man the things that God has prepared for those who love Him. (1 Corinthians 2:9)

Now I see dimly, as in a mirror, but then I shall see face to face. Now I know in part, but then I shall know fully, even as I am fully known. (1 Corinthians 13:12)

4. The Character I Want to Cultivate

I will not worry about tomorrow, for tomorrow will worry about itself. Each day has enough trouble of its own. (Matthew 6:34)

I do not want to be worried and troubled about many things; only one thing is needed. Like Mary, I want to choose the good part, which will not be taken away from me. (Luke 10:41, 42)

5. My Relationship to Others

We must encourage one another daily, as long as it is still called "Today," lest any of us be hardened by the deceitfulness of sin. (Hebrews 3:13)

We should consider how to stir up one another toward love and good works. (Hebrews 10:24)

DAY 7

1. The Attributes of God

I will give thanks to the Lord according to His righteousness, and will sing praise to the name of the LORD Most High. (Psalm 7:17)

My soul magnifies the Lord, and my spirit rejoices in God my Savior, for the Mighty One has done great things for me, and holy is His name. His mercy is on those who fear Him, from generation to generation. (Luke 1:46-47, 49-50)

2. The Works of God

Your hand laid the foundations of the earth, and Your right hand spread out the heavens; when You summon them, they all stand up together. (Isaiah 48:13)

Heaven is Your throne, and the earth is Your footstool. Your hand made all these things, and so they came into being. (Isaiah 66:1-2)

3. My Relationship to God

I believe that it is through the grace of our Lord Jesus that I am saved. (Acts 15:11)

By grace I have been saved through faith, and this is not of myself; it is the gift of God, not of works, so that no one can boast. (Ephesians 2:8-9)

4. The Character I Want to Cultivate

Your word is a lamp to my feet and a light to my path. I have inclined my heart to perform Your statutes to the very end. (Psalm 119:105, 112)

We are all sons of the light and sons of the day. We do not belong to the night or to the darkness. So then, let us not be like others, who are asleep, but let us be alert and self-controlled. (1 Thessalonians 5:5-6)

5. My Relationship to Others

I will accept him whose faith is weak, without passing judgment on his opinions. Who am I to judge another's servant? To his own master he stands or falls, and he will stand, for the Lord is able to make him stand. (Romans 14:1, 4)

Knowledge puffs up, but love builds up. (1 Corinthians 8:1)

DAY 8

1. The Attributes of God

Before Abraham was born, Jesus Christ always exists. (John 8:58)

In Christ all the fullness of the Godhead lives in bodily form. (Colossians 2:9)

2. The Works of God

The Lord said, "Destroy this temple, and I will raise it again in three days." But He was speaking of the temple of His body. After He was raised from the dead, His disciples remembered that He had said this to them, and they believed the Scripture and the words that Jesus had spoken. (John 2:19, 21-22)

Jesus said, "My Father loves Me, because I lay down My life that I may take it up again. No one takes it from Me, but I lay it down of My own accord. I have authority to lay it down and authority to take it up again. This command I received from My Father." (John 10:17-18)

3. My Relationship to God

Everyone who drinks ordinary water will be thirsty again, but whoever drinks the water You give will never thirst. Indeed, the water You give becomes in us a spring of water welling up to eternal life. (John 4:13-14)

Whoever hears the word of Jesus and believes Him who sent Him has eternal life, and will not come into judgment, but has passed over from death to life. (John 5:24)

4. The Character I Want to Cultivate

I want the Lord to establish my heart as blameless and holy before our God and Father at the coming of our Lord Jesus with all His saints. (1 Thessalonians 3:13)

I desire to be diligent to realize the full assurance of hope to the end. I do not want to become sluggish, but to imitate those who through faith and patience inherit the promises. (Hebrews 6:11-12)

5. My Relationship to Others

A righteous man guides his friends, but the way of the wicked leads them astray. (Proverbs 12:26)

I will not give cause for offense in anything, so that my ministry will not be discredited. (2 Corinthians 6:3)

DAY 9

1. The Attributes of God

To the LORD, my God, belong the heavens, even the highest heavens, the earth and everything in it. (Deuteronomy 10:14)

There is none like You, O LORD; You are great, and Your name is mighty in power. Who should not revere You, O King of the nations? It is Your rightful due. For among all the wise men of the nations and in all their kingdoms, there is no one like You. (Jeremiah 10:6-7)

2. The Works of God

There will be no temple in the new Jerusalem, because the Lord God Almighty and the Lamb are its temple. The city will not need the sun or the moon to shine on it, for the glory of God gives it light, and the Lamb is its lamp. The nations will walk by its light, and the kings of the earth will bring their splendor into it. And its gates will never be shut by day, for there will be no night there. (Revelation 21:22-25)

There will no longer be any curse. The throne of God and of the Lamb will be in the new Jerusalem, and His servants will serve Him. They will see His face, and His name will be on their foreheads. And there will be no night there; they will not need the light of a lamp or the light of the sun, for the Lord God will give them light. And they shall reign for ever and ever. (Revelation 22:3-5)

3. My Relationship to God

I lift up my eyes to the hills—where does my help come from? My help comes from the LORD, who made heaven and earth. He will not allow my foot to slip; He who watches over me will not slumber. The LORD is my keeper; the LORD is my shade at my right hand. The sun will not harm me by day, nor the moon by night. The LORD will keep me from all evil; He will preserve my soul. The LORD will watch over my coming and going from this time forth and forever. (Psalm 121:1-3, 5-8)

Even to my old age, You are the same, and even to my gray hairs, You will carry me. You have made me, and You will bear me; You will sustain me, and You will deliver me. (Isaiah 46:4)

4. The Character I Want to Cultivate

I will commit my works to the LORD, and my plans will be established. (Proverbs 16:3)

I want my conscience to testify that I have conducted myself in the world in the holiness and sincerity that are from God, not in fleshly wisdom, but in the grace of God, especially in my relations with others. (2 Corinthians 1:12)

5. My Relationship to Others

If someone is caught in a trespass, we who are spiritual should restore him in a spirit of gentleness, considering ourselves, lest we also be tempted. (Galatians 6:1)

We should let the word of Christ dwell in us richly, as we teach and admonish one another with all wisdom, and as we sing psalms, hymns, and spiritual songs with gratitude in our hearts to God. (Colossians 3:16)

DAY 10

1. The Attributes of God

Righteousness and justice are the foundation of Your throne; lovingkindness and truth go before You. (Psalm 89:14)

I will give thanks to the LORD, for He is good; His lovingkindness endures forever. I will give thanks to the LORD for His unfailing love and His wonderful acts to the children of men, for He satisfies the thirsty soul and fills the hungry soul with good things. (Psalm 107:1, 8-9)

2. The Works of God

Jesus said to Martha, "I am the resurrection and the life. He who believes in Me will live, even though he dies; and whoever lives and believes in Me will never die." (John 11:25-26)

The earnest expectation of the creation eagerly waits for the revealing of the sons of God. (Romans 8:19)

3. My Relationship to God

As the Father has loved You, You also have loved me. I must abide in Your love. If I keep Your commandments, I will abide in Your love, just as You kept Your Father's commandments and abide in His love. You have told me this so that Your joy may be in me and that my joy may be full. (John 15:9-11)

This is eternal life: that I may know You, the only true God, and Jesus Christ, whom You have sent. (John 17:3)

4. The Character I Want to Cultivate

I will keep the pattern of sound teaching that I have heard, in faith and love which are in Christ Jesus. (2 Timothy 1:13)

I will not love with words or tongue but in deed and in truth. By this I will know that I am of the truth and will assure my heart before Him; for if my heart condemns me, God is greater than my heart and knows all things. If my heart does not condemn me, I have confidence before God and receive from Him whatever I ask, because I keep His commandments and do the things that are pleasing in His sight. (1 John 3:18-22)

5. My Relationship to Others

I was called to freedom, but I will not use my freedom to indulge the flesh, but through love I will serve others. For the whole law is summed up in this word: "You shall love your neighbor as yourself." (Galatians 5:13-14)

Concerning brotherly love, we have been taught by God to love each other, and the Lord urges us to increase more and more. (1 Thessalonians 4:9-10)

DAY 11

1. The Attributes of God

Jesus proved through His works that the Father is in Him and that He is in the Father. (John 10:38)

Jesus knew that the Father had given all things into His hands, and that He had come from God and was returning to God. (John 13:3)

2. The Works of God

The LORD stretches out the heavens, lays the foundation of the earth, and forms the spirit of man within him. (Zechariah 12:1)

Since the creation of the world God's invisible attributes — His eternal power and divine nature — have been clearly seen, being understood from what has been made, so that men are without excuse. (Romans 1:20)

3. My Relationship to God

The righteous shall rejoice in the LORD and trust in Him, and all the upright in heart shall glory. (Psalm 64:10)

I will sing to the LORD as long as I live; I will sing praise to my God while I have my being. May my meditation be pleasing to Him; I will be glad in the LORD. (Psalm 104:33-34)

4. The Character I Want to Cultivate

I will guard my heart with all diligence, for out of it flow the issues of life. (Proverbs 4:23)

Whatever is true, whatever is noble, whatever is right, whatever is pure, whatever is lovely, whatever is of good report — if anything is excellent or praiseworthy — I will think about such things. The things I have learned and received and heard and seen in those who walk with Christ I will practice, and the God of peace will be with me. (Philippians 4:8-9)

5. My Relationship to Others

I will avoid foolish and ignorant disputes, knowing that they produce quarrels. The Lord's servant must not quarrel but be gentle toward all, able to teach, and patient. (2 Timothy 2:23-24)

I will not return evil for evil or insult for insult, but blessing instead, because to this I was called, that I may inherit a blessing. (1 Peter 3:9)

DAY 12

1. The Attributes of God

God fashions the hearts of all and understands all their works. (Psalm 33:15)

Death and Destruction lie open before the LORD; how much more, the hearts of men! (Proverbs 15:11)

2. The Works of God

Lord, You said, "Come to Me, all you who labor and are heavy laden, and I will give you rest. Take My yoke upon you and learn from Me, for I am gentle and humble in heart, and you will find rest for your souls. For My yoke is easy and My burden is light." (Matthew 11:28-30)

As Moses lifted up the serpent in the desert, so the Son of Man had to be lifted up, that everyone who believes in Him may have eternal life. (John 3:14-15)

3. My Relationship to God

You have asked the Father, and He has given me another Comforter to be with me forever, even the Spirit of truth, whom the world cannot receive, because it neither sees Him nor knows Him. But I know Him, for He lives in me. (John 14:16-17)

I am not in the flesh but in the Spirit, since the Spirit of God lives in me. And if anyone does not have the Spirit of Christ, he does not belong to Christ. (Romans 8:9)

4. The Character I Want to Cultivate

I will not show partiality in judgment; I will hear both small and great alike. I will not be afraid of any man, for judgment belongs to God. (Deuteronomy 1:17)

I do not want even a hint of immorality, or any impurity, or greed in my life, as is proper for a saint. Nor will I give myself to obscenity, foolish talk, or coarse joking, which are not fitting, but rather to giving of thanks. (Ephesians 5:3-4)

5. My Relationship to Others

As we have opportunity, we should do good to all people, especially to those who belong to the family of faith. (Galatians 6:10)

God is not unjust to be forgetful of our work and the love we have shown toward His name in having ministered and in continuing to minister to the saints. (Hebrews 6:10)

DAY 13

1. The Attributes of God

The LORD is upright; He is my rock, and there is no unrighteousness in Him. (Psalm 92:15)

O Lord of hosts, You judge righteously and test the heart and mind; to You I have committed my cause. (Jeremiah 11:20)

2. The Works of God

Blessed are the dead who die in the Lord from now on. They will rest from their labor, for their works will follow them. (Revelation 14:13)

There will be a new heaven and a new earth, for the first heaven and the first earth will pass away, and there will no longer be any sea. (Revelation 21:1)

3. My Relationship to God

Your grace is sufficient for me, for Your power is made perfect in weakness. Therefore, I will boast all the more gladly in my weaknesses, that the power of Christ may rest upon me. Therefore, I can be content in weaknesses, in insults, in hardships, in persecutions, in difficulties, for Christ's sake. For when I am weak, then I am strong. (2 Corinthians 12:9-10)

Since I have a great high priest who has passed through the heavens, Jesus the Son of God, I will hold firmly to the faith I confess. For I do not have a high priest who is unable to sympathize with my weaknesses, but one who has been tempted in every way, just as I am, yet without sin. Therefore I will approach the throne of grace with confidence, so that I may receive mercy and find grace to help in time of need. (Hebrews 4:14-16)

4. The Character I Want to Cultivate

Better is open rebuke than love that is concealed. (Proverbs 27:5)

Faithful are the wounds of a friend, but the kisses of an enemy are deceitful. (Proverbs 27:6)

5. My Relationship to Others

I will put away all bitterness and anger and wrath and shouting and slander along with all malice. And I will be kind and compassionate to others, forgiving them, just as God in Christ also forgave me. (Ephesians 4:31-32)

I will not slander other believers. Anyone who slanders his brother or judges his brother slanders the law and judges the law. When I judge the law, I am not a doer of the law, but a judge. There is only one Lawgiver and Judge, the One who is able to save and to destroy. Who am I to judge my neighbor? (James 4:11-12)

DAY 14

1. The Attributes of God

Jesus is in the Father, and the Father is in Him. He spoke the words of His Father and did the works of His Father who dwells in Him. He claimed to be in the Father and the Father in Him and proved it through His works. (John 14:10-11)

Jesus is my Lord and my God. (John 20:28)

2. The Works of God

God is able to do immeasurably more than all that we ask or think, according to His power that is at work within us. To Him be glory in the Church and in Christ Jesus throughout all generations, for ever and ever. (Ephesians 3:20-21)

The mystery that has been kept hidden for ages and generations is now disclosed to the saints. To them God has chosen to make known among the Gentiles the glorious riches of this mystery, which is Christ in you, the hope of glory. (Colossians 1:26-27)

3. My Relationship to God

The greatest among us should be like the youngest, and the one who rules like the one who serves. For who is greater, the one who is at the table or the one who serves? Is it not the one who is at the table? But Jesus came among us as the One who serves. (Luke 22:26-27)

If anyone serves You, he must follow You; and where You are, Your servant also will be. If anyone serves You, the Father will honor him. (John 12:26)

4. The Character I Want to Cultivate

I will not trust in myself or in my own righteousness, nor will I view others with contempt. (Luke 18:9)

I will be of the same mind with others; I will not be haughty in mind or wise in my own estimation, but I will associate with the humble. (Romans 12:16)

5. My Relationship to Others

We should love one another, for love is from God, and everyone who loves has been born of God and knows God. Whoever does not love does not know God, for God is love. (1 John 4:7-8)

We love, because God first loved us. If anyone says, "I love God," and hates his brother, he is a liar; for the one who does not love his brother whom he has seen cannot love God whom he has not seen. And we have this commandment from Him, that the one who loves God must also love his brother. (1 John 4:19-21)

DAY 15

1. The Attributes of God

The LORD of hosts has sworn, "Surely, as I have thought, so it will be, and as I have purposed, so it will stand. For the LORD of hosts has purposed, and who can annul it? His hand is stretched out, and who can turn it back?" (Isaiah 14:24, 27)

You are the LORD, and there is no Savior besides You. From ancient days You are He, and no one can deliver out of Your hand; You act, and who can reverse it? (Isaiah 43:11, 13)

2. The Works of God

God gives life to the dead and calls into being things that do not exist. (Romans 4:17)

The whole family in heaven and on earth derives its name from the God and Father of our Lord Jesus Christ. (Ephesians 3:14-15)

3. My Relationship to God

I do not lose heart; even though my outward man is perishing, yet my inner man is being renewed day by day. For this light affliction which is momentary is working for me a far more exceeding and eternal weight of glory, while I do not look at the things which are seen, but at the things which are unseen. For the things which are seen are temporary, but the things which are unseen are eternal. (2 Corinthians 4:16-18)

My citizenship is in heaven, from which I also eagerly await a Savior, the Lord Jesus Christ, who will transform my lowly body and conform it to His glorious body, according to the exertion of His ability to subject all things to Himself. (Philippians 3:20, 21)

4. The Character I Want to Cultivate

I will be anxious for nothing, but in everything by prayer and petition, with thanksgiving, I will let my requests be known to God. And the peace of God, which transcends all understanding will guard my heart and my mind in Christ Jesus. (Philippians 4:6-7)

I will let the peace of Christ rule in my heart, to which I was called as a member of one body, and I will be thankful. (Colossians 3:15)

5. My Relationship to Others

I will give to all what they are due: taxes to whom taxes are due, custom to whom custom, respect to whom respect, honor to whom honor. (Romans 13:7)

I will honor all people, love the brotherhood of believers, fear God, and honor the king. (I Peter 2:17)

DAY 16

1. The Attributes of God
I will express the memory of Your abundant goodness and joyfully sing of Your righteousness. The LORD is gracious and compassionate, slow to anger, and great in lovingkindness. The LORD is good to all, and His tender mercies are over all His works. (Psalm 145:7-9)

The Lord is not slow concerning His promise, as some count slowness, but is patient with us, not wanting anyone to perish, but for all to come to repentance. (2 Peter 3:9)

2. The Works of God
You, Lord GOD, take no pleasure in the death of the wicked, but rather that the wicked turn from their ways and live. (Ezekiel 18:23; 33:11)

Jesus said, "It is not the healthy who need a physician, but those who are sick." He did not come to call the righteous, but sinners. (Matthew 9:12-13)

3. My Relationship to God
I am confident of this, that He who began a good work in me will carry it on to completion until the day of Christ Jesus. (Philippians 1:6)

The God of all grace, who called me to His eternal glory in Christ, after I have suffered a little while, will Himself perfect, confirm, strengthen, and establish me. (1 Peter 5:10)

4. The Character I Want to Cultivate
A hot-tempered man stirs up dissension, but he who is slow to anger calms a quarrel. (Proverbs 15:18)

Everyone should be quick to hear, slow to speak, and slow to anger, for the anger of man does not produce the righteousness of God. (James 1:19-20)

5. My Relationship to Others
Fathers should not provoke their children to wrath but bring them up in the discipline and instruction of the Lord. (Ephesians 6:4)

Fathers should not provoke their children, or they will become discouraged. (Colossians 3:21)

DAY 17

1. The Attributes of God

Jesus is the Christ, the Son of God, who came into the world. (John 11:27)

Anyone who has seen Jesus has seen the Father. (John 14:9)

2. The Works of God

Jesus Christ is the faithful witness, the firstborn from the dead, and the ruler of the kings of the earth. To Him who loves us, and has freed us from our sins by His blood, and has made us to be a kingdom and priests to serve His God and Father; to Him be glory and power for ever and ever. (Revelation 1:5-6)

You are worthy to take the scroll and to open its seals, because You were slain, and with Your blood, You purchased men for God from every tribe and language and people and nation. You have made them to be a kingdom and priests to serve our God, and they will reign on the earth. (Revelation 5:9-10)

3. My Relationship to God

You are the door; whoever enters through You will be saved and will come in and go out and find pasture. The thief comes only to steal and kill and destroy; You have come that we may have life and have it abundantly. (John 10:9-10)

Your sheep hear Your voice, and You know them, and they follow You. You give them eternal life, and they shall never perish; no one can snatch them out of Your hand. The Father, who has given them to You, is greater than all; no one can snatch them out of the Father's hand. (John 10:27-28)

4. The Character I Want to Cultivate

I will fight the good fight, finish the race, and keep the faith, so that there will be laid up for me the crown of righteousness, which the Lord, the righteous Judge, will award to me on that day; and not only to me, but also to all who have longed for His appearing. (2 Timothy 4:7-8)

Since I have a great cloud of witnesses surrounding me, I want to lay aside every impediment and the sin that so easily entangles and run with endurance the race that is set before me, fixing my eyes on Jesus, the author and perfecter of my faith, who for the joy set before Him endured the cross, despising the shame, and sat down at the right hand of the throne of God. I will consider Him who endured such hostility from sinners, so that I will not grow weary and lose heart. (Hebrews 12:1-3)

5. My Relationship to Others

We should always pray for other believers, that our God may count them worthy of His calling, and may fulfill every desire for goodness and every work of faith with power. (2 Thessalonians 1:11)

We should ask that the name of our Lord Jesus may be glorified in others, and they in Him, according to the grace of our God and the Lord Jesus Christ. (2 Thessalonians 1:12)

DAY 18

1. The Attributes of God

Though the LORD is on high, yet He looks upon the lowly, but the proud He knows from afar. (Psalm 138:6)

I know, O LORD, that a man's way is not his own; it is not in a man who walks to direct his steps. (Jeremiah 10:23)

2. The Works of God

You answer us with awesome deeds of righteousness, O God of our salvation, You who are the hope of all the ends of the earth and of the farthest seas; You formed the mountains by Your strength, having armed Yourself with power; and You stilled the roaring of the seas, the roaring of their waves, and the tumult of the peoples. (Psalm 65:5-7)

Christ is the image of the invisible God, the firstborn over all creation. For by Him all things were created that are in heaven and on earth, visible and invisible, whether thrones or dominions or rulers or authorities; all things were created by Him and for Him. And He is before all things, and in Him all things hold together. (Colossians 1:15-17)

3. My Relationship to God

If God is for me, who can be against me? He who did not spare His own Son but delivered Him up for us all; how will He not also with Him freely give us all things? (Romans 8:31-32)

God's divine power has given me all things that pertain to life and godliness, through the knowledge of Him who called me by His own glory and virtue. Through these He has given me His very great and precious promises, so that through them I may be a partaker of the divine nature, having escaped the corruption that is in the world by lust. (2 Peter 1:3-4)

4. The Character I Want to Cultivate

Blessed are those who hunger and thirst for righteousness, for they shall be satisfied. (Matthew 5:6)

The Kingdom of God is not a matter of eating and drinking, but of righteousness and peace and joy in the Holy Spirit. (Romans 14:17)

5. My Relationship to Others

May the Lord make me increase and abound in my love for believers and for unbelievers. (1 Thessalonians 3:12)

The one who loves his brother abides in the light, and there is no cause for stumbling in him. But the one who hates his brother is in the darkness, and walks in the darkness, and does not know where he is going, because the darkness has blinded his eyes. (1 John 2:10-11)

DAY 19

1. The Attributes of God

I will enter the LORD's gates with thanksgiving and His courts with praise; I will give thanks to Him and bless His name. For the LORD is good, and His lovingkindness endures forever; His faithfulness continues through all generations. (Psalm 100:4-5)

Blessed be the God and Father of our Lord Jesus Christ, the Father of mercies and the God of all comfort. (2 Corinthians 1:3)

2. The Works of God

You save the humble but bring low those whose eyes are haughty. (Psalm 18:27)

The LORD guides the humble in what is right and teaches the humble His way. (Psalm 25:9)

3. My Relationship to God

I have set the LORD always before me; because He is at my right hand, I will not be shaken. Therefore my heart is glad and my glory rejoices; my body also will rest in hope. You will make known to me the path of life; in Your presence is fullness of joy; in Your right hand are pleasures forever. (Psalm 16:8-9, 11)

"The LORD is my portion," says my soul, "therefore I will wait for Him." The LORD is good to those who wait for Him, to the soul who seeks Him. It is good to hope silently for the salvation of the LORD. (Lamentations 3:24-26)

4. The Character I Want to Cultivate

The waywardness of the simple will kill them, and the complacency of fools will destroy them, but whoever listens to wisdom will live securely and be at ease from the fear of evil. (Proverbs 1:32-33)

He who trusts in his own heart is a fool, but he who walks in wisdom will be delivered. (Proverbs 28:26)

5. My Relationship to Others

An anxious heart weighs a man down, but a good word makes him glad. (Proverbs 12:25)

God comforts us in all our afflictions, so that we can comfort those in any affliction with the comfort we ourselves have received from God. (2 Corinthians 1:4)

DAY 20

1. The Attributes of God

In his heart a man plans his way, but the LORD determines his steps. (Proverbs 16:9)

Many are the plans in a man's heart, but it is the counsel of the LORD that will stand. (Proverbs 19:21)

2. The Works of God

In the past God spoke to the fathers through the prophets at many times and in various ways, but in these last days He has spoken to us by His Son whom He appointed heir of all things, and through whom He made the universe. (Hebrews 1:1-2)

By faith I understand that the universe was formed by the word of God, so that what is seen was not made out of things which are visible. (Hebrews 11:3)

3. My Relationship to God

To me, to live is Christ and to die is gain. (Philippians 1:21)

Whatever was gain to me I now consider loss for the sake of Christ. What is more, I consider all things loss compared to the surpassing greatness of knowing Christ Jesus, my Lord, for whose sake I have suffered the loss of all things and consider them rubbish, that I may gain Christ and be found in Him, not having a righteousness of my own that comes from the law, but that which is through faith in Christ — the righteousness that comes from God on the basis of faith. (Philippians 3:7-9)

4. The Character I Want to Cultivate

I will flee from sexual immorality. All other sins a man commits are outside his body, but the immoral person sins against his own body. (1 Corinthians 6:18)

I will consider the members of my earthly body as dead to immorality, impurity, passion, evil desires, and greed, which is idolatry. Because of these, the wrath of God is coming, and in them I once walked when I lived in them. (Colossians 3:5-7)

5. My Relationship to Others

If we have any encouragement from being united with Christ, if any comfort from His love, if any fellowship of the Spirit, if any affection and compassion, we should also be like-minded, having the same love, being one in spirit and one in purpose. (Philippians 2:1-2)

We should all be of one mind and be sympathetic, loving as brothers, compassionate, and humble. (1 Peter 3:8)

DAY 21

1. The Attributes of God

Your merciful love is higher than the heavens, and Your truth reaches to the skies. (Psalm 108:4)

I will give thanks to the God of heaven, for His merciful love endures forever. (Psalm 136:26)

2. The Works of God

Jesus rejoiced in the Holy Spirit and said, "I praise You, Father, Lord of heaven and earth, because You have hidden these things from the wise and learned and revealed them to little children. Yes, Father, for this was well-pleasing in Your sight. All things have been delivered to Me by My Father. No one knows the Son except the Father, and no one knows the Father except the Son and those to whom the Son chooses to reveal Him." (Matthew 11:25-27; Luke 10:21-22)

Jesus preached the gospel of the Kingdom of God and said, "The time is fulfilled, and the Kingdom of God is at hand. Repent and believe the good news." (Mark 1:14-15)

3. My Relationship to God

I believe that Jesus is the Christ, the Son of God, and by believing, I have life in His name. (John 20:31)

If I confess with my mouth the Lord Jesus and believe in my heart that God raised Him from the dead, I will be saved. For it is with my heart that I believe unto righteousness, and it is with my mouth that I confess unto salvation. As the Scripture says, "Whoever trusts in Him will not be put to shame." (Romans 10:9-11)

4. The Character I Want to Cultivate

Let him who thinks he stands take heed lest he fall. (1 Corinthians 10:12)

I do not dare to classify or compare myself with other people, for it is unwise to measure or compare myself with others. I will not boast beyond proper limits but within the sphere of the gospel of Christ. "Let him who boasts boast in the LORD." For it is not the one who commends himself who is approved, but the one whom the Lord commends. (2 Corinthians 10:12-14, 17-18)

5. My Relationship to Others

I will remind others to be subject to rulers and authorities, to be obedient, to be ready for every good work, to slander no one, to be peaceable and gentle, and to show true humility toward all men. (Titus 3:1-2)

Young men should be submissive to those who are older, and all of us should clothe ourselves with humility toward one another, for "God opposes the proud but gives grace to the humble." (1 Peter 5:5)

DAY 22

1. The Attributes of God

Ah, Lord GOD! You have made the heavens and the earth by Your great power and outstretched arm. Nothing is too difficult for You. You are the great and mighty God, whose name is the LORD of hosts. You are great in counsel and mighty in deed, and Your eyes are open to all the ways of the sons of men; You reward everyone according to his ways and according to the fruit of his deeds. (Jeremiah 32:17-19)

The word of God is living and active and sharper than any double-edged sword, piercing even to the dividing of soul and spirit, and of joints and marrow, and it judges the thoughts and attitudes of the heart. And there is no creature hidden from His sight, but everything is uncovered and laid bare before the eyes of Him to whom we must give account. (Hebrews 4:12-13)

2. The Works of God

By the word of God the heavens existed long ago, and the earth was formed out of water and by water. By these waters also the world of that time was deluged and destroyed. By the same word the present heavens and earth are reserved for fire, being kept for the day of judgment and destruction of ungodly men. (2 Peter 3:5-7)

You are worthy, our Lord and God, to receive glory and honor and power, for You created all things, and by Your will they were created and have their being. (Revelation 4:11)

3. My Relationship to God

From everyone who has been given much, much will be required; and from the one who has been entrusted with much, much more will be asked. (Luke 12:48)

As a servant of Christ and a steward of His possessions, it is required that I be found faithful. (1 Corinthians 4:1-2)

4. The Character I Want to Cultivate

I will covet no one's money or possessions. (Acts 20:33)

Godliness with contentment is great gain. For I brought nothing into the world, and I can take nothing out of it. But if I have food and clothing, with these I will be content. (1 Timothy 6:6-8)

5. My Relationship to Others

I will remember those who led me, who spoke the word of God to me. I will consider the outcome of their way of life and imitate their faith. (Hebrews 13:7)

I will obey those who lead me and submit to them, for they keep watch over my soul as those who must give an account. I will obey them so that they may do this with joy and not with grief, for this would be unprofitable for me. (Hebrews 13:17)

DAY 23

1. The Attributes of God

The LORD of hosts is wonderful in counsel and great in wisdom. (Isaiah 28:29)

In Christ are hidden all the treasures of wisdom and knowledge. (Colossians 2:2-3)

2. The Works of God

The LORD has said, "If My people who are called by My name will humble themselves and pray and seek My face and turn from their wicked ways, then I will hear from heaven and will forgive their sin and heal their land." (2 Chronicles 7.14)

Blessed is the nation whose God is the LORD, the people whom He has chosen for His inheritance. (Psalm 33:12)

3. My Relationship to God

I know that if my earthly house, or tent, is destroyed, I have a building from God, a house not made with hands, eternal in the heavens. For in this house I groan, longing to be clothed with my heavenly dwelling, because when I am clothed, I will not be found naked. For while I am in this tent, I groan, being burdened, because I do not want to be unclothed but to be clothed, so that what is mortal may be swallowed up by life. Now it is God who has made me for this very purpose and has given me the Spirit as a guarantee. (2 Corinthians 5:1-5)

I make it my ambition to please the Lord, whether I am at home in the body or away from it. For we must all appear before the judgment seat of Christ, that each one may receive what is due for the things done while in the body, whether good or bad. (2 Corinthians 5:9-10)

4. The Character I Want to Cultivate

I will watch and pray so that I will not fall into temptation; the spirit is willing, but the flesh is weak. (Matthew 26:41)

I will devote myself to prayer, being watchful in it with thanksgiving. (Colossians 4:2)

5. My Relationship to Others

I will obey those who are in authority over me in all things, not with external service as a pleaser of men, but with sincerity of heart, fearing the Lord. Whatever I do, I will work at it with all my heart, as to the Lord and not to men, knowing that I will receive the reward of the inheritance from the Lord. It is the Lord Christ I am serving. (Colossians 3:22-24)

I will provide my subordinates with what is just and fair, knowing that I also have a Master in heaven. (Colossians 4:1)

DAY 24

1. The Attributes of God

The Most High is sovereign over the kingdoms of men and gives them to whomever He wishes and sets over them the lowliest of men. I will bless the Most High and praise and honor Him who lives forever. His dominion is an eternal dominion, and His kingdom endures from generation to generation. He regards all the inhabitants of the earth as nothing and does as He pleases with the host of heaven and the inhabitants of the earth. No one can hold back His hand or say to Him: "What have You done?" I praise, exalt, and honor the King of heaven, for all His works are true, and all His ways are just, and He is able to humble those who walk in pride. (Daniel 4:17, 34-35, 37)

All authority in heaven and on earth has been given to the Son of God. (Matthew 28:18)

2. The Works of God

He who comes from above is above all; he who is from the earth belongs to the earth and speaks as one from the earth. He who comes from heaven is above all. He whom God has sent speaks the words of God, for He gives the Spirit without limit. (John 3:31, 34)

The Father judges no one but has given all judgment to the Son, that all may honor the Son just as they honor the Father. He who does not honor the Son does not honor the Father who sent Him. (John 5:22-23)

3. My Relationship to God

The grace of my Lord was poured out on me abundantly, along with the faith and love that are in Christ Jesus. (1 Timothy 1:14)

God has saved me and called me with a holy calling, not according to my works, but according to His own purpose and grace. (2 Timothy 1:9)

4. The Character I Want to Cultivate

I will consider it all joy whenever I fall into various trials, knowing that the testing of my faith produces endurance. And I will let endurance finish its work, so that I may be mature and complete, lacking nothing. (James 1:2-4)

Blessed is the man who perseveres under trial, because when he has been approved, he will receive the crown of life that God has promised to those who love Him. (James 1:12)

5. My Relationship to Others

Each of us must put off falsehood and speak truthfully to his neighbor, for we are members of one another. (Ephesians 4:25)

We ought always to thank God for other believers and pray that their faith would grow more and more and that the love each of them has toward one another would increase. (2 Thessalonians 1:3)

DAY 25

1. The Attributes of God

The LORD is good, a refuge in times of trouble; He knows those who trust in Him. (Nahum 1:7)

God is light; in Him there is no darkness at all. (1 John 1:5)

2. The Works of God

Jesus did not ask that the Father should take us out of the world, but that He protect us from the evil one. He prayed, "Father, I desire those You have given Me to be with Me where I am, that they may behold My glory, the glory You have given Me because You loved Me before the foundation of the world." (John 17:15, 24)

The Lord told the apostles, "You will receive power when the Holy Spirit comes upon you, and you will be My witnesses in Jerusalem and in all Judea and Samaria and to the ends of the earth." (Acts 1:8)

3. My Relationship to God

Since I have been justified by Christ's blood, much more shall I be saved from God's wrath through Him. For if, when I was God's enemy, I was reconciled to Him through the death of His Son, much more, having been reconciled, shall I be saved through His life. And not only this, but I also rejoice in God through my Lord Jesus Christ through whom I have now received the reconciliation. (Romans 5:9-11)

God made Him who knew no sin to be sin for me, so that in Him I might become the righteousness of God. (2 Corinthians 5:21)

4. The Character I Want to Cultivate

I do not want to justify myself in the eyes of men; God knows our hearts, and what is highly esteemed among men is detestable in the sight of God. (Luke 16:15)

I do not want to love praise from men more than praise from God. (John 12:43)

5. My Relationship to Others

"You shall love the LORD, your God, with all your heart and with all your soul and with all your mind." This is the first and great commandment. And the second is like it: "You shall love your neighbor as yourself." All the law and the prophets hang on these two commandments. (Matthew 22:37-40)

This is God's commandment: that we believe in the name of His Son, Jesus Christ, and love one another as He commanded us. (1 John 3:23)

DAY 26

1. The Attributes of God

You declare the end from the beginning and from ancient times things that have not yet been done, saying, "My purpose will stand, and I will do all My pleasure." (Isaiah 46:10)

The word that goes forth from Your mouth will not return to You empty but will accomplish what You desire and achieve the purpose for which You sent it. (Isaiah 55:11)

2. The Works of God

The law was added that the transgression might increase. But where sin increased, grace abounded all the more, so that, just as sin reigned in death, so also grace might reign through righteousness to bring eternal life through Jesus Christ our Lord. (Romans 5:20-21)

Christ is the end of the law for righteousness to everyone who believes. (Romans 10:4)

3. My Relationship to God

The love of Christ compels me, because I am convinced that One died for all, and therefore all died. And He died for all, that those who live should no longer live for themselves but for Him who died for them and was raised again. (2 Corinthians 5:14-15)

When the kindness and love of God my Savior appeared, He saved me, not by works of righteousness which I have done, but according to His mercy. He saved me through the washing of regeneration and renewal by the Holy Spirit whom He poured out on me abundantly through Jesus Christ my Savior, so that, having been justified by His grace, I might become an heir according to the hope of eternal life. (Titus 3:4-7)

4. The Character I Want to Cultivate

There is a way that seems right to a man, but its end is the way of death. (Proverbs 14:12)

I will examine all things, hold fast to the good, and abstain from every form of evil. (1 Thessalonians 5:21-22)

5. My Relationship to Others

I will be hospitable to others without grumbling. (1 Peter 4:9)

As each one has received a gift, he should use it to serve others, as a good steward of the manifold grace of God. (1 Peter 4:10)

DAY 27

1. The Attributes of God

The Son of Man will come with the clouds of heaven. In the presence of the Ancient of Days, He will be given dominion and glory and a kingdom, so that all peoples, nations, and men of every language will worship Him. His dominion is an everlasting dominion that will not pass away, and His kingdom is one that will never be destroyed. (Daniel 7:13-14)

To the only God our Savior, through Jesus Christ our Lord, be glory, majesty, dominion, and authority, before all ages and now and forever. Amen. (Jude 25)

2. The Works of God

Faith comes from hearing, and hearing by the word of Christ. (Romans 10:17)

The faith of those chosen of God and the knowledge of the truth which is according to godliness is a faith and knowledge resting in the hope of eternal life, which God, who does not lie, promised before the beginning of time. At the appointed time, He manifested His word through the preaching entrusted to the apostles by the command of God our Savior. (Titus 1:1-3)

3. My Relationship to God

God, who is rich in mercy, because of His great love with which He loved me, made me alive with Christ even when I was dead in transgressions; it is by grace I have been saved. (Ephesians 2:4-5)

Once I was alienated from God and was an enemy in my mind because of my evil works. But now He has reconciled me by His fleshly body through death to present me holy and blameless in His sight and free from reproach. (Colossians 1:21-22)

4. The Character I Want to Cultivate
I will not set my heart on evil things, or be an idolater, or commit sexual immorality. (1 Corinthians 10:6-8)

This is the will of God, my sanctification, that I abstain from immorality and learn to possess my own vessel in sanctification and honor. For God did not call me to be impure, but to live a holy life. (1 Thessalonians 4:3-4, 7)

5. My Relationship to Others
I will not strive with a man without cause, if he has done me no harm. (Proverbs 3:30)

I will not take revenge, but leave room for the wrath of God, for it is written: "Vengeance is Mine; I will repay," says the Lord. I will not be overcome by evil, but overcome evil with good. (Romans 12:19, 21)

DAY 28

1. The Attributes of God
I will give thanks to the LORD, for He is good; His lovingkindness endures forever. (Psalm 118:1)

Your testimonies, which You have commanded, are righteous and trustworthy. Your righteousness is everlasting, and Your law is truth. (Psalm 119:138, 142)

2. The Works of God
No one can lay a foundation other than the one already laid, which is Jesus Christ. (1 Corinthians 3:11)

Jesus as my high priest meets my needs: He is holy, blameless, undefiled, set apart from sinners, and exalted above the heavens. Unlike the other high priests, He does not need to offer sacrifices day after day, first for His own sins and then for the sins of the people, for He did this once for all when He offered up Himself. (Hebrews 7:26-27)

3. My Relationship to God
The Father has qualified me to share in the inheritance of the saints in the light. For He has rescued me from the dominion of darkness and brought me into the kingdom of the His beloved Son, in whom I have redemption, the forgiveness of sins. (Colossians 1:12-14)

I was not redeemed with perishable things such as silver or gold from the aimless way of life handed down to me from my forefathers, but with the precious blood of Christ, as of a lamb without blemish or defect. (1 Peter 1:18-19)

4. The Character I Want to Cultivate

I will submit myself to God and resist the devil, and he will flee from me. I will humble myself before the Lord, and He will exalt me. (James 4:7, 10)

I will humble myself under the mighty hand of God, that He may exalt me in due time, casting all my anxiety upon Him, because He cares for me. (1 Peter 5:6-7)

5. My Relationship to Others

Wives should submit to their husbands, as is fitting in the Lord. (Colossians 3:18)

Husbands should love their wives and not be bitter toward them. (Colossians 3:19)

DAY 29

1. The Attributes of God

Heaven and earth will pass away, but the words of the Lord Jesus will never pass away. (Matthew 24:35; Luke 21:33)

To the King eternal, immortal, invisible, the only God, be honor and glory forever and ever. (1 Timothy 1:17)

2. The Works of God

God was pleased to have all His fullness dwell in Christ, and through Him to reconcile all things to Himself, whether things on earth or things in heaven, having made peace through the blood of His cross. (Colossians 1:19-20)

During the days of His flesh, Jesus offered up prayers and petitions with loud cries and tears to the One who could save Him from death, and He was heard because of His devoutness. Although He was a Son, He learned obedience by the things which He suffered; and being perfected, He became the source of eternal salvation for all who obey Him, being designated by God as a high priest according to the order of Melchizedek. (Hebrews 5:7-10)

3. My Relationship to God

Those God foreknew, He also predestined to be conformed to the likeness of His Son, that He might be the firstborn among many brothers. And those He predestined, He also called; those He called, He also justified; those He justified, He also glorified. (Romans 8:29-30)

When I was dead in my trespasses and in the uncircumcision of my flesh, God made me alive with Christ. He forgave me all my trespasses, having canceled the written code, with its regulations, that was against me and was contrary to me; He took it away, nailing it to the cross. And having disarmed the powers and authorities, He made a public spectacle of them, triumphing over them by the cross. (Colossians 2:13-15)

4. The Character I Want to Cultivate

I greatly rejoice in my salvation, though now for a little while, if necessary, I have been grieved by various trials, so that the proving of my faith, being much more precious than gold that perishes, even though refined by fire, may be found to result in praise, glory, and honor at the revelation of Jesus Christ. (1 Peter 1:6-7)

I will be self-controlled and alert; my adversary the devil prowls around like a roaring lion looking for someone to devour. But I will resist him, standing firm in the faith, knowing that my brothers throughout the world are undergoing the same kind of sufferings. (1 Peter 5:8-9)

5. My Relationship to Others

I will lay up Your words in my heart and in my soul and teach them to my children, talking about them when I sit in my house and when I walk along the way and when I lie down and when I rise up. (Deuteronomy 11:18-19)

A fool despises his father's discipline, but whoever heeds correction is prudent. (Proverbs 15:5)

DAY 30

1. The Attributes of God

Before You formed me in the womb, You knew me; before I was born, You set me apart. (Jeremiah 1:5)

God numbers even the very hairs of my head. (Matthew 10:30; Luke 12:7)

2. The Works of God

Because Jesus lives forever, He has a permanent priesthood. There-fore, He is also able to save completely those who come to God through Him, since He always lives to intercede for them. (Hebrews 7:24-25)

By the will of God, I have been sanctified through the offering of the body of Jesus Christ, once for all. And every priest stands daily minister-ing and offering again and again the same sacrifices which can never take away sins. But when this Priest had offered for all time one sacrifice for sins, He sat down at the right hand of God, waiting from that time for His enemies to be made a footstool for His feet. For by one offering, He has made perfect forever those who are being sanctified. (Hebrews 10:10-14)

3. My Relationship to God

I do not want to be conformed to the pattern of this world but to be transformed by the renewing of my mind, that I may prove that the will of God is good and acceptable and perfect. (Romans 12:2)

May the God of my Lord Jesus Christ, the Father of glory, give me a spirit of wisdom and of revelation in the full knowledge of Him, and may the eyes of my heart be enlightened, in order that I may know what is the hope of His calling, what are the riches of His glorious inheritance in the saints, and what is the incomparable greatness of His power toward us who believe. (Ephesians 1:17-19)

4. The Character I Want to Cultivate

Since the day of the Lord will come like a thief—in which the heav-ens will pass away with a roar, and the elements will be destroyed by intense heat, and the earth and its works will be laid bare—what kind of person should I be in holy conduct and godliness, as I look for and hasten the coming of the day of God? But according to His promise, I am looking for new heavens and a new earth in which righteousness dwells. Therefore, since I am looking for these things, I will be diligent to be found by Him in peace, spotless and blameless. (2 Peter 3:10-14)

I will abide in Christ, so that when He appears, I may have confi-dence and not be ashamed before Him at His coming. (1 John 2:28)

5. My Relationship to Others

Better a meal of vegetables where there is love, than a fattened calf with hatred. (Proverbs 15:17)

He who covers a transgression seeks love, but he who repeats a mat-ter separates close friends. (Proverbs 17:9)

DAY 31

1. The Attributes of God

Long ago You ordained Your plan, and now You are bringing it to pass. (2 Kings 19:25; Isaiah 37:26)

With the Lord one day is like a thousand years, and a thousand years are like one day. (2 Peter 3:8)

2. The Works of God

Every good and perfect gift is from above, coming down from the Father of lights, with whom there is no variation or shifting shadow. Of His own will, He brought us forth by the word of truth, that we might be a kind of firstfruits of His creatures. (James 1:17-18)

Christ died for sins once for all, the righteous for the unrighteous, to bring me to God. Having been put to death in the body but made alive by the Spirit, He has gone into heaven and is at the right hand of God, after angels and authorities and powers were made subject to Him. (1 Peter 3:18, 22)

3. My Relationship to God

I trusted in Christ when I heard the word of truth, the gospel of my salvation. Having believed, I was sealed in Him with the Holy Spirit of promise, who is a deposit guaranteeing my inheritance until the redemption of those who are God's possession, to the praise of His glory. (Ephesians 1:13-14)

Since I have been raised with Christ, I should seek the things above, where Christ is seated at the right hand of God. I will set my mind on the things above, not on the things on the earth, for I died, and my life is now hidden with Christ in God. When Christ who is my life appears, then I also will appear with Him in glory. (Colossians 3:1-4)

4. The Character I Want to Cultivate

I will work out my salvation with fear and trembling, for it is God who works in me to will and to act according to His good purpose. (Philippians 2:12-13)

Whatever I do, whether in word or in deed, I will do all in the name of the Lord Jesus, giving thanks to God the Father through Him. (Colossians 3:17)

5. My Relationship to Others

All things are for our sakes, so that the grace that is reaching more and more people may cause thanksgiving to abound to the glory of God. (2 Corinthians 4:15)

I should offer petitions, prayers, intercessions, and thanksgivings on behalf of all men, for kings and all those who are in authority, that we may live peaceful and quiet lives in all godliness and reverence. This is good and acceptable in the sight of God our Savior who desires all men to be saved and to come to a knowledge of the truth. (1 Timothy 2:1-4)

PART TWO

TOPICAL AFFIRMATIONS GUIDE

FOUR

THE ATTRIBUTES
OF GOD

The Person of God

You are the God of Abraham, the God of Isaac, and the God of Jacob. (Exodus 3:6)

You revealed Yourself to Moses as "I AM WHO I AM." (Exodus 3:14)

You are the LORD, the God of our fathers — the God of Abraham, the God of Isaac, and the God of Jacob. This is Your name forever, the name by which You are to be remembered from generation to generation. (Exodus 3:15)

I will sing to the LORD, for He is highly exalted. The LORD is my strength and my song; He has become my salvation. He is my God, and I will praise him, my father's God, and I will exalt Him. (Exodus 15:1-2)

I acknowledge this day and take it to my heart that the LORD is God in heaven above and on the earth below; there is no other. (Deuteronomy 4:39)

I will proclaim the name of the LORD and praise the greatness of my God. (Deuteronomy 32:3)

There is no one holy like the LORD; there is no one besides You, nor is there any rock like our God. (1 Samuel 2:2)

O Sovereign Lord, You are God! Your words are true, and You have promised good things to Your servant. (2 Samuel 7:28)

The LORD lives! Blessed be my rock! Exalted be God, the rock of my salvation! (2 Samuel 22:47)

I will arise and bless the LORD, my God, who is from everlasting to everlasting. Blessed be Your glorious name, which is exalted above all blessing and praise! (Nehemiah 9:5)

God is exalted beyond our understanding; the number of His years is unsearchable. (Job 36:26)

O LORD, our Lord, how majestic is Your name in all the earth! You have set Your glory above the heavens! (Psalm 8:1)

I will be still and know that You are God; You will be exalted among the nations; You will be exalted in the earth. (Psalm 46:10)

The LORD Most High is awesome, the great King over all the earth! God is the King of all the earth, and I will sing His praise. God reigns over the nations; God is seated on His holy throne. (Psalm 47:2, 7-8)

Great is the LORD and most worthy of praise in the city of our God, His holy mountain. As is Your name, O God, so is Your praise to the ends of the earth; Your right hand is filled with righteousness. (Psalm 48:1, 10)

Your righteousness, O God, reaches to the heavens, You who have done great things. O God, who is like You? (Psalm 71:19)

I know that You alone, whose name is the LORD, are the Most High over all the earth. (Psalm 83:18)

Great is the LORD and most worthy of praise; He is to be feared above all gods. For all the gods of the nations are idols, but the LORD made the heavens. Splendor and majesty are before Him; strength and beauty are in His sanctuary. I will ascribe to the LORD glory and strength. I will ascribe to the LORD the glory due His name and worship the LORD in the beauty of holiness. (Psalm 96:4-9)

Bless the LORD, O my soul. O LORD, my God, You are very great; You are clothed with splendor and majesty. (Psalm 104:1)

Who can express the mighty acts of the Lord or fully declare His praise? (Psalm 106:2)

Blessed be the LORD, the God of Israel, from everlasting to everlasting. Praise the Lord. (Psalm 106:48)

You are my God, and I will give thanks to You; You are my God, and I will exalt You. I will give thanks to the LORD, for He is good; His loyal love endures forever. (Psalm 118:28-29)

My flesh trembles for fear of You; I stand in awe of Your judgments. (Psalm 119:120)

Your name, O LORD, endures forever, Your renown, O LORD, through all generations. (Psalm 135:13)

I will exalt You, my God and King; I will bless Your name for ever and ever. Every day I will bless You, and I will praise Your name for ever and ever. Great is the LORD and most worthy of praise; His greatness is unsearchable. (Psalm 145:1-3)

Holy, Holy, Holy is the LORD of hosts; the whole earth is full of His glory. (Isaiah 6:3)

I will regard the LORD of hosts as holy; He shall be my fear, and He shall be my dread. (Isaiah 8:13)

I will trust in the LORD forever, for in Yahweh, the LORD, I have an everlasting rock. (Isaiah 26:4)

You are the LORD, that is Your name. You will not give Your glory to another or Your praise to idols. (Isaiah 42:8)

You have chosen me as Your witness and servant, so that I may know and believe You and understand that You are the LORD. Before You no God was formed, nor will there be one after You. (Isaiah 43:10)

You are the LORD, and there is no other; apart from You there is no God. From the rising to the setting of the sun, we know there is none besides You. You are the LORD, and there is no other. (Isaiah 45:5-6)

You, the LORD, alone have declared what is to come from the distant past. There is no God apart from You, a righteous God and a Savior; there is none besides You. You are God, and there is no other. (Isaiah 45:21-22)

I will recall to mind the former things, those of long ago; You are God, and there is no other; You are God, and there is none like You. (Isaiah 46:9)

My Redeemer, the LORD of hosts is Your name; You are the Holy One of Israel. (Isaiah 47:4)

You are He; You are the first, and You are also the last. (Isaiah 48:12)

The LORD is the true God; He is the living God and the everlasting King. At His wrath, the earth trembles, and the nations cannot endure His indignation. (Jeremiah 10:10)

The LORD is in His holy temple; let all the earth be silent before Him. (Habakkuk 2:20)

You are the LORD; You do not change. (Malachi 3:6)

Jesus is Your beloved Son in whom You are well pleased. (Matthew 3:17; Mark 1:11; Luke 3:22)

Jesus is the Christ, the Son of the living God. (Matthew 16:16)

Glory to God in the highest, and on earth peace to those on whom His favor rests. (Luke 2:14)

Jesus is Your Son, whom You have chosen. (Luke 9:35)

In the beginning was the Word, and the Word was with God, and the Word was God. He was in the beginning with God. (John 1:1-2)

The Word became flesh and dwelt among us. We have seen His glory, the glory of the only begotten of the Father, full of grace and truth. (John 1:14)

No one has ever seen God, but the only begotten God, who is in the bosom of the Father, has made Him known. (John 1:18)

Jesus of Nazareth, the son of Joseph, is the Messiah (that is, the Christ). He is the One Moses wrote about in the law and about whom the prophets also wrote. (John 1:41, 45)

Jesus is the Son of God; He is the King of Israel. (John 1:49)

No one has seen the Father, except the One who is from God; only He has seen the Father. (John 6:46)

Before Abraham was born, Jesus Christ always exists. (John 8:58)

Jesus and the Father are one. (John 10:30)

Jesus proved through His works that the Father is in Him, and that He is in the Father. (John 10:38)

Jesus is the Christ, the Son of God, who came into the world. (John 11:27)

Jesus knew that the Father had given all things into His hands and that He had come from God and was returning to God. (John 13:3)

Jesus is the way and the truth and the life. No one comes to the Father except through Him. (John 14:6)

Anyone who has seen Jesus has seen the Father. (John 14:9)

Jesus is in the Father, and the Father is in Him. He spoke the words of His Father and did the works of His Father who dwells in Him. He claimed to be in the Father and the Father in Him and proved it through His works. (John 14:10-11)

Jesus is my Lord and my God. (John 20:28)

There is but one God, the Father, from whom all things came and for whom I live; and there is but one Lord, Jesus Christ, through whom all things came and through whom I live. (1 Corinthians 8:6)

The Lord is the Spirit, and where the Spirit of the Lord is, there is freedom. (2 Corinthians 3:17)

The God and Father of the Lord Jesus is blessed forever. (2 Corinthians 11:31)

In Christ all the fullness of the Godhead lives in bodily form. (Colossians 2:9)

God is the blessed and only Sovereign, the King of kings and Lord of lords, who alone has immortality and dwells in unapproachable light, whom no one has seen or can see. To Him be honor and eternal dominion. (1 Timothy 6:15-16)

The Son is the radiance of God's glory and the exact representation of His being, upholding all things by His powerful word. After He cleansed our sins, He sat down at the right hand of the Majesty on high, having become as much superior to the angels as the name He has inherited is more excellent than theirs. (Hebrews 1:3-4)

Jesus Christ is the same yesterday, today, and forever. (Hebrews 13:8)

The Lord Jesus Christ received honor and glory from God the Father when the voice came to Him from the Majestic Glory who said, "This is My beloved Son, with whom I am well pleased." (2 Peter 1:17)

The Lord God is the Alpha and the Omega, who is, and who was, and who is to come, the Almighty. (Revelation 1:8)

The Lord Jesus is the first and the last, and the Living One; He was dead, and behold, He is alive forevermore and holds the keys of death and of Hades. (Revelation 1:17-18)

Every creature, in heaven and on earth and under the earth and on the sea and all that is in them, will sing: "To Him who sits on the throne and to the Lamb be blessing and honor and glory and power for ever and ever!" (Revelation 5:13)

The Powers of God

Nothing is too difficult for the LORD. (Genesis 18:14)

The LORD shall reign for ever and ever. (Exodus 15:18)

The LORD will be gracious to whom He will be gracious, and He will have compassion on whom He will have compassion. (Exodus 33:19)

No one can see the LORD and live. (Exodus 33:20)

God is not a man, that He should lie, nor a son of man, that He should change his mind. Has He spoken and not done it? Has He promised and not fulfilled it? (Numbers 23:19)

O Lord GOD, You have shown Your servants Your greatness and Your strong hand, for what god is there in heaven or on earth who can do the works and mighty deeds You do? (Deuteronomy 3:24)

To the LORD, my God, belong the heavens, even the highest heavens, the earth and everything in it. (Deuteronomy 10:14)

You are the living God, and there is no god besides You. You put to death, and You bring to life, You have wounded, and You will heal, and no one can deliver from Your hand. (Deuteronomy 32:39)

The LORD is the God of knowledge, and by Him actions are weighed. (1 Samuel 2:3)

The LORD brings death and makes alive; He brings down to the grave and raises up. The LORD sends poverty and wealth; He humbles and He exalts. He raises the poor from the dust and lifts the needy from the ash heap, to seat them with princes and make them inherit a throne of honor. For the foundations of the earth are the LORD's, and He has set the world upon them. (1 Samuel 2:6-8)

The LORD will guard the feet of His saints, but the wicked will be silenced in darkness. It is not by strength that one prevails; those who contend with the LORD will be shattered. He will thunder against them from heaven; the LORD will judge the ends of the earth. He will give strength to His king and exalt the horn of His anointed. (1 Samuel 2:9-10)

He who is the Glory of Israel does not lie or change His mind, for He is not a man, that He should change His mind. (1 Samuel 15:29)

The LORD does not see as man sees. Man looks at the outward appearance, but the LORD looks at the heart. (1 Samuel 16:7)

Will God indeed dwell on earth? Heaven and the highest heaven cannot contain You. (1 Kings 8:27)

Long ago You ordained Your plan, and now You are bringing it to pass. (2 Kings 19:25; Isaiah 37:26)

The LORD is great and greatly to be praised; He is to be feared above all gods. For all the gods of the nations are idols, but the LORD made the heavens. Splendor and majesty are before Him; strength and joy are in His place. I will ascribe to the LORD glory and strength. I will ascribe to the LORD the glory due His name and worship the LORD in the beauty of holiness. (1 Chronicles 16:25-29)

Yours, O LORD, is the greatness and the power and the glory and the victory and the majesty, for everything in heaven and earth is Yours. Yours, O LORD, is the kingdom, and You are exalted as head over all. Both riches and honor come from You, and You are the ruler of all things. In Your hand is power and might to exalt and to give strength to all. Therefore, my God, I give You thanks and praise Your glorious name. All things come from You, and I can only give You what comes from Your hand. (1 Chronicles 29:11-14)

The heavens and the highest heavens cannot contain the LORD. (2 Chronicles 2:6; 6:18)

O LORD, the God of our fathers, are You not the God who is in heaven? Are You not the ruler over all the kingdoms of the nations? Power and might are in Your hand, and no one is able to withstand You. (2 Chronicles 20:6)

You are the great, the mighty, and the awesome God, who keeps His covenant of lovingkindness. (Nehemiah 9:32)

God is wise in heart and mighty in strength. Who has resisted Him without harm? (Job 9:4)

God alone stretches out the heavens and treads on the waves of the sea. (Job 9:8)

God reveals deep things out of darkness and brings the shadow of death into the light. He makes nations great and destroys them; He enlarges nations and disperses them. (Job 12:22-23)

God's voice thunders in marvelous ways; He does great things which we cannot comprehend. (Job 37:5)

The Almighty is beyond our reach; He is exalted in power and in His justice and great righteousness, He does not oppress. (Job 37:23)

I know that You can do all things and that no purpose of Yours can be thwarted. (Job 42:2)

You are the righteous God, who searches the hearts and secret thoughts. (Psalm 7:9)

The LORD is in His holy temple; the LORD is on His heavenly throne. He observes the sons of men; His eyes examine them. (Psalm 11:4)

I will ascribe to the LORD glory and strength. I will ascribe to the LORD the glory due His name and worship the Lord in the beauty of holiness. (Psalm 29:1-2)

The counsel of the LORD stands firm forever, the plans of His heart through all generations. (Psalm 33:11)

God fashions the hearts of all and understands all their works. (Psalm 33:15)

Your throne, O God, is forever and ever; a scepter of righteousness is the scepter of Your kingdom. (Psalm 45:6)

LORD, You have been our dwelling place throughout all generations. Before the mountains were born or You brought forth the earth and the world, from everlasting to everlasting, You are God. You turn men back into dust and say, "Return, O children of men." For a thousand years in Your sight are like yesterday when it passes by or like a watch in the night. (Psalm 90:1-4)

You have set our iniquities before You, our secret sins in the light of Your presence. (Psalm 90:8)

The LORD reigns; He is clothed with majesty; the LORD is robed in majesty and is armed with strength. Indeed, the world is firmly established; it cannot be moved. Your throne is established from of old; You are from everlasting. Your testimonies stand firm; holiness adorns Your house, O LORD, forever. (Psalm 93:1-2, 5)

My days are like a lengthened shadow, and I wither away like grass. But You, O LORD, will endure forever, and the remembrance of Your name to all generations. Of old, You laid the foundations of the earth, and the heavens are the work of Your hands. They will perish, but You will endure; they will all wear out like a garment. Like clothing, You will change them, and they will be discarded. But You are the same, and Your years will have no end. (Psalm 102:11-12, 25-27)

The LORD has established His throne in heaven, and His kingdom rules over all. (Psalm 103:19)

From the rising of the sun to its setting, the name of the LORD is to be praised. The LORD is high above all nations, His glory above the heavens. Who is like the LORD, our God, the One who is enthroned on high, who humbles Himself to behold the things that are in the heavens and in the earth? (Psalm 113:3-6)

Whatever the LORD pleases He does, in the heavens and on the earth, in the seas and all their depths. (Psalm 135:6)

Though the LORD is on high, yet He looks upon the lowly, but the proud He knows from afar. (Psalm 138:6)

O LORD, You have searched me and You know me. You know when I sit down and when I rise up; You understand my thoughts from afar. You scrutinize my path and my lying down and are acquainted with all my ways. Before a word is on my tongue, O LORD, You know it completely. (Psalm 139:1-4)

Where can I go from Your Spirit? Or where can I flee from Your presence? If I ascend to heaven, You are there; if I make my bed in Sheol, You are there. If I take the wings of the dawn, if I dwell in the furthest part of the sea, even there Your hand will lead me; Your right hand will lay hold of me. If I say, "Surely the darkness will cover me," even the night will be light around me. The darkness is not dark to You, and the night shines as the day; darkness and light are alike to You. (Psalm 139:7-12)

All Your works will praise you, O LORD, and Your saints will bless You. They will speak of the glory of Your kingdom and talk of Your power, so that all men may know of Your mighty acts and the glorious majesty of Your kingdom. Your kingdom is an everlasting kingdom, and Your dominion endures through all generations. The LORD is righteous in all His ways and gracious in all His works. (Psalm 145:10-13, 17)

Great is our Lord and mighty in power; His understanding is infinite. (Psalm 147:5)

The eyes of the LORD are everywhere, keeping watch on the evil and the good. (Proverbs 15:3)

Death and Destruction lie open before the LORD, how much more the hearts of men! (Proverbs 15:11)

In his heart a man plans his way, but the LORD determines his steps. (Proverbs 16:9)

The refining pot is for silver and the furnace for gold, but the LORD tests the hearts. (Proverbs 17:3)

Many are the plans in a man's heart, but it is the counsel of the LORD that will stand. (Proverbs 19:21)

The spirit of a man is the lamp of the LORD, searching the inward depths of his being. (Proverbs 20:27)

All a man's ways are right in his own eyes, but the LORD weighs the hearts. (Proverbs 21:2)

I know that whatever God does will remain forever; nothing can be added to it and nothing taken from it. God does it so that men will revere Him. (Ecclesiastes 3:14)

For God will bring every work into judgment, including every hidden thing, whether it is good or evil. (Ecclesiastes 12:14)

The LORD of hosts has sworn, "Surely, as I have thought, so it will be, and as I have purposed, so it will stand. For the LORD of hosts has purposed, and who can annul it? His hand is stretched out, and who can turn it back?" (Isaiah 14:24, 27)

All men are like grass, and all their glory is like the flower of the field. The grass withers and the flower fades, because the breath of the LORD blows on it. Surely the people are grass. The grass withers and the flower fades, but the word of our God stands forever. (Isaiah 40:6-8)

Who has directed the Spirit of the LORD or instructed Him as His counselor? Whom did the Lord consult to enlighten Him, and who taught Him the path of justice? Who taught Him knowledge or showed Him the way of understanding? Surely the nations are like a drop in a bucket and are regarded as dust on the scales; He weighs the islands as though they were fine dust. Before Him all the nations are as nothing; they are regarded by Him as less than nothing and worthless. To whom, then, will I compare God? Or what likeness will I compare with Him? (Isaiah 40:13-15, 17-18)

God sits enthroned above the circle of the earth, and its inhabitants are like grasshoppers. He stretches out the heavens like a curtain and spreads them out like a tent to dwell in. He reduces rulers to nothing and makes the judges of this world meaningless. (Isaiah 40:22-23)

You are the LORD, and there is no savior besides You. From ancient days You are He, and no one can deliver out of Your hand; You act, and who can reverse it? (Isaiah 43:11, 13)

You have sworn by Yourself; the word has gone out of Your mouth in righteousness and will not return. Every knee will bow before You, and every tongue will acknowledge You. (Isaiah 45:23)

To whom can I liken You or count You equal? To whom can I compare You that You may be alike? (Isaiah 46:5)

You declare the end from the beginning, and from ancient times things that have not yet been done, saying, "My purpose will stand, and I will do all My pleasure." (Isaiah 46:10)

The word that goes forth from Your mouth will not return to You empty but will accomplish what You desire and achieve the purpose for which You sent it. (Isaiah 55:11)

You are the high and lofty One who inhabits eternity, whose name is holy. You live in a high and holy place but also with him who is contrite and lowly in spirit, to revive the spirit of the lowly and to revive the heart of the contrite. (Isaiah 57:15)

Before You formed me in the womb, You knew me; before I was born, You set me apart. (Jeremiah 1:5)

There is none like You, O LORD; You are great, and Your name is mighty in power. Who should not revere You, O King of the nations? It is Your rightful due. For among all the wise men of the nations and in all their kingdoms, there is no one like You. (Jeremiah 10:6-7)

I know, O LORD, that a man's way is not his own; it is not in a man who walks to direct his steps. (Jeremiah 10:23)

You know me, O LORD; You see me and test my thoughts about You. (Jeremiah 12:3)

The heart is deceitful above all things and incurably sick. Who can understand it? You, the LORD, search the heart and test the mind to reward a man according to his ways, according to the fruit of his deeds. (Jeremiah 17:9-10)

Are You a God nearby, and not a God far away? Can anyone hide in secret places so that You cannot see him? Do You not fill heaven and earth? (Jeremiah 23:23-24)

Ah, Lord GOD! You have made the heavens and the earth by Your great power and outstretched arm. Nothing is too difficult for You. You are the great and mighty God, whose name is the LORD of hosts. You are great in counsel and mighty in deed, and Your eyes are open to all the ways of the sons of men; You reward everyone according to his ways and according to the fruit of his deeds. (Jeremiah 32:17-19)

You are the LORD, the God of all mankind. Nothing is too difficult for You. (Jeremiah 32:27)

In Your majesty, You dwell in the likeness of a throne of sapphire above the expanse that is over the cherubim. (Ezekiel 10:1)

Blessed be the name of God for ever and ever, for wisdom and power belong to Him. He changes the times and the seasons; He raises up kings and deposes them. He gives wisdom to the wise and knowledge to those who have understanding. He reveals deep and hidden things; He knows what is in the darkness, and light dwells with Him. (Daniel 2:20-22)

How great are God's signs, and how mighty are His wonders! His kingdom is an eternal kingdom; His dominion endures from generation to generation. (Daniel 4:3)

The Most High is sovereign over the kingdoms of men and gives them to whomever He wishes and sets over them the lowliest of men. I will bless the Most High and praise and honor Him who lives forever. His dominion is an eternal dominion, and His kingdom endures from generation to generation. He regards all the inhabitants of the earth as nothing and does as He pleases with the host of heaven and the inhabitants of the earth. No one can hold back His hand or say to Him: "What have You done?" I praise, exalt, and honor the King of heaven, for all His works are true, and all His ways are just, and He is able to humble those who walk in pride. (Daniel 4:17, 34-35, 37)

The Son of Man will come with the clouds of heaven. In the presence of the Ancient of Days, He will be given dominion and glory and a kingdom, so that all peoples, nations, and men of every language will worship Him. His dominion is an everlasting dominion that will not pass away, and His kingdom is one that will never be destroyed. (Daniel 7:13-14)

I will be silent before the LORD, for He is aroused from His holy dwelling place. (Zechariah 2:13)

God numbers even the very hairs of my head. (Matthew 10:30; Luke 12:7)

Where two or three come together in the name of Jesus, He is there in their midst. (Matthew 18:20)

All things are possible with God. (Matthew 19:26; Mark 10:27)

Heaven and earth will pass away, but the words of the Lord Jesus will never pass away. (Matthew 24:35; Luke 21:33)

All authority in heaven and on earth has been given to the Son of God. (Matthew 28:18)

Nothing is impossible with God. (Luke 1:37)

It is easier for heaven and earth to disappear than for a stroke of a letter of God's law to fail. (Luke 16:17)

The Father loves the Son and has given all things into His hand. (John 3:35)

To the King eternal, immortal, invisible, the only God, be honor and glory forever and ever. (1 Timothy 1:17)

The word of God is living and active and sharper than any double-edged sword, piercing even to the dividing of soul and spirit and of joints and marrow, and it judges the thoughts and attitudes of the heart. And there is no creature hidden from His sight, but everything is uncovered and laid bare before the eyes of Him to whom we must give account. (Hebrews 4:12-13)

With the Lord one day is like a thousand years, and a thousand years are like one day. (2 Peter 3:8)

To the only God our Savior, through Jesus Christ our Lord, be glory, majesty, dominion, and authority, before all ages and now and forever. Amen. (Jude 1:25)

The Lord Jesus, who is holy and true, holds the key of David. What He opens no one can shut, and what He shuts no one can open. (Revelation 3:7)

The Perfections of God

Far be it from You to kill the righteous with the wicked, treating the righteous and the wicked alike. Far be it from You! Will not the Judge of all the earth do right? (Genesis 18:25)

Who is like You, O LORD? Who is like You — majestic in holiness, awesome in praises, working wonders? (Exodus 15:11)

The LORD is a jealous God, punishing the children for the sin of the fathers to the third and fourth generation of those who hate Him, but showing lovingkindness to a thousand generations of those who love Him and keep His commandments. (Exodus 20:5-6)

The LORD, the LORD God, is compassionate and gracious, slow to anger, and abounding in lovingkindness and truth, maintaining love to thousands, and forgiving iniquity, transgression, and sin. (Exodus 34:6-7)

I will not worship any other god, for the LORD, whose name is Jealous, is a jealous God. (Exodus 34:14)

You must be treated as holy by those who come near You, and before all people, You will be honored. (Leviticus 10:3)

The LORD, my God, is a consuming fire, a jealous God (Deuteronomy 4:24)

The LORD, my God, is the faithful God, who keeps His covenant and His lovingkindness to a thousand generations of those who love Him and keep His commands. (Deuteronomy 7:9)

The LORD, my God, is God of gods and Lord of lords, the great God, mighty and awesome, who shows no partiality and accepts no bribes. He executes justice for the fatherless and the widow and loves the alien, giving him food and clothing. (Deuteronomy 10:17-18)

God is the rock; His work is perfect, for all His ways are just. A God of faithfulness and without injustice, upright and just is He. (Deuteronomy 32:4)

As for God, His way is perfect; the word of the Lord is proven. He is a shield for all who take refuge in Him. For who is God besides the LORD? And who is the rock except our God? (2 Samuel 22:31-32)

O LORD, God of Israel, there is no God like You in heaven above or on earth below; You keep Your covenant and mercy with Your servants who walk before You with all their heart. (1 Kings 8:23; 2 Chronicles 6:14)

I will give thanks to the LORD, for He is good; His love endures forever. (1 Chronicles 16:34)

Let me fall into the hands of the LORD, for His mercies are very great; but do not let me fall into the hands of men. (1 Chronicles 21:13)

O LORD, God of heaven, You are the great and awesome God, keeping Your covenant of loyal love with those who love You and obey Your commands. (Nehemiah 1:5)

You have been just in all that has happened to us; You have acted faithfully, while we did wrong. (Nehemiah 9:33)

To God belong wisdom and power; counsel and understanding are His. (Job 12:13)

Where does wisdom come from? Where does understanding dwell? It is hidden from the eyes of every living thing and concealed from the birds of the air. Destruction and Death say, "Only a rumor of it has reached our ears." God understands its way, and He knows its place. For He looks to the ends of the earth and sees everything under the heavens. (Job 28:20-24)

You are not a God who takes pleasure in wickedness; evil cannot dwell with You. (Psalm 5:4)

I will give thanks to the Lord according to His righteousness and will sing praise to the name of the LORD Most High. (Psalm 7:17)

The Lord reigns forever; He has established His throne for judgment. He will judge the world in righteousness, and He will govern the peoples with justice. The LORD will also be a refuge for the oppressed, a stronghold in times of trouble. Those who know Your name will trust in You, for You, LORD, have never forsaken those who seek You. (Psalm 9:7-10)

The LORD is righteous; He loves righteousness; the upright will see His face. (Psalm 11:7)

As for God, His way is perfect; the word of the Lord is proven. He is a shield to all who take refuge in Him. For who is God besides the LORD? And who is the rock except our God? (Psalm 18:30-31)

The law of the LORD is perfect, restoring the soul. The testimony of the LORD is sure, making wise the simple. The precepts of the LORD are right, rejoicing the heart. The commandment of the LORD is pure, enlightening the eyes. The fear of the LORD is clean, enduring forever. The judgments of the LORD are true and altogether righteous. They are more desirable than gold, than much pure gold; they are sweeter than honey, than honey from the comb. Moreover, by them is Your servant warned; in keeping them there is great reward. (Psalm 19:7-11)

Good and upright is the LORD; therefore He instructs sinners in His ways. (Psalm 25:8)

The word of the LORD is upright, and all His work is done in faithfulness. He loves righteousness and justice; the earth is full of the lovingkindness of the LORD. (Psalm 33:4-5)

Your lovingkindness, O LORD, reaches to the heavens, Your faithfulness to the skies. Your righteousness is like the mountains of God; Your judgments are like a great deep. O LORD, You preserve man and beast. How priceless is Your lovingkindness, O God! The children of men find refuge in the shadow of Your wings. For with You is the fountain of life; in Your light we see light. (Psalm 36:5-7, 9)

Be exalted, O God, above the heavens; let Your glory be over all the earth. For Your mercy reaches to the heavens, and Your faithfulness reaches to the skies. (Psalm 57:5, 10)

Once God has spoken; twice I have heard this: that power belongs to God, and that You, O Lord, are loving. For You reward each person according to what he has done. (Psalm 62:11-12)

Lovingkindness and truth have met together; righteousness and peace have kissed each other. Truth shall spring forth from the earth, and righteousness looks down from heaven. (Psalm 85:10-11)

You, Lord, are good and ready to forgive and abundant in mercy to all who call upon You. (Psalm 86:5)

You, O Lord, are a compassionate and gracious God, slow to anger, and abounding in lovingkindness and truth. (Psalm 86:15)

I will sing of the mercies of the LORD forever; with my mouth I will make Your faithfulness known through all generations. I will declare that Your lovingkindness will be built up forever, that you will establish Your faithfulness in the heavens. And the heavens will praise Your wonders, O LORD, Your faithfulness also in the assembly of the holy ones. For who in the heavens can be compared with the LORD? Who is like the LORD among the sons of the mighty? God is greatly feared in the council of the holy ones and more awesome than all who surround Him. O LORD God of hosts, who is like You, O mighty LORD? Your faithfulness also surrounds You. (Psalm 89:1-2, 5-8)

Righteousness and justice are the foundation of Your throne; lovingkindness and truth go before You. (Psalm 89:14)

It is good to give thanks to the LORD and to sing praises to Your name, O Most High, to declare Your lovingkindness in the morning and Your faithfulness at night. (Psalm 92:1-2)

The LORD is upright; He is my rock, and there is no unrighteousness in Him. (Psalm 92:15)

I will exalt the LORD, my God, and worship Him, for the LORD God is holy. (Psalm 99:9)

I will enter the LORD's gates with thanksgiving and His courts with praise; I will give thanks to Him and bless His name. For the LORD is good, and His lovingkindness endures forever; His faithfulness continues through all generations. (Psalm 100:4-5)

I will sing of Your lovingkindness and justice; to you, O LORD, I will sing praises. (Psalm 101:1)

The LORD executes righteousness and justice for all who are oppressed. The LORD is compassionate and gracious, slow to anger, and abounding in lovingkindness. (Psalm 103:6, 8)

I will give thanks to the LORD, for He is good; His lovingkindness endures forever. I will give thanks to the LORD for His unfailing love and His wonderful acts to the children of men, for He satisfies the thirsty soul and fills the hungry soul with good things. (Psalm 107:1, 8-9)

Your merciful love is higher than the heavens, and Your truth reaches to the skies. (Psalm 108:4)

Great are the works of the LORD; they are pondered by all who delight in them. Splendid and majestic is His work, and His righteousness endures forever. He has caused His wonderful acts to be remembered; the LORD is gracious and compassionate. (Psalm 111:2-4)

The LORD's lovingkindness is great toward us, and the truth of the LORD endures forever. Praise the LORD! (Psalm 117:2)

I will give thanks to the LORD, for He is good; His lovingkindness endures forever. (Psalm 118:1)

Your word is settled in heaven forever, O LORD. Your faithfulness continues through all generations; You established the earth, and it stands. They continue to this day according to Your ordinances, for all things serve You. (Psalm 119:89-91)

Your testimonies, which You have commanded, are righteous and trustworthy. Your righteousness is everlasting, and Your law is truth. (Psalm 119:138, 142)

The sum of Your words is truth, and all of Your righteous judgments are eternal. (Psalm 119:160)

I will give thanks to the God of heaven, for His merciful love endures forever. (Psalm 136:26)

How precious are Your thoughts to me, O God! How vast is the sum of them! If I should count them, they would outnumber the grains of sand. When I awake, I am still with You. (Psalm 139:17-18)

I know that the Lord will maintain the cause of the afflicted and justice for the poor. (Psalm 140:12)

I will express the memory of Your abundant goodness and joyfully sing of Your righteousness. The LORD is gracious and compassionate, slow to anger, and great in lovingkindness. The LORD is good to all, and His tender mercies are over all His works. (Psalm 145:7-9)

The LORD is righteous in all His ways and gracious in all His works. (Psalm 145:17)

The LORD of hosts will be exalted in judgment, and the holy God will show Himself holy in righteousness. (Isaiah 5:16)

The LORD of hosts is wonderful in counsel and great in wisdom. (Isaiah 28:29)

The LORD longs to be gracious and rises to show compassion. For the LORD is a God of justice; blessed are all those who wait for Him! (Isaiah 30:18)

The LORD is our judge; the LORD is our lawgiver; the LORD is our king; it is He who will save us. (Isaiah 33:22)

It pleased the LORD for the sake of His righteousness to make His law great and glorious. (Isaiah 42:21)

Only in the LORD are righteousness and strength. (Isaiah 45:24)

"My thoughts are not your thoughts, neither are your ways My ways," declares the LORD. "As the heavens are higher than the earth, so are My ways higher than your ways, and My thoughts than your thoughts." (Isaiah 55:8-9)

You, LORD, love justice; You hate robbery and iniquity. (Isaiah 61:8)

O Lord of hosts, You judge righteously and test the heart and mind; to You I have committed my cause. (Jeremiah 11:20)

I call this to mind, and therefore I have hope: The LORD's mercies never cease, for His compassions never fail. They are new every morning; great is Your faithfulness. (Lamentations 3:21-23)

I know that You are a gracious and compassionate God, slow to anger, and abounding in lovingkindness, a God who relents from sending calamity. (Jonah 4:2)

The LORD is good, a refuge in times of trouble; He knows those who trust in Him. (Nahum 1:7)

Your eyes are too pure to look at evil; You cannot look on wickedness. (Habakkuk 1:13)

My soul magnifies the Lord, and my spirit rejoices in God my Savior, for the Mighty One has done great things for me, and holy is His name. His mercy is on those who fear Him from generation to generation. (Luke 1:46-47, 49-50)

Your word is truth. (John 17:17)

Oh, the depth of the riches both of the wisdom and knowledge of God! How unsearchable are His judgments, and His ways past finding out! For who has known the mind of the LORD? Or who has been His counselor? Or who has first given to Him, that He should repay him? For from Him and through Him and to Him are all things. To Him be the glory forever! Amen. (Romans 11:33-36)

Blessed be the God and Father of our Lord Jesus Christ, the Father of mercies and the God of all comfort. (2 Corinthians 1:3)

In Christ are hidden all the treasures of wisdom and knowledge. (Colossians 2:2-3)

The Lord is not slow concerning His promise, as some count slowness, but is patient with us, not wanting anyone to perish but for all to come to repentance. (2 Peter 3:9)

God is light; in Him there is no darkness at all. (1 John 1:5)

Great and marvelous are Your works, Lord God Almighty! Righteous and true are Your ways, King of the nations! Who will not fear you, O Lord, and glorify Your name? For You alone are holy. All nations will come and worship before You, for Your righteous acts have been revealed. (Revelation 15:3-4)

Hallelujah! Salvation and glory and power belong to our God, because His judgments are true and righteous. (Revelation 19:1-2)

THE WORKS OF GOD

Creation

In the beginning God created the heavens and the earth. Now the earth was formless and empty, and darkness was over the surface of the deep, and the Spirit of God was hovering over the face of the waters. And God said, "Let there be light," and there was light. And God saw that the light was good, and He separated the light from the darkness. God called the light "day," and the darkness He called "night." So the evening and the morning were the first day. Then God said, "Let there be an expanse in the midst of the waters, and let it separate the waters from waters." So God made the expanse and separated the waters under the expanse from the waters above it, and it was so. And God called the expanse "heaven." So the evening and the morning were the second day. Then God said, "Let the waters under the heavens be gathered into one place, and let dry ground appear"; and it was so. And God called the dry ground "earth," and the gathered waters He called "seas." And God saw that it was good. (Genesis 1:1-10)

God said, "Let the earth produce vegetation: seed-bearing plants and trees that yield fruit with seed in it, according to their various kinds"; and it was so. And the earth produced vegetation: plants bearing seed according to their kinds and trees bearing fruit with seed in it according to their kinds. And God saw that it was good. So the evening and the morning were the third day. (Genesis 1:11-13)

God said, "Let there be lights in the expanse of the heavens to separate the day from the night, and let them serve as signs to mark seasons and days and years, and let them be lights in the expanse of the heavens to give light on the earth"; and it was so. God made two great lights— the greater light to govern the day and the lesser light to govern the night. He also made the stars. God set them in the expanse of the heavens to give light on the earth, and to govern the day and the night, and to separate the light from the darkness. And God saw that it was good. So the evening and the morning were the fourth day. (Genesis 1:14-19)

God said, "Let the waters teem with an abundance of living creatures, and let birds fly above the earth across the expanse of the heavens." So God created great sea creatures and every living creature with which the waters abounded, according to their kinds, and every winged bird according to its kind. And God saw that it was good. God blessed them and said, "Be fruitful and multiply, and fill the waters in the seas, and let the birds multiply on the earth." So the evening and the morning were the fifth day. (Genesis 1:20-23)

God said, "Let the earth produce living creatures according to their kinds: livestock, creatures that creep on the earth, and beasts of the earth, each according to its kind"; and it was so. God made the beasts of the earth according to their kinds, the livestock according to their kinds, and all the creatures that creep on the earth according to their kinds. And God saw that it was good. (Genesis 1:24-25)

God said, "Let Us make man in Our image, in Our likeness, and let them rule over the fish of the sea and the birds of the air and over the livestock and over all the earth and over all the creatures that creep on the earth." So God created man in His own image; in the image of God He created him; male and female He created them. Then God blessed them and said to them, "Be fruitful and multiply; fill the earth and subdue it; and rule over the fish of the sea and the birds of the air and over every living creature that moves on the earth." Then God said, "Behold, I have given you every seed-bearing plant on the face of the whole earth and every tree that has fruit with seed in it; they will be yours for food. And to all the beasts of the earth and all the birds of the air and all the creatures that move on the ground, in which there is life, I have given every green plant for food"; and it was so. God saw all that he had made, and it was very good. So the evening and the morning were the sixth day. (Genesis 1:26-31)

God completed the heavens and the earth in all their vast array. By the seventh day God finished the work which He had done, and He rested on the seventh day from all His creative work. And God blessed the seventh day and sanctified it, because on it He rested from all the work of creating that He had done. (Genesis 2:1-3)

The LORD God formed man from the dust of the ground and breathed into his nostrils the breath of life; and man became a living being. And out of the ground the LORD God made every tree grow that is pleasing to the eye and good for food. In the middle of the garden were the tree of life and the tree of the knowledge of good and evil. Then the LORD God took the man and put him in the Garden of Eden to cultivate it and take care of it. (Genesis 2:7, 9, 15)

In the day that God created man, He made him in the likeness of God. (Genesis 5:1)

In six days the LORD made the heavens and the earth, the sea, and all that is in them, and rested on the seventh day. Therefore the LORD blessed the Sabbath day and made it holy. (Exodus 20:11)

O LORD, God of Israel, enthroned between the cherubim, You alone are God over all the kingdoms of the earth. You have made heaven and earth. (2 Kings 19:15)

You alone are the LORD. You made the heavens, even the heaven of heavens, and all their starry host, the earth and all that is on it, the seas and all that is in them. You give life to all that is in them, and the host of heaven worships You. (Nehemiah 9:6)

God is the maker of the Bear and Orion, the Pleiades, and the constellations of the south. (Job 9:9)

He does great things that cannot be fathomed and wonderful works that cannot be counted. (Job 9:10)

When I consider Your heavens, the work of Your fingers, the moon and the stars, which You have set in place, what is man that You are mindful of him, and the son of man that You care for him? You made him a little lower than the heavenly beings and crowned him with glory and honor. You made him ruler over the works of Your hands, and You put everything under his feet. (Psalm 8:3-6)

The heavens declare the glory of God, and the skies proclaim the work of His hands. Day after day they pour forth speech; night after night they reveal knowledge. (Psalm 19:1-2)

The earth is the LORD's and everything in it, the world and all who dwell in it. For He founded it upon the seas and established it upon the waters. (Psalm 24:1-2)

By the word of the LORD the heavens were made, and by the breath of His mouth their starry host. (Psalm 33:6)

The Mighty One, God, the LORD, has spoken and summoned the earth from the rising of the sun to the place where it sets. (Psalm 50:1)

Every animal of the forest is Yours, and the cattle on a thousand hills. You know every bird in the mountains, and everything that moves in the field is Yours. (Psalm 50:10-11)

You answer us with awesome deeds of righteousness, O God of our salvation, You who are the hope of all the ends of the earth and of the farthest seas; You formed the mountains by Your strength, having armed Yourself with power; and You stilled the roaring of the seas, the roaring of their waves, and the tumult of the peoples. (Psalm 65:5-7)

The day is Yours; the night also is Yours; You established the sun and moon. It was You who set all the boundaries of the earth; You made both summer and winter. (Psalm 74:16-17)

The heavens are Yours; the earth also is Yours; You founded the world and all its fullness. (Psalm 89:11)

The LORD is the great God, the great King above all gods. In His hand are the depths of the earth, and the summits of the mountains are His also. The sea is His, for He made it, and His hands formed the dry land. He is our God, and we are the people of His pasture and the sheep under His care. (Psalm 95:3-5, 7)

The LORD, He is God. It is He who made us, and not we ourselves; we are His people and the sheep of His pasture. (Psalm 100:3)

The LORD covers Himself in light as with a garment; He stretches out the heavens like a tent curtain and lays the beams of His upper chambers in the waters. He makes the clouds His chariot and walks on the wings of the wind. He makes the winds His messengers, flames of fire His servants. He set the earth on its foundations, so that it can never be moved. You covered it with the deep as with a garment; the waters stood above the mountains. At Your rebuke the waters fled; at the sound of Your thunder they hurried away. They flowed over the mountains and went down into the valleys to the place You assigned for them. You set a boundary they cannot cross, that they will not return to cover the earth. O Lord, how manifold are Your works! In wisdom You made them all; the earth is full of Your possessions. (Psalm 104:2-9, 24)

Your hands made me and fashioned me. (Psalm 119:73)

You formed my inward parts; You wove me together in my mother's womb. I thank You because I am fearfully and wonderfully made; Your works are wonderful, and my soul knows it full well. My frame was not hidden from You when I was made in secret and skillfully wrought in the depths of the earth. Your eyes saw my embryo, and all the days ordained for me were written in Your book before one of them came to be. (Psalm 139:13-16)

The LORD appoints the number of the stars and calls them each by name. (Psalm 147:4)

The LORD by wisdom founded the earth; by understanding He established the heavens; by His knowledge the deeps were divided, and the clouds drop down the dew. (Proverbs 3:19-20)

God has made everything beautiful in its time. He has also set eternity in the hearts of men, yet they cannot fathom what God has done from beginning to end. (Ecclesiastes 3:11)

O LORD of hosts, God of Israel, enthroned between the cherubim, You alone are God over all the kingdoms of the earth. You have made heaven and earth. (Isaiah 37:16)

Who has measured the waters in the hollow of his hand or marked off the heavens with the breadth of his hand? Who has calculated the dust of the earth in a measure or weighed the mountains in the balance and the hills in scales? (Isaiah 40:12)

"To whom will you compare Me? Or who is My equal?" says the Holy One. Lift your eyes to the heavens and see who has created them, He who brings out the starry host by number and calls them each by name. Because of His great might and the strength of His power, not one of them is missing. Do you not know? Have you not heard? The everlasting God, the LORD, the Creator of the ends of the earth, does not grow tired or weary. No one can fathom His understanding. (Isaiah 40:25-26, 28)

It is God the LORD who created the heavens and stretched them out, who spread out the earth and all that comes out of it, who gives breath to its people and spirit to those who walk on it. (Isaiah 42:5)

You form the light and create darkness; You bring prosperity and create disaster; You, the LORD, do all these things. (Isaiah 45:7)

You made the earth and created man upon it. Your own hands stretched out the heavens, and You ordered their starry hosts. (Isaiah 45:12)

The Lord who created the heavens, He is God. He fashioned and made the earth and established it; He did not create it to be empty but formed it to be inhabited. He is the LORD, and there is no other. (Isaiah 45:18)

Your hand laid the foundations of the earth, and Your right hand spread out the heavens; when You summon them, they all stand up together. (Isaiah 48:13)

Heaven is Your throne, and the earth is Your footstool. Your hand made all these things, and so they came into being. (Isaiah 66:1-2)

God made the earth by His power; He established the world by His wisdom and stretched out the heavens by His understanding. (Jeremiah 10:12)

The LORD gives the sun for light by day and decrees the moon and stars for light by night; He stirs up the sea so that its waves roar—the LORD of hosts is His name. (Jeremiah 31:35)

The LORD made the earth by His power; He established the world by His wisdom and stretched out the heavens by His understanding. (Jeremiah 51:15)

The Lord GOD of hosts—He who touches the earth and it melts, and all who live in it mourn; He who builds His staircase in the heavens and founded the expanse over the earth; He who calls for the waters of the sea and pours them out over the face of the earth—the LORD is His name. (Amos 9:5-6)

The LORD stretches out the heavens, lays the foundation of the earth, and forms the spirit of man within him. (Zechariah 12:1)

Through Christ all things were made, and without Him nothing was made that has been made. In Him was life, and the life was the light of men. (John 1:3-4)

God, who made the world and everything in it, since He is Lord of heaven and earth, does not dwell in temples built by hands. And He is not served by human hands, as though He needed anything, since He Himself gives all men life and breath and everything else. (Acts 17:24-25)

Since the creation of the world God's invisible attributes—His eternal power and divine nature—have been clearly seen, being understood from what has been made, so that men are without excuse. (Romans 1:20)

God gives life to the dead and calls into being things that do not exist. (Romans 4:17)

The whole family in heaven and on earth derives its name from the God and Father of our Lord Jesus Christ. (Ephesians 3:14-15)

Christ is the image of the invisible God, the firstborn over all creation. For by Him all things were created that are in heaven and on earth, visible and invisible, whether thrones or dominions or rulers or authorities; all things were created by Him and for Him. And He is before all things, and in Him all things hold together. (Colossians 1:15-17)

Everything God created is good, and nothing is to be rejected if it is received with thanksgiving, because it is sanctified by the word of God and prayer. (1 Timothy 4:4-5)

In the past God spoke to the fathers through the prophets at many times and in various ways, but in these last days He has spoken to us by His Son, whom He appointed heir of all things and through whom He made the universe. (Hebrews 1:1-2)

By faith I understand that the universe was formed by the word of God, so that what is seen was not made out of things which are visible. (Hebrews 11:3)

By the word of God the heavens existed long ago, and the earth was formed out of water and by water. By these waters also the world of that time was deluged and destroyed. By the same word the present heavens and earth are reserved for fire, being kept for the day of judgment and destruction of ungodly men. (2 Peter 3:5-7)

You are worthy, our Lord and God, to receive glory and honor and power, for You created all things, and by Your will they were created and have their being. (Revelation 4:11)

Redemption

B ecause Adam listened to the voice of his wife and ate from the tree about which God commanded him, "You must not eat of it," the ground was cursed; through painful toil he ate of it all the days of his life. It produced thorns and thistles for him, and he ate the plants of the field. By the sweat of his brow he ate his food until he returned to the ground, because from it he was taken; "For dust you are, and to dust you will return." (Genesis 3:17-19)

The earth became corrupt in God's sight and was filled with violence. God looked upon the earth and saw how corrupt it had become, for all the people on earth had corrupted their ways. (Genesis 6:11-12)

In the judgment of the flood, every living thing that moved on the earth perished — birds, livestock, wild animals, all the creatures that swarm over the earth, and all mankind. Everything on dry land that had the breath of life in its nostrils died. Every living thing on the face of the earth was wiped out; men and animals and the creatures that move along the ground and the birds of the air were destroyed from the earth. Only Noah was left, and those with him in the ark. (Genesis 7:21-23)

After the flood, Noah brought out every kind of living creature that was with him — the birds, the animals, and all the creatures that move along the ground — so they could multiply on the earth and be fruitful and increase in number upon it. All the animals and all the creatures that move along the ground and all the birds — everything that moves on the earth—went out according to their families from the ark. (Genesis 8:17, 19)

When Noah made an offering after the flood, the Lord smelled the pleasing aroma and said in His heart: "I will never again curse the ground because of man, even though every inclination of his heart is evil from childhood; nor will I again destroy all living creatures, as I have done. While the earth remains, seedtime and harvest, cold and heat, summer and winter, day and night, will never cease." (Genesis 8:21-22)

God blessed Noah and his sons and told them to be fruitful and multiply and fill the earth. He established His covenant with them and with their descendants after them and with every living creature that was with them—the birds, the livestock, and all the beasts of the earth, all those that came out of the ark with them—every living creature on earth. God established His covenant that never again will all life be cut off by the waters of a flood; never again will there be a flood to destroy the earth. The sign of God's covenant for all generations to come is the rainbow that He set in the clouds; whenever a rainbow appears in the clouds, He will remember His everlasting covenant with mankind and every living creature of every kind on the earth. (Genesis 9:1, 9-16)

The LORD said to Abram, "Leave your country, your people and your father's household, and go to the land I will show you. I will make you into a great nation, and I will bless you; I will make your name great, and you will be a blessing. I will bless those who bless you, and whoever curses you I will curse; and all the families of the earth will be blessed through you." (Genesis 12:1-3)

The Lord said to Abram after Lot had separated from him, "Now lift up your eyes and look from the place where you are north and south, east and west. All the land that you see I will give to you and to your descendants forever. I will make your descendants like the dust of the earth, so that if anyone could count the dust, then your offspring also could be counted." (Genesis 13:14-16)

After Abram rescued Lot, Melchizedek, king of Salem, brought out bread and wine; he was a priest of God Most High, and he blessed him and said, "Blessed be Abram of God Most High, Possessor of heaven and earth. And blessed be God Most High, who delivered your enemies into your hand." Then Abram gave him a tenth of everything. (Genesis 14:18-20)

God took Abram outside and said, "Look up at the heavens and count the stars, if you are able to count them." Then He said to him,

"So shall your descendants be." And Abram believed in the LORD, and He credited it to him as righteousness. (Genesis 15:5-6)

The LORD appeared to Abram and said to him, "I am El Shaddai; walk before Me and be blameless. And I will confirm My covenant between me and you and will greatly increase your numbers." Then Abram fell on his face, and God talked with him, saying, "As for Me, My covenant is with you, and you will be the father of many nations. No longer will you be called Abram; your name will be Abraham, for I have made you a father of many nations. I will make you exceedingly fruitful; I will make nations of you, and kings will come from you. And I will establish My covenant as an everlasting covenant between Me and you and your descendants after you for the generations to come, to be your God and the God of your descendants after you." (Genesis 17:1-7)

The LORD confirmed that Abraham would surely become a great and powerful nation, and all nations on earth would be blessed through him. (Genesis 18:18)

The LORD said to Abraham, "By Myself I have sworn, that because you have not withheld your son, your only son, I will surely bless you and make your descendants as numerous as the stars in the sky and as the sand on the seashore. Your descendants will take possession of the cities of their enemies, and through your offspring all nations on earth will be blessed, because you have obeyed My voice." (Genesis 22:16-18)

The LORD appeared to Isaac and said, "Do not go down to Egypt; dwell in the land of which I shall tell you. Sojourn in this land, and I will be with you and will bless you. For to you and your descendants I will give all these lands and will confirm the oath I swore to your father Abraham. I will make your descendants as numerous as the stars in the sky and will give them all these lands, and through your offspring all nations on earth will be blessed, because Abraham obeyed me and kept My charge, My commands, My statutes, and My laws." (Genesis 26:2-5)

Jacob had a dream in which he saw a ladder resting on the earth, with its top reaching to heaven; and the angels of God were ascending and descending on it. Above it stood the LORD, and He said, "I am the LORD, the God of your father Abraham and the God of Isaac. I will give you and your descendants the land on which you are lying. Your descendants will also be like the dust of the earth, and you will spread out to the west and to the east, to the north and to the south; and all the families of the earth will be blessed through you and your offspring. (Genesis 28:12-14)

After Jacob returned from Paddan Aram, God appeared to him again and blessed him. And God said to him, "Your name is Jacob, but you will no longer be called Jacob; your name will be Israel." So He called his name Israel. And God said to him, "I am El Shaddai; be fruitful and increase in number. A nation and a company of nations will proceed from you, and kings will come from your body. The land I gave to Abraham and Isaac I also give to you, and I will give this land to your descendants after you." (Genesis 35:9-12)

Joseph said to his brothers, "Do not be grieved or angry with yourselves for selling me here, for God sent me before you to save lives. He sent me ahead of you to preserve for you a remnant on earth and to save your lives by a great deliverance. So it was not you who sent me here, but God. (Genesis 45:5, 7-8)

You raised up Pharaoh for this purpose, that You might show him Your power and that Your name might be proclaimed through all the earth. (Exodus 9:16)

In Your unfailing love You have led the people You have redeemed. In your strength You have guided them to Your holy dwelling. You brought them in and planted them in the mountain of Your inheritance — the place, O LORD, You made for Your dwelling; the sanctuary, O LORD, Your hands have established. (Exodus 15:13, 17)

You overwhelmed the Egyptians and carried Your people on eagles' wings and brought them to Yourself. (Exodus 19:4)

You are the LORD, our God, who brought Your people out of Egypt, out of the land of slavery. (Exodus 20:2)

You are the LORD, our God, who brought Your people out of Egypt so that they would no longer be their slaves; You broke the bars of their yoke and enabled them to walk with heads held high. (Leviticus 26:13)

Has any other people heard the voice of God speaking out of the midst of the fire, as the children of Israel have, and lived? Has any god ever tried to take for himself one nation from the midst of another nation, by trials, by miraculous signs and wonders, by war, by a mighty hand and an outstretched arm, and by great and awesome deeds, like all the things the LORD God did for Israel in Egypt before their very eyes? The Israelites were shown these things so that they might know that the LORD, He is God; there is no other besides Him. Out of heaven He made the children of Israel hear His voice to discipline them. On earth He showed them His great fire, and they heard His words out of the midst of the fire. Because He loved their fathers, He chose their descendants after them, and He brought them out of Egypt by His presence and His great power; He drove out from before the Israelites nations greater and mightier than they, to bring them in and to give them their land as an inheritance. (Deuteronomy 4:33-38)

The children of Israel were a people holy to the LORD their God. The Lord God chose them out of all the peoples on the face of the earth to be His people, His treasured possession. The LORD did not set His love on them and choose them because they were more numerous than other peoples, for they were the fewest of all peoples. But it was because the LORD loved them and kept the oath He swore to their fathers that He brought them out with a mighty hand and redeemed them from the house of slavery, from the hand of Pharaoh king of Egypt. (Deuteronomy 7:6-8)

The LORD led His people all the way in the wilderness for forty years, to humble them and to test them in order to know what was in their heart, whether or not they would keep His commands. He humbled them, allowing them to hunger and then feeding them with manna, which neither they nor their fathers had known, to teach them that man does not live on bread alone; but man lives by every word that proceeds from the mouth of the LORD. (Deuteronomy 8:2-3)

The LORD set His affection on the forefathers of Israel to love them, and He chose their descendants above all peoples. (Deuteronomy 10:15)

The LORD is our praise, and He is our God, who performed for the children of Israel those great and awesome wonders which they saw with their own eyes. (Deuteronomy 10:21)

The children of Israel were a people holy to the LORD their God. Out of all the peoples on the face of the earth, the Lord chose them to be His treasured possession. (Deuteronomy 14:2)

The LORD God is the One who went with Israel to fight for them against their enemies, to save them. (Deuteronomy 20:4)

You set before Your people life and prosperity, death and destruction; and You commanded them to love You, the LORD their God, to walk in Your ways, and to keep Your commandments, statutes, and judgments, so that they would live and multiply and that You would bless them in the land they were entering to possess. You called heaven and earth as witnesses against them that You set before them life and death, blessings and curses, and told them to choose life, so that they and their children would live by loving You, listening to Your voice, and holding fast to You. (Deuteronomy 30:15-16, 19-20)

Joshua said to Israel, "Now I am about to go the way of all the earth. You know with all your hearts and souls that not one of all the good promises the LORD, your God, gave you has failed. Every promise has been fulfilled; not one has failed." (Joshua 23:14)

Blessed is the LORD, who has not left His people without a kinsman-redeemer. (Ruth 4:14)

The LORD does not save by sword or by spear, for the battle is the LORD's. (1 Samuel 17:47)

With the kind, You show Yourself kind; with the blameless You show Yourself blameless; with the pure You show Yourself pure; but to the crooked You show Yourself shrewd. You save the humble, but Your eyes are on the haughty to bring them low. (2 Samuel 22:26-28)

The LORD has said, "If My people who are called by My name will humble themselves and pray and seek My face and turn from their wicked ways, then I will hear from heaven and will forgive their sin and heal their land." (2 Chronicles 7:14)

When the children of Judah were victorious, it was because they relied on the LORD, the God of their fathers. (2 Chronicles 13:18)

The eyes of the LORD move to and fro throughout the whole earth to strengthen those whose hearts are fully committed to Him. (2 Chronicles 16:9)

You save the humble but bring low those whose eyes are haughty. (Psalm 18:27)

The LORD guides the humble in what is right and teaches the humble His way. (Psalm 25:9)

Blessed is the nation whose God is the LORD, the people whom He has chosen for His inheritance. (Psalm 33:12)

I will praise You forever for what You have done; I will hope in Your name, for it is good. I will praise You in the presence of Your saints. (Psalm 52:9)

Blessed be the LORD God, the God of Israel, who alone does wonderful things. (Psalm 72:18)

I will remember the works of the LORD; surely, I will remember Your wonders of long ago. I will meditate on all Your works and consider all Your mighty deeds. Your way, O God, is holy. What god is so great as our God? You are the God who works wonders; You have revealed Your strength among the peoples. You redeemed your people with Your power, the descendants of Jacob and Joseph. (Psalm 77:11-15)

How great are Your works, O LORD! Your thoughts are very deep. The senseless man does not know; fools do not understand that when the wicked spring up like grass and all the evildoers flourish, they will be destroyed forever. But You, O LORD, are exalted forever. (Psalm 92:5-7)

O LORD, what is man that You know him or the son of man that You think of him? Man is like a breath; his days are like a passing shadow. (Psalm 144:3-4)

One generation shall praise Your works to another and shall declare Your mighty acts. I will meditate on the glorious splendor of Your majesty and on Your wonderful works. Men shall speak of the might of Your awesome works, and I will proclaim Your great deeds. (Psalm 145:4-6)

The LORD upholds all who fall and lifts up all who are bowed down. The eyes of all look to You, and You give them their food at the proper time. You open Your hand and satisfy the desire of every living thing. (Psalm 145:14-16)

The LORD is near to all who call upon Him, to all who call upon Him in truth. He fulfills the desire of those who fear Him; He hears their cry and saves them. The LORD preserves all who love Him, but all the wicked He will destroy. (Psalm 145:18-20)

The LORD watches over the strangers; He sustains the orphan and the widow, but He thwarts the way of the wicked. (Psalm 146:9)

The Lord relieves the humble, but He casts the wicked to the ground. (Psalm 147:6)

A Shoot will come forth from the stump of Jesse; from his roots a Branch will bear fruit. The Spirit of the LORD will rest on Him — the Spirit of wisdom and of understanding, the Spirit of counsel and of power, the Spirit of knowledge and of the fear of the LORD — and He will delight in the fear of the LORD. He will not judge by what He sees with His eyes or decide by what He hears with His ears, but with righteousness He will judge the poor and decide with fairness for the meek of the earth. And He will strike the earth with the rod of His mouth; with the breath of His lips He will slay the wicked. Righteousness will be His belt, and faithfulness the sash around His waist. (Isaiah 11:1-5)

O LORD, You are my God; I will exalt You and praise Your name, for You have done wonderful things, things planned long ago in perfect faithfulness. (Isaiah 25:1)

The LORD humbles those who dwell on high and lays the lofty city low; He levels it to the ground and casts it down to the dust. (Isaiah 26:5)

God gives strength to the weary and increases the power of the weak. Even youths grow tired and weary, and young men stumble and fall; but those who wait for the LORD will renew their strength; they will mount up with wings like eagles; they will run and not grow weary; they will walk and not be faint. (Isaiah 40:29-31)

Shout for joy, O heavens! Rejoice, O earth! Break out into singing, O mountains! For the LORD has comforted His people and will have compassion on His afflicted. (Isaiah 49:13)

Was it not You who dried up the sea, the waters of the great deep; who made the depths of the sea a road so that the redeemed might cross over? (Isaiah 51:10)

The LORD has bared His holy arm in the sight of all the nations, and all the ends of the earth will see the salvation of our God. (Isaiah 52:10)

The Servant of God was despised and rejected by men, a man of sorrows, and acquainted with grief. And like one from whom men hide their faces, He was despised, and we esteemed Him not. Surely He has borne our infirmities and carried our sorrows; yet we considered Him stricken, smitten by God, and afflicted. But He was pierced for our transgressions, He was crushed for our iniquities; the punishment that brought us peace was upon Him, and by His wounds we are healed. All of us like sheep have gone astray; each of us has turned to his own way, and the LORD has laid on Him the iniquity of us all. He was oppressed and afflicted, yet He did not open His mouth; He was led like a lamb to the slaughter, and as a sheep before her shearers is silent, so He did not open His mouth. By oppression and judgment He was taken away. And who can speak of His descendants? For He was cut off from the land of the living; He was stricken for the transgression of God's people. He was assigned a grave with the wicked, yet with a rich man in His death, though He had done no violence, nor was any deceit in His mouth. Yet it was the LORD's will to crush Him and cause Him to suffer. When He makes His soul a guilt offering, He will see His offspring and prolong His days, and the pleasure of the LORD will prosper in His hand. He will see the fruit of the travail of His soul and be satisfied; by His knowledge God's righteous Servant will justify many, and He will bear their iniquities. Therefore God will give Him a portion among the great, and He will divide the spoils with the strong, because He poured out His life unto death, and was numbered with the transgressors. For He bore the sin of many and made intercession for the transgressors. (Isaiah 53:3-12)

Surely the LORD's hand is not too short to save, nor His ear too dull to hear. But our iniquities have separated us from our God; our sins have hidden His face from us, so that He will not hear. Yet the LORD saw that there was no one to intervene; so His own arm worked salvation for Him, and His righteousness sustained Him. He put on righteousness as His breastplate and the helmet of salvation on His head; He put on the garments of vengeance and wrapped Himself in zeal as a cloak. From the west, men will fear the name of the LORD, and from the rising of the sun, they will revere His glory. For He will come like a flood that the breath of the LORD drives along. (Isaiah 59:1-2, 16-19)

Nations will come to Your light and kings to the brightness of your dawning. (Isaiah 60:3)

As the earth brings forth its sprouts and as a garden causes that which is sown to spring up, so the Lord GOD will make righteousness and praise spring up before all nations. (Isaiah 61:11)

I will tell of the lovingkindnesses of the LORD, the praises of the LORD, according to all the LORD has done for us, and the great goodness toward the house of Israel, which He has bestowed on them according to His mercies, and according to the multitude of His lovingkindnesses. (Isaiah 63:7)

I will sing to the LORD and give praise to the LORD, for He has rescued the life of the needy from the hands of evildoers. (Jeremiah 20:13)

When You promised to make a new covenant with the house of Israel, You said, "I will put My law within them and write it on their hearts. I will be their God, and they will be My people. No longer will each one teach his neighbor, or each one his brother, saying, 'Know the LORD,' because they shall all know Me, from the least of them to the greatest of them. For I will forgive their iniquity and will remember their sins no more." (Jeremiah 31:33-34)

You promised to restore the children of Israel and Judah, saying, "They shall be My people, and I will be their God. And I will give them one heart and one way, so that they will always fear Me for their own good and the good of their children after them." (Jeremiah 32:38-39)

When the glory of the LORD departed from the temple, it rose from above the cherubim and moved to the threshold of the temple. The cloud filled the temple, and the court was full of the radiance of the glory of the LORD. The sound of the wings of the cherubim could be heard as far away as the outer court, like the voice of El Shaddai when He speaks. Then the glory of the LORD departed from over the threshold of the temple and stood over the cherubim. While Ezekiel watched, the cherubim spread their wings and rose from the ground, and as they went, their wheels went with them, and they stood still at the entrance to the east gate of the LORD's house, and the glory of the God of Israel was above them. Each of the cherubim had four faces and four wings, and under their wings was what looked like the hands of a man. Each one went straight ahead. Then the cherubim spread their wings with the wheels beside them, and the glory of the God of Israel was high above them. And the glory of the LORD went up from the midst of the city and stood over the Mount of Olives which is east of the city. (Ezekiel 10:4-5, 18-22; 11:22-23)

The Lord GOD promised to gather the children of Israel from the nations and bring them back from the countries where they were scattered. "And I will give them the land of Israel. They will return to it and remove all its detestable images and abominations. I will give them one heart and put a new spirit within them, and I will remove the stony heart out of their flesh and give them a heart of flesh, that they may walk in My statutes and keep My ordinances. They shall be My people, and I will be their God." (Ezekiel 11:17-20)

Although the glory of the LORD departed because of the unfaithfulness of Israel, God has promised that because of His faithfulness, He will redeem His people, and His glory will return. Ezekiel was given a vision of the glory of the God of Israel coming from the east. His voice was like the roar of rushing waters, and the earth was radiant with His glory. The glory of the LORD entered the temple through the gate facing toward the east. Then the Spirit lifted him up and brought him into the inner court, and the glory of the LORD filled the temple. The LORD said to him, "Son of Man, this is the place of My throne and the place for the soles of My feet. This is where I will dwell among the children of Israel forever. And the house of Israel will never again defile My holy name, neither they nor their kings, by their harlotry and idolatry." (Ezekiel 43:2, 4-7)

You, Lord GOD, take no pleasure in the death of the wicked but rather that the wicked turn from their ways and live. (Ezekiel 18:23; 33:11)

You led Your people with cords of human kindness, with bands of love; You lifted the yoke from their neck and bent down to feed them. (Hosea 11:4)

Who is a God like You, who pardons iniquity and passes over the transgression of the remnant of His inheritance? You do not stay angry forever but delight to show mercy. You will have compassion on Your people; You will tread their iniquities underfoot and hurl all their sins into the depths of the sea. (Micah 7:18-19)

LORD, I have heard of Your fame, and I stand in awe of Your deeds. O LORD, revive Your work in the midst of the years, in our time make them known, in wrath remember mercy. (Habakkuk 3:2)

Rejoice greatly, O daughter of Zion! Shout, O daughter of Jerusalem! Behold, Your King is coming to you; He is just and having salvation, humble and riding on a donkey, on a colt, the foal of a donkey. He will proclaim peace to the nations; His dominion will extend from sea to sea and from the River to the ends of the earth. (Zechariah 9:9-10)

The LORD of hosts warned the priests of Israel, "If you do not listen, and if you do not set your heart to honor My name, I will send a curse upon you, and I will curse your blessings; indeed, I have already cursed them, because you have not set your heart to honor Me." (Malachi 2:2)

For those who revere Your name, the Sun of righteousness will rise with healing in His wings. And they will go out and leap like calves released from the stall. (Malachi 4:2)

Behold, a virgin shall be with child and will give birth to a son, and they will call His name Immanuel, which means, "God with us." (Matthew 1:23)

After His baptism and temptation, Jesus began to preach and say, "Repent, for the kingdom of heaven is at hand." (Matthew 4:17)

The Son of Man has authority on earth to forgive sins. (Matthew 9:6)

Jesus said, "It is not the healthy who need a physician, but those who are sick." He did not come to call the righteous, but sinners. (Matthew 9:12-13)

Where Jesus went, the blind received sight, the lame walked, the lepers were cured, the deaf heard, the dead were raised up, and the good news was preached to the poor. (Matthew 11:5)

Jesus said, "I praise You, Father, Lord of heaven and earth, because You have hidden these things from the wise and learned and revealed them to little children. Yes, Father, for this was well-pleasing in Your sight. All things have been delivered to Me by My Father. No one knows the Son except the Father, and no one knows the Father except the Son and those to whom the Son wills to reveal Him." (Matthew 11:25-27)

Lord, You said, "Come to Me, all you who labor and are heavy laden, and I will give you rest. Take My yoke upon you and learn from Me, for I am gentle and humble in heart, and you will find rest for your souls. For My yoke is easy, and My burden is light." (Matthew 11:28-30)

The Son of Man did not come to be served, but to serve, and to give His life as a ransom for many. (Matthew 20:28)

The gospel of the kingdom will be preached in the whole world as a witness to all the nations, and then the end will come. (Matthew 24:14)

Jesus took bread, gave thanks, and broke it, and gave it to His disciples, saying, "Take and eat; this is My body." Then He took the cup, gave thanks, and offered it to them, saying, "Drink from it, all of you. This is My blood of the new covenant, which is poured out for many for the forgiveness of sins." (Matthew 26:26-28)

Jesus fell with His face to the ground and prayed, "My Father, if it is possible, let this cup pass from Me. Yet not as I will but as You will." (Matthew 26:39)

Jesus preached the gospel of the Kingdom of God and said, "The time is fulfilled, and the Kingdom of God is at hand. Repent and believe the good news." (Mark 1:14-15)

When Jesus said to the paralytic, "My son, your sins are forgiven," the scribes were sitting there and reasoned in their hearts, "Why does this man speak blasphemies like this? Who can forgive sins but God alone?" (Mark 2:5-7)

Jesus said to the scribes and Pharisees, "It is not the healthy who need a physician, but the sick. I have not come to call the righteous, but sinners." (Mark 2:17)

Jesus had compassion on the crowds, because they were like sheep without a shepherd. So He began to teach them many things. (Mark 6:34)

Jesus did all things well. He made the deaf hear and the mute speak. (Mark 7:37)

If anyone is ashamed of You and Your words in this adulterous and sinful generation, the Son of Man will be ashamed of him when He comes in the glory of His Father with the holy angels. (Mark 8:38)

The Son of Man went up to Jerusalem where He was delivered to the chief priests and to the scribes. They condemned Him to death and handed Him over to the Gentiles, who mocked Him and spat upon Him and scourged Him and killed Him. But on the third day He rose again. (Mark 10:33-34)

The Son of Man did not come to be served, but to serve, and to give His life as a ransom for many. (Mark 10:45)

While Jesus was eating His last Passover meal with His disciples, He took bread, blessed it, and broke it, and gave it to His disciples, saying, "Take it; this is My body." Then He took the cup, and when He had given thanks, He gave it to them, and they all drank from it. And He said to them, "This is My blood of the covenant, which is poured out for many." (Mark 14:22-24)

In Gethsemane, Jesus prayed, "Abba, Father, all things are possible for You; take this cup from Me. Yet not what I will, but what You will." (Mark 14:36)

During His trials, some began to spit at Jesus and blindfold Him and strike Him with their fists and say to Him, "Prophesy!" And the guards received Him with slaps in the face. The soldiers put a purple robe on Him then twisted together a crown of thorns and set it on Him. And they began to call out to Him, "Hail, king of the Jews!" Again and again they struck Him on the head with a staff and spit on Him, and bending their knees, they paid mock homage to Him. When they crucified Him, those who passed by hurled insults at Him, wagging their heads and saying, "Ha! You who are going to destroy the temple and build it in three days, save Yourself and come down from the cross!" And at the ninth hour, Jesus cried out in a loud voice, "Eloi, Eloi, lama sabachthani?" which means, "My God, My God, why have You forsaken Me?" (Mark 14:65; 15:17-19, 29-30, 34)

The Lord has performed mighty deeds with His arm; He has scattered those who are proud in the thoughts of their heart. He has brought down rulers from their thrones and has lifted up the humble. (Luke 1:51-52)

Blessed be the Lord, the God of Israel, because He has visited us and has redeemed His people. He has raised up a horn of salvation for us in the house of His servant David (as He spoke by the mouth of His holy prophets of long ago), salvation from our enemies and from the hand of all who hate us — to show mercy to our fathers and to remember His holy covenant, the oath He swore to our father Abraham, to rescue us from the hand of our enemies, and to enable us to serve Him without fear in holiness and righteousness before Him all our days. (Luke 1:68-75)

John was called a prophet of the Most High; for he went on before the Lord to prepare the way for Him, and to give His people the knowledge of salvation through the forgiveness of their sins — because of the tender mercy of our God, with which the Sunrise from on high came from heaven to shine on those living in darkness and in the shadow of death — to guide their feet into the path of peace. (Luke 1:76-79)

The angel said to the shepherds, "Do not be afraid. I bring you good news of great joy that will be for all the people. For today in the city of David a Savior has been born to you, who is Christ the Lord." (Luke 2:10-11)

Jesus fulfilled the words of the prophet Isaiah: "The Spirit of the LORD is upon Me, because He has anointed Me to preach good news to the poor. He has sent Me to proclaim freedom for the captives and recovery of sight to the blind, to set free those who are downtrodden, to proclaim the acceptable year of the LORD." (Luke 4:18-19)

Those who had anyone sick with various kinds of diseases brought them to Jesus, and laying His hands on each one, He healed them. (Luke 4:40)

Jesus was sent for the purpose of preaching the good news of the Kingdom of God. (Luke 4:43)

Many came to hear Jesus and to be healed of their diseases, and those who were tormented by evil spirits were healed. (Luke 6:18)

Jesus cured many who had diseases, sicknesses, and evil spirits, and gave sight to many who were blind. So he replied to the messengers sent from John the Baptist, "Go back and report to John what you have seen and heard: The blind receive sight, the lame walk, the lepers are cured, the deaf hear, the dead are raised, and the good news is preached to the poor. And blessed is he who does not fall away on account of Me." (Luke 7:21-23)

The Lord gave the knowledge of the mysteries of the Kingdom of God to His disciples, but to others He spoke in parables, that "seeing they may not see and hearing they may not understand." (Luke 8:10)

The Son of Man knew that He must suffer many things and be rejected by the elders, chief priests, and scribes, and be killed and be raised on the third day. (Luke 9:22)

Jesus rejoiced in the Holy Spirit and said, "I praise You, Father, Lord of heaven and earth, because You have hidden these things from the wise and learned and revealed them to little children. Yes, Father, for this was Your good pleasure. All things have been delivered to Me by My Father, and no one knows who the Son is except the Father, and no one knows who the Father is except the Son and those to whom the Son chooses to reveal Him." (Luke 10:21-22)

When He was asked by the Pharisees when the Kingdom of God would come, Jesus replied, "The Kingdom of God does not come with observation, nor will people say, 'Here it is,' or 'There it is,' for behold, the Kingdom of God is within you." (Luke 17:20-21)

Jesus took the twelve aside and told them, "We are going up to Jerusalem, and everything that is written by the prophets about the Son of Man will be fulfilled. He will be handed over to the Gentiles and will be mocked, insulted, and spit upon; and when they have scourged Him, they will put Him to death. And on the third day He will rise again." (Luke 18:31-33)

The Son of Man came to seek and to save that which was lost. (Luke 19:10)

Blessed is the King who comes in the name of the Lord! Peace in heaven and glory in the highest! (Luke 19:38)

On the cross, Jesus said, "Father, forgive them, for they do not know what they are doing." One of the criminals who hung there hurled insults at Him: "Are You not the Christ? Save yourself and us!" But the other, answering, rebuked him and said, "Do you not even fear God, since you are under the same sentence? We are punished justly, for we are getting what our deeds deserve. But this man has done nothing wrong." Then he said, "Jesus, remember me when You come into Your kingdom." Jesus answered him, "I tell you the truth: today you will be with Me in paradise." (Luke 23:34, 39-43)

After His resurrection, Jesus said to the two disciples on the road to Emmaus, "Did not the Christ have to suffer these things and then enter His glory?" And beginning with Moses and all the Prophets, He explained to them what was said in all the Scriptures concerning Himself. Later, He appeared to His disciples and said to them, "These are the words I spoke to you while I was still with you, that everything must be fulfilled that is written about Me in the law of Moses, the Prophets and the Psalms." (Luke 24:26-27, 44)

The Scriptures predicted that the Christ should suffer and rise from the dead on the third day, and that repentance and forgiveness of sins should be preached in His name to all nations, beginning at Jerusalem. (Luke 24:46-47)

Christ was in the world, and the world was made through Him, and the world did not know Him. He came to His own, but His own did not receive Him. (John 1:10-11)

From Christ's fullness we have all received, and grace upon grace. For the law was given through Moses; grace and truth came through Jesus Christ. (John 1:16-17)

Jesus is the Lamb of God, who takes away the sin of the world. (John 1:29)

Jesus told Nathanael, "I tell you the truth: you shall see heaven open and the angels of God ascending and descending on the Son of Man." (John 1:51)

Jesus performed the first of His miraculous signs in Cana of Galilee and manifested His glory, and His disciples believed in Him. (John 2:11)

The Lord said, "Destroy this temple, and I will raise it again in three days." But He was speaking of the temple of His body. After He was raised from the dead, His disciples remembered that He had said this to them, and they believed the Scripture and the words that Jesus had spoken. (John 2:19, 21-22)

Jesus knew all men and had no need for anyone's testimony about man, for He knew what was in man. (John 2:24-25)

As Moses lifted up the serpent in the desert, so the Son of Man had to be lifted up, that everyone who believes in Him may have eternal life. (John 3:14-15)

God so loved the world that He gave His only begotten Son, that whoever believes in Him should not perish but have eternal life. For God did not send His Son into the world to condemn the world, but to save the world through Him. (John 3:16-17)

The light has come into the world, but men loved darkness rather than light because their deeds were evil. For everyone who does evil hates the light and will not come into the light for fear that his deeds will be exposed. But whoever practices the truth comes into the light, so that his deeds may be clearly seen as having been done through God. (John 3:19-21)

He who comes from above is above all; he who is from the earth belongs to the earth and speaks as one from the earth. He who comes from heaven is above all. He whom God has sent speaks the words of God, for He gives the Spirit without limit. (John 3:31, 34)

Just as the Father raises the dead and gives them life, even so the Son gives life to whom He wishes. (John 5:21)

The Father judges no one but has given all judgment to the Son, that all may honor the Son just as they honor the Father. He who does not honor the Son does not honor the Father who sent Him. (John 5:22-23)

All these testified that Jesus is the Son of God: John the Baptist, the works that Jesus did, the Father, and the Scriptures. (John 5:31-39)

It is the Spirit who gives life; the flesh counts for nothing. The words Jesus spoke are spirit and are life. (John 6:63)

Never did a man speak the way Jesus did. (John 7:46)

Jesus told His opponents, "You are from below; I am from above. You are of this world; I am not of this world. I told you, therefore, that you would die in your sins, for if you do not believe that I AM, you will die in your sins." (John 8:23-24)

Jesus told His opponents, "You are of your father, the devil, and you want to carry out your father's desire. He was a murderer from the beginning and did not stand in the truth, for there is no truth in him.

When he lies, he speaks his native language, for he is a liar and the father of lies. But because I tell the truth, you do not believe Me." (John 8:44-45)

While Jesus was in the world, He was the light of the world. For judgment He came into this world, that those who do not see may see, and that those who see may become blind. (John 9:5, 39)

He who enters by the door is the shepherd of his sheep. To him the doorkeeper opens, and the sheep listen to his voice, and he calls his own sheep by name and leads them out. When he brings out his own, he goes before them, and his sheep follow him because they know his voice. And they will never follow a stranger but will run away from him because they do not recognize the voice of strangers. Jesus used this figure of speech, but His hearers did not understand what He was telling them. Therefore Jesus said again, "I tell you the truth: I am the door of the sheep. All who came before Me were thieves and robbers, but the sheep did not listen to them. I am the good Shepherd; the good Shepherd lays down His life for the sheep. I am the good Shepherd; I know My sheep and My sheep know Me — just as the Father knows Me and I know the Father — and I lay down My life for the sheep." (John 10:2-8, 11, 14-15)

Jesus said, "My Father loves Me because I lay down My life that I may take it up again. No one takes it from Me, but I lay it down of My own accord. I have authority to lay it down and authority to take it up again. This command I received from My Father." (John 10:17-18)

Jesus said to Martha, "I am the resurrection and the life. He who believes in Me will live, even though he dies, and whoever lives and believes in Me will never die." (John 11:25-26)

The Lord said, "I have come as a light into the world, that whoever believes in Me should not stay in darkness. And if anyone hears My words but does not keep them, I do not judge him; for I did not come to judge the world, but to save the world." (John 12:46-47)

When Judas went out to betray Him, Jesus said, "Now is the Son of Man glorified, and God is glorified in Him. If God is glorified in Him, God will glorify the Son in Himself and will glorify Him immediately." (John 13:31-32)

The Lord said, "In My Father's house are many dwellings; if it were not so, I would have told you. I am going there to prepare a place for you. And if I go and prepare a place for you, I will come again and receive you to Myself, that you also may be where I am." (John 14:2-3)

Greater love has no one than this, that he lay down his life for his friends. (John 15:13)

He who hates Jesus hates His Father as well. (John 15:23)

The Holy Spirit convicts the world concerning sin and righteousness and judgment. (John 16:8)

Jesus told His disciples, "The Spirit will glorify Me by taking from what is Mine and making it known to you. All that belongs to the Father is Mine. Therefore I said that He will take from what is Mine and make it known to you." (John 16:14-15)

Jesus told His disciples, "I came from the Father and entered the world; now I am leaving the world and going back to the Father." (John 16:28)

The Father granted the Son authority over all people that He might give eternal life to as many as He has given Him. (John 17:2)

The Lord prayed, "I glorified You on the earth by completing the work You gave Me to do. And now, Father, glorify Me in Your presence with the glory I had with You before the world began." (John 17:4-5)

Jesus did not ask that the Father should take us out of the world, but that He protect us from the evil one. He prayed, "Father, I desire those You have given Me to be with Me where I am, that they may behold My glory, the glory You have given Me because You loved Me before the foundation of the world." (John 17:15, 24)

The Lord Jesus was taken up to heaven, after He gave instructions through the Holy Spirit to the apostles He had chosen. (Acts 1:2)

After His suffering, Jesus showed Himself to the apostles and gave many convincing proofs that He was alive. He appeared to them over a period of forty days and spoke of the things concerning the Kingdom of God. (Acts 1:3)

The Lord told the apostles, "You will receive power when the Holy Spirit comes upon you; and you will be My witnesses in Jerusalem, and in all Judea and Samaria, and to the ends of the earth." (Acts 1:8)

God raised Jesus from the dead, freeing Him from the agony of death, because it was impossible for Him to be held by it. (Acts 2:24)

The believers in Jerusalem continually devoted themselves to the apostles' teaching and to the fellowship, the breaking of bread, and to prayer. (Acts 2:42)

Jesus is the stone which was rejected by the builders, but which has become the chief cornerstone. Salvation is found in no one else, for there is no other name under heaven given to men by which we must be saved. (Acts 4:11-12)

Peter told the council, "The God of our fathers raised up Jesus whom you had killed by hanging Him on a tree. God exalted Him to His own right hand as Prince and Savior, that He might give repentance and forgiveness of sins to Israel." (Acts 5:30-31)

The Church throughout all Judea and Galilee and Samaria enjoyed a time of peace and was edified. And living in the fear of the Lord and in the comfort of the Holy Spirit, it multiplied (Acts 9:31)

God does not show favoritism but accepts those from every nation who fear Him and do what is right. (Acts 10:34-35)

God sent His word to the children of Israel, telling the good news of peace through Jesus Christ, who is Lord of all. He commanded the apostles to preach to the people and to testify that He is the One whom God appointed as judge of the living and the dead. To Him all the prophets witness that through His name, everyone who believes in Him receives forgiveness of sins. (Acts 10:36, 42-43)

Through Jesus the forgiveness of sins is proclaimed, that through Him everyone who believes is justified from all things from which they could not be justified by the law of Moses. (Acts 13:38-39)

As the gospel spread to the Gentiles, many rejoiced and glorified the word of the Lord, and all who were appointed for eternal life believed. (Acts 13:48)

In the past God overlooked the times of ignorance, but now He commands all people everywhere to repent. For He has set a day when He will judge the world with justice by the man He has appointed. He has given assurance of this to all men by raising Him from the dead. (Acts 17:30-31)

Both Jews and Greeks must turn to God in repentance and have faith in our Lord Jesus Christ. (Acts 20:21)

God promised the gospel beforehand through His prophets in the Holy Scriptures, concerning His Son—who was a descendant of David according to the flesh, and who was declared with power to be the Son of God, according to the Spirit of holiness, by His resurrection from the dead—Jesus Christ our Lord. (Romans 1:2-4)

The wrath of God is revealed from heaven against all the godlessness and unrighteousness of men who suppress the truth by their unrighteousness, since what may be known about God is manifest in them, because God has manifested it to them. (Romans 1:18-19)

Men exchanged the truth of God for a lie and worshiped and served the creation rather than the Creator, who is blessed forever. (Romans 1:25)

God's judgment against those who judge others and practice the same things themselves is based on truth. (Romans 2:1-2)

Those who show contempt for the riches of God's kindness, forbearance, and patience do not realize that the kindness of God leads toward repentance. (Romans 2:4)

There is no one righteous, not even one; there is no one who understands, no one who seeks God. All have turned away; they have together become useless; there is no one who does good, not even one. (Romans 3:10-12)

We know that whatever the law says, it says to those who are under the law, that every mouth may be silenced, and the whole world held accountable to God; because no one will be justified in His sight by the works of the law, for through the law comes the knowledge of sin. (Romans 3:19-20)

Apart from law the righteousness of God has been made known, being witnessed by the law and the prophets, even the righteousness of God through faith in Jesus Christ to all who believe. For there is no difference, for all have sinned and fall short of the glory of God, being justified freely by His grace through the redemption that is in Christ Jesus. (Romans 3:21-24)

God set forth Christ to be a propitiation through faith in His blood. He did this to demonstrate His righteousness, because in His forbearance He passed over the sins committed beforehand; He did it to demonstrate His righteousness at the present time, that He might be just and the justifier of those who have faith in Jesus. Where, then, is boasting? It is excluded. By what law? Of works? No, but by a law of faith. For we maintain that a man is justified by faith apart from works of the law. (Romans 3:25-28)

God will impute righteousness to us who believe in Him who raised Jesus our Lord from the dead, who was delivered over to death because of our sins and was raised because of our justification. (Romans 4:24-25)

When we were helpless, at the right time, Christ died for the ungodly. For rarely will anyone die for a righteous man, though perhaps for a good man someone would even dare to die. But God demonstrates His own love for us in that while we were still sinners, Christ died for us. (Romans 5:6-8)

If the many died by the trespass of the one man, how much more did the grace of God and the gift that came by the grace of the one man, Jesus Christ, abound to the many. And the gift of God is not like the result of the one man's sin, for the judgment followed one sin and brought condemnation, but the gift followed many trespasses and brought justification. (Romans 5:15-16)

If by the trespass of the one man, death reigned through that one man, much more will those who receive the abundance of grace and of the gift of righteousness reign in life through the one man, Jesus Christ. Consequently, just as the result of one trespass was condemnation for all men, so also the result of one act of righteousness was justification that brings life for all men. For just as through the disobedience of the one man the many were made sinners, so also through the obedience of the one man the many will be made righteous. (Romans 5:17-19)

The law was added that the transgression might increase. But where sin increased, grace abounded all the more, so that just as sin reigned in death, so also grace might reign through righteousness to bring eternal life through Jesus Christ our Lord. (Romans 5:20-21)

The wages of sin is death, but the gift of God is eternal life in Christ Jesus our Lord. (Romans 6:23)

What the law was powerless to do in that it was weakened through the flesh, God did by sending His own Son in the likeness of sinful flesh, on account of sin; He condemned sin in the flesh, in order that the requirement of the law might be fully met in us, who do not walk according to the flesh, but according to the Spirit. (Romans 8:3-4)

The earnest expectation of the creation eagerly waits for the revealing of the sons of God. (Romans 8:19)

God will have mercy on whom He has mercy, and He will have compassion on whom He has compassion. It does not depend on human desire or effort, but on God's mercy. (Romans 9:15-16)

Christ is the end of the law for righteousness to everyone who believes. (Romans 10:4)

Faith comes from hearing, and hearing by the word of Christ. (Romans 10:17)

Christ died and returned to life, that He might be the Lord of both the dead and the living. (Romans 14:9)

Where is the wise man? Where is the scholar? Where is the disputer of this age? Has not God made foolish the wisdom of the world? But to those whom God has called, both Jews and Greeks, Christ is the power of God and the wisdom of God. (1 Corinthians 1:20, 24)

The foolishness of God is wiser than men, and the weakness of God is stronger than men. But God chose the foolish things of the world to shame the wise, and God chose the weak things of the world to shame the strong; and the lowly things of this world and the despised things God has chosen, and the things that are not, to nullify the things that are, so that no one may boast before Him. (1 Corinthians 1:25, 27-29)

No one can lay a foundation other than the one already laid, which is Jesus Christ. (1 Corinthians 3:11)

Christ, our Passover lamb, has been sacrificed for us. (1 Corinthians 5:7)

The things that happened to the Israelites in the wilderness were examples and were written for our admonition, upon whom the fulfillment of the ages has come. (1 Corinthians 10:11)

Christ died for our sins according to the Scriptures; He was buried, and He was raised on the third day according to the Scriptures. (1 Corinthians 15:3-4)

The god of this age has blinded the minds of unbelievers, so that they cannot see the light of the gospel of the glory of Christ, who is the image of God. (2 Corinthians 4:4)

We know the grace of our Lord Jesus Christ, that though He was rich, yet for our sakes He became poor, that we through His poverty might become rich. (2 Corinthians 8:9)

Thanks be to God for His indescribable gift! (2 Corinthians 9:15)

Satan himself masquerades as an angel of light. It is not surprising, then, if his servants masquerade as servants of righteousness, whose end will be according to their works. (2 Corinthians 11:14-15)

Our Lord Jesus Christ gave Himself for our sins to rescue us from the present evil age, according to the will of our God and Father, to whom be glory for ever and ever. (Galatians 1:3-5)

If righteousness could be gained through the law, Christ died for nothing. (Galatians 2:21)

Clearly no one is justified before God by the law, for "The righteous will live by faith." (Galatians 3:11)

Christ redeemed us from the curse of the law by becoming a curse for us, for it is written: "Cursed is everyone who hangs on a tree." (Galatians 3:13)

Is the law opposed to the promises of God? Certainly not! For if a law had been given that could impart life, then righteousness would indeed have been by the law. But the Scripture has confined all under sin, so that the promise by faith in Jesus Christ might be given to those who believe. (Galatians 3:21-22)

Before faith in Christ came, we were guarded by the law, confined for the faith which was later to be revealed. So the law has become our tutor to lead us to Christ, that we might be justified by faith. Now that faith has come, we are no longer under a tutor. (Galatians 3:23-25)

When the fullness of time had come, God sent forth His Son, born of a woman, born under law, to redeem those under law, that we might receive the adoption as sons. (Galatians 4:4-5)

God's power toward us who believe is according to the working of His mighty strength, which He exerted in Christ when He raised Him from the dead and seated Him at His right hand in the heavenly realms, far above all rule and authority, power and dominion, and every title that can be given, not only in the present age but also in the one to come. (Ephesians 1:19-21)

God placed all things under Christ's feet and gave Him to be head over all things to the Church, which is His body, the fullness of Him who fills all in all. (Ephesians 1:22-23)

Through the gospel, the Gentiles are fellow heirs with Israel, fellow members of the same body, and fellow partakers of the promise in Christ Jesus. (Ephesians 3:6)

God is able to do immeasurably more than all that we ask or think, according to His power that is at work within us. To Him be glory in the Church and in Christ Jesus throughout all generations, for ever and ever. (Ephesians 3:20-21)

There is one body and one Spirit, just as we were called in one hope of our calling; one Lord, one faith, one baptism, one God and Father of all, who is over all and through all and in all. (Ephesians 4:4-6)

My attitude should be the same as that of Christ Jesus, who, being in the form of God, did not consider equality with God something to be grasped but emptied Himself, taking the form of a servant, being made in the likeness of men. And being found in appearance as a man, He humbled Himself and became obedient to death, even death on a cross. (Philippians 2:5-8)

Christ is the head of the body, the Church; He is the beginning and the firstborn from among the dead, so that in everything He might have the supremacy. (Colossians 1:18)

God was pleased to have all His fullness dwell in Christ and through Him to reconcile all things to Himself, whether things on earth or things in heaven, having made peace through the blood of His cross. (Colossians 1:19-20)

The mystery that has been kept hidden for ages and generations is now disclosed to the saints. To them God has chosen to make known among the Gentiles the glorious riches of this mystery, which is Christ in you, the hope of glory. (Colossians 1:26-27)

In Christ there is neither Greek or Jew, circumcised or uncircumcised, barbarian, Scythian, slave or free, but Christ is all and in all. (Colossians 3:11)

There is one God and one Mediator between God and men, the man Christ Jesus, who gave Himself as a ransom for all, the testimony given in its proper time. (1 Timothy 2:5-6)

By common confession, great is the mystery of godliness: He who was revealed in the flesh, vindicated in the Spirit, seen by angels, preached among the nations, believed on in the world, taken up in glory. (1 Timothy 3:16)

God's grace was given to us in Christ Jesus before the beginning of time and has now been revealed through the appearing of our Savior, Christ Jesus, who abolished death and brought life and immortality to light through the gospel. (2 Timothy 1:9-10)

The faith of those chosen of God and the knowledge of the truth, which is according to godliness, is a faith and knowledge resting in the hope of eternal life, which God, who does not lie, promised before the beginning of time. At the appointed time, He manifested His word through the preaching entrusted to the apostles by the command of God our Savior. (Titus 1:1-3)

How shall we escape if we ignore God's great salvation? This salvation, which was first announced by the Lord, was confirmed by those who heard Him. God also bore witness to it by signs and wonders and various miracles and gifts of the Holy Spirit distributed according to His will. (Hebrews 2:3-4)

I see Jesus, who was made a little lower than the angels, now crowned with glory and honor because He suffered death, that by the grace of God He might taste death for everyone. For it was fitting for Him, for whom are all things and through whom are all things, in bringing many sons to glory, to make the author of their salvation perfect through sufferings. (Hebrews 2:9-10)

Since God's children have partaken of flesh and blood, He too shared in their humanity so that by His death He might destroy him who holds the power of death, that is, the devil, and free those who all their lives were held in slavery by their fear of death. (Hebrews 2:14-15)

Christ had to be made like His brothers in every way, in order that He might become a merciful and faithful high priest in things pertaining to God, to make propitiation for the sins of the people. Because He Himself suffered when He was tempted, He is able to help those who are being tempted. (Hebrews 2:17-18)

During the days of His flesh, Jesus offered up prayers and petitions with loud cries and tears to the One who could save Him from death, and He was heard because of His devoutness. Although He was a Son, He learned obedience by the things which He suffered; and being perfected, He became the source of eternal salvation for all who obey Him, being designated by God as a high priest according to the order of Melchizedek. (Hebrews 5:7-10)

Because Jesus lives forever, He has a permanent priesthood. Therefore He is also able to save completely those who come to God through Him, since He always lives to intercede for them. (Hebrews 7:24-25)

Jesus as my high priest meets my needs: He is holy, blameless, undefiled, set apart from sinners, and exalted above the heavens. Unlike the other high priests, He does not need to offer sacrifices day after day, first for His own sins, and then for the sins of the people, for He did this once for all when He offered up Himself. (Hebrews 7:26-27)

When Christ came as high priest of the good things that have come, He went through the greater and more perfect tabernacle that is not made with hands, that is to say, not a part of this creation. Not through the blood of goats and calves but through His own blood, He entered the Most Holy Place once for all, having obtained eternal redemption. (Hebrews 9:11-12)

If the blood of goats and bulls and the ashes of a heifer sprinkled on those who are ceremonially unclean sanctify them so that they are outwardly clean, how much more will the blood of Christ, who through the eternal Spirit offered Himself unblemished to God, cleanse our consciences from acts that lead to death, so that we may serve the living God? (Hebrews 9:13-14)

Christ is the mediator of a new covenant, by means of death, for the redemption of the transgressions committed under the first covenant, that those who are called may receive the promise of the eternal inheritance. (Hebrews 9:15)

Christ has appeared once for all at the end of the ages to do away with sin by the sacrifice of Himself. And as it is appointed for man to die once and after that to face judgment, so Christ was offered once to bear the sins of many; and He will appear a second time, not to bear sin but to bring salvation to those who eagerly wait for Him. (Hebrews 9:26-28)

By the will of God, I have been sanctified through the offering of the body of Jesus Christ once for all. And every priest stands daily ministering and offering again and again the same sacrifices, which can never take away sins. But when this Priest had offered for all time one sacrifice for sins, He sat down at the right hand of God, waiting from that time for His enemies to be made a footstool for His feet. For by one offering, He has made perfect forever those who are being sanctified. (Hebrews 10:10-14)

I have come to Mount Zion, to the heavenly Jerusalem, the city of the living God, to myriads of angels, and to the assembly and Church of the firstborn, who are enrolled in heaven. I have come to God, the Judge of all men, to the spirits of righteous men made perfect, to Jesus the mediator of a new covenant, and to the sprinkled blood that speaks better things than the blood of Abel. (Hebrews 12:22-24)

Every good and perfect gift is from above, coming down from the Father of lights, with whom there is no variation, or shifting shadow. Of His own will He brought us forth by the word of truth, that we might be a kind of firstfruits of His creatures. (James 1:17-18)

As living stones, we are being built into a spiritual house to be a holy priesthood, offering spiritual sacrifices acceptable to God through Jesus Christ. We are a chosen people, a royal priesthood, a holy nation, a people for God's own possession, that we may declare the praises of Him who called us out of darkness into His marvelous light. (1 Peter 2:5, 9)

Christ suffered for me, leaving me an example that I should follow in His steps. "He committed no sin, and no deceit was found in his mouth." When He was reviled, He did not retaliate; when He suffered, He made no threats but entrusted Himself to Him who judges right-eously, and He Himself bore our sins in His body on the tree, so that I might die to sins and live for righteousness; by His wounds I have been healed. For I was like a sheep going astray, but now I have returned to the Shepherd and Overseer of my soul. (1 Peter 2:21-25)

Christ died for sins once for all, the righteous for the unrighteous, to bring me to God. Having been put to death in the body but made alive by the Spirit, He has gone into heaven and is at the right hand of God, after angels and authorities and powers were made subject to Him. (1 Peter 3:18, 22)

By this the love of God was manifested to me, that God has sent His only begotten Son into the world that I might live through Him. In this is love, not that I loved God, but that He loved me and sent His Son to be the propitiation for my sins. (1 John 4:9-10)

The Father has sent the Son to be the Savior of the world. Whoever confesses that Jesus is the Son of God, God abides in him, and he in God. (1 John 4:14-15)

Jesus Christ is the faithful witness, the firstborn from the dead, and the ruler of the kings of the earth. To Him who loves us and has freed us from our sins by His blood and has made us to be a kingdom and priests to serve His God and Father; to Him be glory and power for ever and ever. (Revelation 1:5-6)

The Lord said, "Behold, I stand at the door and knock. If anyone hears My voice and opens the door, I will come in to him and dine with him, and he with Me. To him who overcomes, I will give the right to sit with Me on My throne, just as I overcame and sat down with My Father on His throne." (Revelation 3:20-21)

You are worthy to take the scroll and to open its seals, because You were slain, and with Your blood You purchased men for God from every tribe and language and people and nation. You have made them to be a kingdom and priests to serve our God, and they will reign on the earth. (Revelation 5:9-10)

John looked and heard the voice of many angels encircling the throne and the living creatures and the elders; and their number was myriads of myriads, and thousands of thousands, saying with a loud voice, "Worthy is the Lamb, who was slain, to receive power and riches and wisdom and strength and honor and glory and blessing!" (Revelation 5:11-12)

A great multitude, which no one could number, from all nations and tribes and peoples and languages will stand before the throne and before the Lamb, clothed with white robes, with palm branches in their hands, and will cry out with a loud voice, "Salvation belongs to our God, who sits on the throne, and to the Lamb!" (Revelation 7:9-10)

Consummation

To us a child is born, to us a son is given, and the government will be on His shoulders. And He will be called Wonderful Counselor, Mighty God, Everlasting Father, Prince of Peace. Of the increase of His government and peace there will be no end. He will reign on the throne of David and over His kingdom, establishing and upholding it with justice and righteousness from that time on and forever. The zeal of the LORD of hosts will accomplish this. (Isaiah 9:6-7)

The wolf will dwell with the lamb, and the leopard will lie down with the goat, and the calf and the lion and the yearling together, and a little child will lead them. The cow will feed with the bear; their young will lie down together, and the lion will eat straw like the ox. The infant will play near the hole of the cobra, and the young child will put his hand into the viper's hole. They will neither harm nor destroy on all My holy mountain, for the earth will be full of the knowledge of the LORD as the waters cover the sea. (Isaiah 11:6-9)

You will punish the world for its evil, the wicked for their iniquity. You will put an end to the arrogance of the haughty and will humble the pride of the ruthless. (Isaiah 13:11)

The LORD of hosts has planned it to bring low the pride of all glory and to humble all who are renowned on the earth. (Isaiah 23:9)

The Lord GOD will swallow up death forever, and He will wipe away the tears from all faces; He will remove the reproach of His people from all the earth. For the LORD has spoken. And it will be said in that day, "Behold, this is our God; we have waited for Him, and He will save us. This is the LORD; we have trusted in Him; let us rejoice and be glad in His salvation." (Isaiah 25:8-9)

Behold, the Lord GOD will come with power, and His arm will rule for Him. Behold, His reward is with Him, and His recompense accompanies Him. He will feed His flock like a shepherd; He will gather the lambs in His arms and carry them close to His heart; He will gently lead those that have young. (Isaiah 40:10-11)

The heavens will vanish like smoke; the earth will wear out like a garment, and its inhabitants will die in the same way. But Your salvation will last forever, and Your righteousness will never fail. (Isaiah 51:6)

You will create new heavens and a new earth. The former things will not be remembered, nor will they come to mind. (Isaiah 65:17)

The wolf and the lamb will feed together, and the lion will eat straw like the ox, and dust will be the serpent's food. They will neither harm nor destroy in all Your holy mountain. (Isaiah 65:25)

The LORD will come with fire and with His chariots like a whirlwind; He will render His anger with fury and His rebuke with flames of fire. (Isaiah 66:15)

You will magnify Yourself and sanctify Yourself, and You will make Yourself known in the sight of many nations, and they will know that You are the LORD. (Ezekiel 38:23)

Multitudes who sleep in the dust of the earth will awake, some to everlasting life, others to shame and everlasting contempt. Those who are wise will shine like the brightness of the heavens, and those who lead many to righteousness like the stars for ever and ever. (Daniel 12:2-3)

God is jealous and the LORD avenges; the LORD takes vengeance and is filled with wrath. The LORD takes vengeance on His adversaries, and He reserves wrath against His enemies. The LORD is slow to anger and great in power and will not leave the guilty unpunished. His way is in the whirlwind and the storm, and clouds are the dust of His feet. (Nahum 1:2-3)

The earth will be filled with the knowledge of the glory of the LORD, as the waters cover the sea. (Habakkuk 2:14)

From the rising to the setting of the sun, Your name will be great among the nations. In every place incense and pure offerings will be brought to Your name, for Your name will be great among the nations. (Malachi 1:11)

The Son of Man is going to come in the glory of His Father with His angels, and then He will reward each person according to his works. (Matthew 16:27)

As the lightning comes from the east and flashes to the west, so will be the coming of the Son of Man. The sign of the Son of Man will appear in the sky, and all the nations of the earth will mourn, and they will see the Son of Man coming on the clouds of the sky with power and great glory. (Matthew 24:27, 30)

I must be ready, for the Son of Man will come at an hour when I do not expect Him. (Matthew 24:44; Luke 12:40)

When the Son of Man comes in His glory, and all the angels with Him, He will sit on His glorious throne. All the nations will be gathered before Him, and He will separate the people one from another as a shepherd separates the sheep from the goats. He will put the sheep on His right and the goats on His left. Then the King will say to those on His right, "Come, you who are blessed by My Father; inherit the kingdom prepared for you since the foundation of the world." (Matthew 25:31-34)

Men will see the Son of Man coming in clouds with great power and glory. And He will send His angels and gather His elect from the four winds, from the ends of the earth to the ends of the heavens. We must take heed and be watchful, for we do not know when that time will come. (Mark 13:26-27, 33)

Jesus will be great and will be called the Son of the Most High. The Lord God will give Him the throne of His father David, and He will reign over the house of Jacob forever, and His kingdom will never end. (Luke 1:32-33)

Nothing is hidden that will not be revealed, and nothing is secret that will not be known and come out into the open. (Luke 8:17)

Whoever is ashamed of Jesus and His words, the Son of Man will be ashamed of him when He comes in His glory and in the glory of the Father and of the holy angels. (Luke 9:26)

The children of this age marry and are given in marriage, but those who are considered worthy to attain that age and the resurrection from the dead will neither marry nor be given in marriage. They can no longer die, for they are like the angels and are sons of God, being sons of the resurrection. (Luke 20:34-36)

An hour is coming, and now is, when the dead will hear the voice of the Son of God; and those who hear will live. For as the Father has life in Himself, so He has granted the Son to have life in Himself, and He has given Him authority to execute judgment, because He is the Son of Man. (John 5:25-27)

An hour is coming when all who are in the graves will hear the voice of the Son of Man and will come out — those who have done good to a resurrection of life, and those who have done evil to a resurrection of judgment. (John 5:28-29)

God will judge the secrets of men through Jesus Christ, according to the gospel. (Romans 2:16)

We will all stand before the judgment seat of God. For it is written, "As I live, says the LORD, every knee will bow before Me, and every tongue will confess to God." So then, each of us will give an account of himself to God. (Romans 14:10-12)

Christ has been raised from the dead, the firstfruits of those who have fallen asleep. For since death came through a man, the resurrection of the dead comes also through a man. For as in Adam all die, so in Christ all will be made alive. But each in his own order: Christ, the firstfruits; afterward, those who are Christ's at His coming. Then the end will come, when He delivers the kingdom to God the Father, when He has abolished all rule and all authority and power. For He must reign until He has put all his enemies under His feet. The last enemy that will be destroyed is death. (1 Corinthians 15:20-26)

In the resurrection of the dead, the body that is sown is perishable, but it is raised imperishable; it is sown in dishonor, but it is raised in glory; it is sown in weakness, but it is raised in power; it is sown a natural body, but it is raised a spiritual body. If there is a natural body, there is also a spiritual body. (1 Corinthians 15:42-44)

The first man is of the dust of the earth; the second man is from heaven. As was the earthly man, so are those who are of the earth; and as is the man from heaven, so also are those who are of heaven. And just as we have borne the image of the earthly man, so shall we bear the likeness of the heavenly man. (1 Corinthians 15:47-49)

We will not all sleep, but we will all be changed, in a moment, in the twinkling of an eye, at the last trumpet. For the trumpet will sound, and the dead will be raised imperishable, and we shall be changed. For this perishable must clothe itself with the imperishable, and this mortal with immortality. (1 Corinthians 15:51-53)

Everything exposed by the light becomes visible, for it is light that makes everything visible. For this reason it says, "Awake, you who sleep; arise from the dead, and Christ will shine on you." (Ephesians 5:13-14)

God highly exalted Christ Jesus and gave Him the name that is above every name, that at the name of Jesus every knee should bow, in heaven and on earth and under the earth, and every tongue should confess that Jesus Christ is Lord, to the glory of God the Father. (Philippians 2:9-11)

We should not be ignorant about those who fall asleep or grieve like the rest of men, who have no hope. For if we believe that Jesus died and rose again, even so God will bring with Him those who have fallen asleep in Jesus. According to the Lord's own word, we who are alive and remain until the coming of the Lord will not precede those who have fallen asleep. For the Lord Himself will come down from heaven, with a loud command, with the voice of the archangel, and with the trumpet of God, and the dead in Christ will rise first. Then we who are alive and remain will be caught up together with them in the clouds to meet the Lord in the air. And so we will be with the Lord forever. (1 Thessalonians 4:13-17)

The Lord will give relief to His own who are afflicted when the Lord Jesus is revealed from heaven in blazing fire with His powerful angels, punishing those who do not know God and do not obey the gospel of our Lord Jesus. (2 Thessalonians 1:7-8)

We must keep God's commandment without blemish or reproach until the appearing of our Lord Jesus Christ, which God will bring about in His own time. (1 Timothy 6:14-15)

We are looking for the blessed hope and the glorious appearing of our great God and Savior, Christ Jesus, who gave Himself for us to redeem us from all iniquity and to purify for Himself a people for His own possession, zealous for good works. (Titus 2:13-14)

The day of the Lord will come like a thief, in which the heavens will pass away with a roar, and the elements will be destroyed by intense heat, and the earth and its works will be laid bare. The day of God will bring about the destruction of the heavens by fire, and the elements will melt with intense heat. (2 Peter 3:10, 12)

Jesus Christ is coming with the clouds, and every eye will see Him, even those who pierced Him; and all the peoples of the earth will mourn because of Him. Even so, Amen. (Revelation 1:7)

The kingdom of the world has become the kingdom of our Lord and of His Christ, and He will reign for ever and ever. (Revelation 11:15)

Blessed are the dead who die in the Lord from now on. They will rest from their labor, for their works will follow them. (Revelation 14:13)

Like the roar of rushing waters and like loud peals of thunder, a great multitude will shout, "Hallelujah! For the Lord God Almighty reigns. Let us rejoice and be glad and give Him glory! For the marriage of the Lamb has come, and His bride has made herself ready." Blessed are those who are invited to the marriage supper of the Lamb. (Revelation 19:6-7, 9)

John saw heaven opened, and there before him was a white horse, whose rider is called Faithful and True; and in righteousness He judges and makes war. His eyes are like a flame of fire, and on His head are many crowns. He has a name written on Him that no one knows except Himself. He is clothed in a robe dipped in blood, and His name is the Word of God. And the armies of heaven, riding on white horses and dressed in fine linen, white and clean, were following Him. And out of His mouth goes a sharp sword with which He will strike down the nations, and He will rule them with a rod of iron. He treads the winepress of the fury of the wrath of God Almighty. And on His robe and on His thigh He has a name written: KING OF KINGS AND LORD OF LORDS. (Revelation 19:11-16)

There will be a new heaven and a new earth, for the first heaven and the first earth will pass away, and there will no longer be any sea. (Revelation 21:1)

The Holy City, new Jerusalem, will come down out of heaven from God, prepared as a bride adorned for her husband. A loud voice from the throne will say, "Behold, the tabernacle of God is with men, and He will dwell with them, and they will be His people, and God Himself will be with them and be their God, and He will wipe every tear from their eyes. There will be no more death or mourning or crying or pain, for the first things have passed away." He who is seated on the throne will say, "Behold, I make all things new." (Revelation 21:2-5)

You are the Alpha and the Omega, the Beginning and the End. To him who is thirsty, You will give to drink without cost from the spring of the water of life. He who overcomes will inherit all this, and You will be his God, and he will be Your son. (Revelation 21:6-7)

There will be no temple in the new Jerusalem, because the Lord God Almighty and the Lamb are its temple. The city will not need the sun or the moon to shine on it, for the glory of God gives it light, and the Lamb is its lamp. The nations will walk by its light, and the kings of the earth will bring their splendor into it. And its gates will never be shut by day, for there will be no night there. (Revelation 21:22-25)

There will no longer be any curse. The throne of God and of the Lamb will be in the new Jerusalem, and His servants will serve Him. They will see His face, and His name will be on their foreheads. And there will be no night there; they will not need the light of a lamp or the light of the sun, for the Lord God will give them light. And they shall reign for ever and ever. (Revelation 22:3-5)

The Lord Jesus is coming quickly. His reward is with Him, and He will give to everyone according to what he has done. He is the Alpha and the Omega, the First and the Last, the Beginning and the End. Yes, He is coming quickly. Amen. Come, Lord Jesus. (Revelation 22:12-13, 20)

MY RELATIONSHIP
TO GOD

God's Grace and Love

I am unworthy of all the lovingkindness and faithfulness You have shown Your servant. (Genesis 32:10)

You have blessed me and kept me; You have made Your face shine upon me and have been gracious to me; You have turned Your face toward me and given me peace. (Numbers 6:24-26)

You, O LORD, are a shield around me; You bestow glory on me and lift up my head. (Psalm 3:3)

My shield is God Most High, who saves the upright in heart. (Psalm 7:10)

I will be glad and rejoice in Your love, for You saw my affliction and have known the anguish of my soul. (Psalm 31:7)

How great is Your goodness, which You have stored up for those who fear You, which You have prepared for those who take refuge in You before the sons of men! (Psalm 31:19)

Many are the sorrows of the wicked, but he who trusts in the LORD, lovingkindness shall surround him. (Psalm 32:10)

The eye of the LORD is on those who fear Him, on those whose hope is in His unfailing love. (Psalm 33:18)

Many, O LORD my God, are the wonders You have done, and Your thoughts toward us no one can recount to You; were I to speak and tell of them, they would be too many to declare. (Psalm 40:5)

Blessed is the one You choose and bring near to live in Your courts. We will be satisfied with the goodness of Your house, of Your holy temple. (Psalm 65:4)

In the day of my trouble I will call upon You, for You will answer me. You are great and do wondrous deeds; You alone are God. (Psalm 86:7, 10)

Because I love You, You will deliver me; You will protect me, for I acknowledge Your name. I will call upon You, and You will answer me; You will be with me in trouble, You will deliver me and honor me. (Psalm 91:14-15)

You know how I am formed; You remember that I am dust. As for man, his days are like grass; he flourishes like a flower of the field. The wind passes over it, and it is gone, and its place remembers it no more. But the lovingkindness of the LORD is from everlasting to everlasting on those who fear Him, and His righteousness with their children's children, to those who keep His covenant and remember to obey His precepts. (Psalm 103:14-18)

May Your merciful kindness be my comfort, according to Your promise to Your servant. (Psalm 119:76)

The LORD will judge His people and have compassion on His servants. (Psalm 135:14)

You have loved me with an everlasting love; You have drawn me with lovingkindness. (Jeremiah 31:3)

No one can come to Jesus unless it has been granted him from the Father. (John 6:65)

I believe that it is through the grace of our Lord Jesus that I am saved. (Acts 15:11)

I have been set apart for the gospel of God — I am among those who are called to belong to Jesus Christ. (Romans 1:1, 6)

I have been loved by God and called to be a saint; grace and peace have been given to me from God our Father and the Lord Jesus Christ. (Romans 1:7)

Having been justified by faith, I have peace with God through the Lord Jesus Christ, through whom I have gained access by faith into this grace in which I stand; and I rejoice in the hope of the glory of God. (Romans 5:1-2)

Who shall separate me from the love of Christ? Shall tribulation, or distress, or persecution, or famine, or nakedness, or danger, or sword? As it is written: "For Your sake we face death all day long; we are considered as sheep to be slaughtered." Yet in all these things, I am more than a conqueror through Him who loved me. (Romans 8:35-37)

I am convinced that neither death nor life, nor angels nor principalities, nor things present nor things to come, nor powers, nor height nor depth, nor anything else in all creation, will be able to separate me from the love of God that is in Christ Jesus, my Lord. (Romans 8:38-39)

Grace and peace come from God our Father and the Lord Jesus Christ. (1 Corinthians 1:3; 2 Corinthians 1:2; Galatians 1:3)

I thank God because of His grace in Christ Jesus. In Him we have been enriched in every way, in all speech and in all knowledge. We do not lack any spiritual gift, as we eagerly wait for the revelation of our Lord Jesus Christ. (1 Corinthians 1:4-5, 7)

God will keep me strong to the end, so that I will be blameless on the day of our Lord Jesus Christ. God is faithful, through whom I was called into fellowship with His Son, Jesus Christ, our Lord. (1 Corinthians 1:8-9)

Thanks be to God, who always leads us in triumph in Christ and through us spreads everywhere the fragrance of the knowledge of Him. (2 Corinthians 2:14)

The grace of the Lord Jesus Christ and the love of God and the fellowship of the Holy Spirit are with me. (2 Corinthians 13:14)

God set me apart from my mother's womb and called me through His grace. (Galatians 1:15)

God chose me in Christ before the foundation of the world to be holy and blameless in His sight. In love He predestined me to be adopted as His son through Jesus Christ, according to the good pleasure of His will, to the praise of the glory of His grace, which He bestowed upon me in the One He loves. (Ephesians 1:4-6)

In Christ I have obtained an inheritance, having been predestined according to the plan of Him who works all things according to the counsel of His will, that we who have trusted in Christ should be to the praise of His glory. (Ephesians 1:11-12)

By grace I have been saved through faith, and this is not of myself; it is the gift of God, not of works, so that no one can boast. (Ephesians 2:8-9)

I am confident of this, that He who began a good work in me will carry it on to completion until the day of Christ Jesus. (Philippians 1:6)

The grace of the Lord Jesus Christ is with my spirit. (Philippians 4:23)

The grace of my Lord was poured out on me abundantly, along with the faith and love that are in Christ Jesus. (1 Timothy 1:14)

God has saved me and called me with a holy calling, not according to my works but according to His own purpose and grace. (2 Timothy 1:9)

The God of all grace, who called me to His eternal glory in Christ, after I have suffered a little while, will Himself perfect, confirm, strengthen, and establish me. (1 Peter 5:10)

We have known and have believed the love God has for us. God is love, and he who abides in love abides in God, and God in him. In this way, love has been perfected among us so that we may have confidence in the day of judgment; because as He is, so are we in this world. There is no fear in love, but perfect love casts out fear, because fear involves punishment, and the one who fears has not been perfected in love. (1 John 4:16-18)

I have been called, having been loved by God the Father and kept by Jesus Christ. (Jude 1)

God's Salvation and Forgiveness

This poor man cried out, and the LORD heard him and saved him out of all his troubles. (Psalm 34:6)

The LORD is close to the brokenhearted and saves those who are crushed in spirit. (Psalm 34:18)

The salvation of the righteous comes from the LORD; He is their stronghold in time of trouble. The LORD helps them and delivers them; He delivers them from the wicked and saves them, because they take refuge in Him. (Psalm 37:39-40)

God lifted me out of the slimy pit, out of the mud and mire; He set my feet on a rock and gave me a firm place to stand. He put a new song in my mouth, a hymn of praise to our God. Many will see and fear and put their trust in the LORD. (Psalm 40:2-3)

The sacrifices of God are a broken spirit; a broken and contrite heart, O God, You will not despise. (Psalm 51:17)

Have mercy on me, O God, have mercy on me, for in You my soul takes refuge. I will take refuge in the shadow of Your wings, until destruction passes by. I cry out to God Most High, to God who fulfills His purpose for me. (Psalm 57:1-2)

My soul silently waits for God alone; my salvation comes from Him. He alone is my rock and my salvation; He is my stronghold; I will never be shaken. (Psalm 62:1-2)

Blessed be the Lord; day by day He bears our burdens, the God of our salvation. Our God is the God of salvation, and to GOD the Lord belong escapes from death. (Psalm 68:19-20)

My mouth will tell of Your righteousness and of Your salvation all day long, though I know not its measure. I will come in the strength of the Lord GOD; I will proclaim Your righteousness, Yours alone. Since my youth, O God, You have taught me, and to this day I declare Your wondrous deeds. (Psalm 71:15-17)

Surely Your salvation is near to those who fear You. (Psalm 85:9)

God will not always strive with us, nor will He harbor His anger forever; He does not treat us as our sins deserve or repay us according to our iniquities. For as high as the heavens are above the earth, so great is His love for those who fear Him; as far as the east is from the west, so far has He removed our transgressions from us. As a father has compassion on His children, so the LORD has compassion on those who fear Him. (Psalm 103:9-13)

I love the LORD, because He has heard my voice and my supplications. Because He turned His ear to me, I will call on Him as long as I live. (Psalm 116:1-2)

The LORD is my strength and my song; He has become my salvation. (Psalm 118:14)

There is not a righteous man on earth who continually does good and never sins. (Ecclesiastes 7:20)

"Come now, let us reason together," says the LORD. "Though your sins are like scarlet, they shall be as white as snow; though they are red as crimson, they shall be like wool." (Isaiah 1:18)

Surely God is my salvation; I will trust and not be afraid. For the Lord GOD is my strength and my song, and He has become my salvation. (Isaiah 12:2)

This is what the Lord GOD, the Holy One of Israel, says: "In repentance and rest is your salvation; in quietness and trust is your strength." (Isaiah 30:15)

Let the wicked forsake his way and the unrighteous man his thoughts; let him return to the LORD, and He will have mercy on him, and to our God, for He will abundantly pardon. (Isaiah 55:7)

I will greatly rejoice in the LORD; my soul will be joyful in my God. For He has clothed me with garments of salvation and arrayed me in a robe of righteousness, as a bridegroom decks himself with ornaments, and as a bride adorns herself with her jewels. (Isaiah 61:10)

All of us have become like one who is unclean, and all our righteous acts are like filthy rags; we all shrivel up like a leaf, and our iniquities, like the wind, sweep us away. But now, O LORD, You are our Father.

We are the clay; You are the potter; we are all the work of Your hand. (Isaiah 64:6, 8)

Heal me, O LORD, and I will be healed; save me, and I will be saved, for You are my praise. (Jeremiah 17:14)

Why should any living man complain when punished for his sins? Let us search out and examine our ways, and let us return to the LORD. (Lamentations 3:39-40)

"Even now," declares the LORD, "return to Me with all your heart, with fasting and weeping and mourning." So rend your heart and not your garments. Return to the LORD, your God, for He is gracious and compassionate, slow to anger and abounding in lovingkindness, and He relents from sending calamity. (Joel 2:12-13)

From within, out of the heart of men, proceed evil thoughts, sexual immorality, thefts, murders, adulteries, greed, wickedness, deceit, lewdness, envy, slander, arrogance, and folly. All these evil things come from within and defile a man. (Mark 7:21-23)

I do not rejoice that the spirits are subject to me, but I rejoice that my name is written in heaven. (Luke 10:20)

As many as received Christ, to them He gave the right to become children of God, to those who believe in His name, who were born not of blood, nor of the will of the flesh, nor of the will of man, but of God. (John 1:12-13)

Unless one is born again, he cannot see the Kingdom of God; unless one is born of water and the Spirit, he cannot enter into the Kingdom of God. That which is born of the flesh is flesh, and that which is born of the Spirit is spirit. The wind blows wherever it pleases, and we hear its sound, but we cannot tell where it comes from, or where it is going. So it is with everyone born of the Spirit. (John 3:3, 5-6, 8)

Whoever believes in the Son has eternal life, but whoever rejects the Son will not see life, for the wrath of God remains on him. (John 3:36)

Everyone who drinks ordinary water will be thirsty again, but whoever drinks the water You give will never thirst. Indeed, the water You give becomes in us a spring of water welling up to eternal life. (John 4:13-14)

Whoever hears the word of Jesus and believes Him who sent Him has eternal life and will not come into judgment but has passed over from death to life. (John 5:24)

I should not work for the food that perishes, but for the food that endures to eternal life, which the Son of Man gives me, for God, the Father, has set His seal on Him. (John 6:27)

Lord Jesus, all that the Father gives You will come to You, and who-ever comes to You, You will never cast out. For You have come down from heaven not to do Your own will, but the will of Him who sent You. And this is the will of Him who sent You, that You will lose none of all that He has given You, but raise them up at the last day. For Your Father's will is that everyone who looks to the Son and believes in Him may have eternal life, and You will raise him up at the last day. (John 6:37-40)

I shall know the truth, and the truth shall set me free. Everyone who commits sin is a slave of sin. And a slave has no permanent place in the family, but a son belongs to it forever. So if the Son sets me free, I shall be free indeed. (John 8:32, 34-36)

You are the door; whoever enters through You will be saved and will come in and go out and find pasture. The thief comes only to steal and kill and destroy; You have come that we may have life and have it abun-dantly. (John 10:9-10)

Your sheep hear Your voice, and You know them, and they follow You. You give them eternal life, and they shall never perish; no one can snatch them out of Your hand. The Father, who has given them to You, is greater than all; no one can snatch them out of the Father's hand. (John 10:27-28)

Blessed are those who have not seen Jesus and yet have believed in Him. (John 20:29)

Since I have been justified by Christ's blood, much more shall I be saved from God's wrath through Him. For if, when I was God's enemy, I was reconciled to Him through the death of His Son, much more, hav-ing been reconciled, shall I be saved through His life. And not only this, but I also rejoice in God through my Lord Jesus Christ, through whom I have now received the reconciliation. (Romans 5:9-11)

Sin shall not be my master, because I am not under law, but under grace. I have been set free from sin and have become a slave of right-eousness. (Romans 6:14, 18)

Those God foreknew, He also predestined to be conformed to the likeness of His Son, that He might be the firstborn among many broth-ers. And those He predestined, He also called; those He called, He also justified; those He justified, He also glorified. (Romans 8:29-30)

The message of the cross is foolishness to those who are perishing, but to us who are being saved, it is the power of God. (1 Corinthians 1:18)

I was washed, I was sanctified, I was justified in the name of the Lord Jesus Christ and by the Spirit of our God. (1 Corinthians 6:11)

The love of Christ compels me, because I am convinced that One died for all, and therefore all died. And He died for all, that those who live should no longer live for themselves but for Him who died for them and was raised again. (2 Corinthians 5:14-15)

God made Him who knew no sin to be sin for me, so that in Him I might become the righteousness of God. (2 Corinthians 5:21)

I must not receive God's grace in vain. For He says, "In the acceptable time I heard you, and in the day of salvation I helped you." Now is the time of God's favor; now is the day of salvation. (2 Corinthians 6:1-2)

Godly sorrow brings repentance that leads to salvation and leaves no regret, but worldly sorrow brings death. (2 Corinthians 7:10)

In Christ I have redemption through His blood, the forgiveness of sins, in accordance with the riches of God's grace that He lavished on me with all wisdom and understanding. (Ephesians 1:7-8)

We were dead in our trespasses and sins, in which we used to live when we followed the course of this world and of the ruler of the kingdom of the air, the spirit who is now at work in the sons of disobedience. All of us also lived among them at one time, gratifying the cravings of our flesh and of the mind, and were by nature children of wrath. (Ephesians 2:1-3)

God, who is rich in mercy because of His great love with which He loved me, made me alive with Christ, even when I was dead in transgressions; it is by grace I have been saved. (Ephesians 2:4-5)

I am no longer a stranger and alien, but a fellow citizen with God's people and a member of God's household, built on the foundation of the apostles and prophets, with Christ Jesus Himself as the chief cornerstone. (Ephesians 2:19-20)

The Father has qualified me to share in the inheritance of the saints in the light. For He has rescued me from the dominion of darkness and brought me into the kingdom of the His beloved Son, in whom I have redemption, the forgiveness of sins. (Colossians 1:12-14)

Once I was alienated from God and was an enemy in my mind because of my evil works. But now He has reconciled me by His fleshly body through death to present me holy and blameless in His sight and free from reproach. (Colossians 1:21-22)

When I was dead in my trespasses and in the uncircumcision of my flesh, God made me alive with Christ. He forgave me all my trespasses, having canceled the written code, with its regulations, that was against me and was contrary to me; He took it away, nailing it to the cross. And having disarmed the powers and authorities, He made a public spectacle of them, triumphing over them by the cross. (Colossians 2:13-15)

God did not appoint me to suffer wrath but to obtain salvation through my Lord Jesus Christ. He died for me, so that, whether I am awake or asleep, I may live together with Him. (1 Thessalonians 5:9-10)

From the beginning, God chose me for salvation through sanctification by the Spirit and through belief in the truth. He called me to this through the gospel, that I might obtain the glory of my Lord Jesus Christ. (2 Thessalonians 2:13-14)

It is a trustworthy saying, that deserves full acceptance, that Christ Jesus came into the world to save sinners. I obtained mercy as the worst of sinners, so that Christ Jesus might display His unlimited patience as an example for those who would believe on Him for eternal life. (1 Timothy 1:15-16)

When the kindness and love of God, my Savior, appeared, He saved me, not by works of righteousness which I have done, but according to His mercy. He saved me through the washing of regeneration and renewal by the Holy Spirit whom He poured out on me abundantly through Jesus Christ my Savior, so that having been justified by His grace, I might become an heir according to the hope of eternal life. (Titus 3:4-7)

I was not redeemed with perishable things such as silver or gold from the aimless way of life handed down to me from my forefathers, but with the precious blood of Christ, as of a lamb without blemish or defect. (1 Peter 1:18-19)

If I claim to be without sin, I deceive myself, and the truth is not in me. If I confess my sins, He is faithful and just and will forgive me my sins and purify me from all unrighteousness. If I claim I have not sinned, I make Him a liar, and His word is not in me. (1 John 1:8-10)

Those whom You love You rebuke and discipline. Therefore I will be zealous and repent. (Revelation 3:19)

God's Care, Guidance, and Provision

Blessed be the LORD, the God of Abraham, who has not abandoned His lovingkindness and His truth. (Genesis 24:27)

As you said to Jacob, "Behold, I am with you and will watch over you wherever you go; I will not leave you until I have done what I have promised you." (Genesis 28:15)

I have waited for Your salvation, O LORD. (Genesis 49:18)

Others may intend evil, but God can use it for good to accomplish His loving purposes. (Genesis 50:20)

You sent an angel before Your people to guard them along the way and to bring them to the place You prepared for them. (Exodus 23:20)

Your presence will go with me, and You will give me rest. (Exodus 33:14)

I know in my heart that as a man disciplines his son, so the LORD, my God, disciplines me. (Deuteronomy 8:5)

The secret things belong to the LORD, our God, but the things revealed belong to us and to our children forever, that we may observe Your words. (Deuteronomy 29:29)

The LORD Himself goes before me and will be with me; He will never leave me nor forsake me. I will not be afraid or be dismayed. (Deuteronomy 31:8)

The LORD is my rock and my fortress and my deliverer; my God is my rock; I will take refuge in Him, my shield and the horn of my salvation, my stronghold and my refuge — my Savior, You save me from violence. I call on the LORD, who is worthy of praise, and I am saved from my enemies. (2 Samuel 22:2-4)

You are my lamp, O LORD; the LORD turns my darkness into light. With Your help I can advance against a troop; with my God I can leap over a wall. (2 Samuel 22:29-30)

God is my strong fortress, and He sets the blameless free in His way. He makes my feet like the feet of a deer; He enables me to stand on the heights. He trains my hands for battle, so that my arms can bend a bow of bronze. He gives me His shield of victory; He stoops down to make me great. He broadens the path beneath me, and my feet have not slipped. (2 Samuel 22:33-37)

Jabez cried out to the God of Israel, "Oh, that You would bless me and enlarge my territory! Let Your hand be with me and keep me from evil, so it may not grieve me." And God granted his request. (1 Chronicles 4:10)

LORD, there is no one besides You to help the powerless against the mighty. Help us, O LORD, our God, for we rest on You. O LORD, You are our God; do not let man prevail against You. (2 Chronicles 14:11)

I will both lie down in peace and sleep, for You alone, O LORD, make me dwell in safety. (Psalm 4:8)

You will light my lamp; the LORD, my God, will make my darkness light. (Psalm 18:28)

It is God who arms me with strength and makes my way perfect. (Psalm 18:32)

The LORD is my shepherd; I shall not be in want. He makes me lie down in green pastures; He leads me beside quiet waters; He restores my soul. He guides me in the paths of righteousness for His name's sake. Even though I walk through the valley of the shadow of death, I will fear no evil, for You are with me; Your rod and Your staff, they comfort me. You prepare a table before me in the presence of my enemies. You anoint my head with oil; my cup overflows. Surely goodness and mercy will follow me all the days of my life, and I will dwell in the house of the LORD forever. (Psalm 23:1-6)

Who is the man that fears the LORD? He will instruct him in the way he should choose. (Psalm 25:12)

In You, O LORD, I have taken refuge; let me never be ashamed; deliver me in Your righteousness. Since You are my rock and my fortress, for Your name's sake, lead me and guide me. Into Your hands I commit my spirit; redeem me, O LORD, God of truth. (Psalm 31:1, 3, 5)

My times are in Your hand; deliver me from the hand of my enemies and from those who pursue me. (Psalm 31:15)

You are my hiding place; You will preserve me from trouble and surround me with songs of deliverance. (Psalm 32:7)

You will instruct me and teach me in the way I should go; You will counsel me and watch over me. (Psalm 32:8)

God is my refuge and strength, an ever-present help in trouble. Therefore I will not fear, though the earth changes and the mountains slip into the heart of the sea. (Psalm 46:1-2)

I will call upon You in the day of trouble, and You will deliver me, and I will honor You. (Psalm 50:15)

Surely God is my helper; the Lord is the sustainer of my soul. (Psalm 54:4)

You have been a shelter for me and a strong tower against the enemy. (Psalm 61:3)

I am continually with You; You hold me by my right hand. You guide me with Your counsel, and afterward You will take me to glory. (Psalm 73:23-24)

Blessed is the man You discipline, O LORD, the man You teach from Your word. (Psalm 94:12)

If Your law had not been my delight, I would have perished in my affliction. (Psalm 119:92)

I lift up my eyes to the hills — where does my help come from? My help comes from the LORD, who made heaven and earth. He will not allow my foot to slip; He who watches over me will not slumber. The LORD is my keeper; the LORD is my shade at my right hand. The sun will not harm me by day, nor the moon by night. The LORD will keep me from all evil; He will preserve my soul. The LORD will watch over my coming and going from this time forth and forever. (Psalm 121:1-3, 5-8)

My help is in the name of the LORD, who made heaven and earth. (Psalm 124:8)

I will not despise the discipline of the LORD nor resent His correction, for the LORD disciplines those He loves; as a father, the son he delights in. (Proverbs 3:11-12)

I will not fear, for You are with me; I will not be dismayed, for You are my God. You will strengthen me and help me; You will uphold me with Your righteous right hand. For You are the LORD, my God, who takes hold of my right hand and says to me, "Do not fear; I will help you." (Isaiah 41:10, 13)

Even to my old age, You are the same, and even to my gray hairs, You will carry me. You have made me, and You will bear me; You will sustain me, and You will deliver me. (Isaiah 46:4)

Thus says the LORD, my Redeemer, the Holy One of Israel: "I am the LORD, your God, who teaches you to profit, who leads you in the way you should go." (Isaiah 48:17)

The Lord GOD has given me the tongue of the learned, to know the word that sustains the weary. He awakens me morning by morning; He awakens my ear to hear as the learned. (Isaiah 50:4)

I called to the LORD in my distress, and He answered me. From the depths of the grave, I called for help, and You heard my voice. (Jonah 2:2)

My Father knows what I need before I ask Him. (Matthew 6:8)

The Spirit helps me in my weakness, for I do not know what I ought to pray for, but the Spirit Himself intercedes for me with groans that words cannot express. And He who searches the hearts knows the mind of the Spirit, because the Spirit intercedes for the saints according to the will of God. (Romans 8:26-27)

I know that all things work together for good to those who love God, to those who have been called according to His purpose. (Romans 8:28)

If God is for me, who can be against me? He who did not spare His own Son but delivered Him up for us all, how will He not, also with Him, freely give us all things? (Romans 8:31-32)

Who will bring a charge against those whom God has chosen? It is God who justifies. Who is he who condemns? It is Christ Jesus who died, who was furthermore raised to life, who is at the right hand of God and is also interceding for me. (Romans 8:33-34)

The gifts and the calling of God are irrevocable. (Romans 11:29)

No temptation has overtaken me except what is common to man. And God is faithful, who will not let me be tempted beyond what I am able but with the temptation will also provide a way out, so that I may be able to endure it. (1 Corinthians 10:13)

As the sufferings of Christ abound in me, so also my comfort abounds through Christ. (2 Corinthians 1:5)

The Lord is faithful, who will strengthen me and protect me from the evil one. (2 Thessalonians 3:3)

May the Lord of peace Himself give me peace always and in every way. The Lord be with all of us. (2 Thessalonians 3:16)

May the God of peace, who through the blood of the eternal covenant brought back from the dead our Lord Jesus, that great Shepherd of the sheep, equip me in every good thing to do His will, working in me what is pleasing in His sight, through Jesus Christ, to whom be glory forever and ever. (Hebrews 13:20-21)

God's divine power has given me all things that pertain to life and godliness, through the knowledge of Him who called me by His own glory and virtue. Through these He has given me His very great and precious promises, so that through them I may be a partaker of the divine nature, having escaped the corruption that is in the world by lust. (2 Peter 1:3-4)

Knowing and Loving God

Like Noah, I want to find favor in the eyes of the LORD. (Genesis 6:8) If I have found grace in Your sight, teach me Your ways, so that I may know You and continue to find favor with You. (Exodus 33:13)

I pray You, show me Your glory. (Exodus 33:18)

When I seek the Lord my God, I will find Him if I seek Him with all my heart and with all my soul. (Deuteronomy 4:29)

The LORD, my God, the LORD is one. I want to love the LORD, my God, with all my heart and with all my soul and with all my strength. (Deuteronomy 6:4-5)

The LORD, my God, wants me to fear Him, to walk in all His ways, to love Him, and to serve the LORD, my God, with all my heart and with all my soul. (Deuteronomy 10:12)

I want to love the LORD, my God, and to serve Him with all my heart and with all my soul. (Deuteronomy 11:13)

I will carefully observe all the commandment to love the LORD, my God, to walk in all His ways and to hold fast to Him. (Deuteronomy 11:22)

I want to love the LORD, my God, obey His voice, and hold fast to Him. For the Lord is my life and the length of my days. (Deuteronomy 30:20)

I will set my heart and my soul to seek the LORD, my God. (1 Chronicles 22:19)

I want to know God and serve Him with a whole heart and with a willing mind; for the LORD searches all hearts and understands every motive behind the thoughts. (1 Chronicles 28:9)

The joy of the Lord is my strength. (Nehemiah 8:10)

It is the spirit in a man, the breath of the Almighty, that gives him understanding. (Job 32:8)

I have set the LORD always before me; because He is at my right hand, I will not be shaken. Therefore my heart is glad, and my glory rejoices; my body also will rest in hope. You will make known to me the path of life; in Your presence is fullness of joy; in Your right hand are pleasures forever. (Psalm 16:8-9, 11)

I love You, O LORD, my strength. The LORD is my rock and my fortress and my deliverer; my God is my rock, in whom I take refuge. He is my shield and the horn of my salvation, my stronghold. I call upon the LORD, who is worthy of praise, and I am saved from my enemies. (Psalm 18:1-3)

As the deer pants for the water brooks, so my soul pants for You, O God. My soul thirsts for God, for the living God. When shall I come and appear before God? (Psalm 42:1-2)

O God, You are my God; earnestly I seek You; my soul thirsts for You; my body longs for You, in a dry and weary land where there is no water. (Psalm 63:1)

Whom have I in heaven but You? And there is nothing on earth I desire besides You. My flesh and my heart may fail, but God is the strength of my heart and my portion forever. Those who are far from You will perish; You have cut off all who are unfaithful to You. But as for me, the nearness of God is my good. I have made the Lord GOD my refuge, that I may tell of all Your works. (Psalm 73:25-28)

How lovely are Your dwellings, O LORD of hosts! My soul longs and even faints for the courts of the LORD; my heart and my flesh cry out for the living God. (Psalm 84:1-2)

Blessed are those whose strength is in You, who have set their hearts on pilgrimage. (Psalm 84:5)

Better is one day in Your courts than a thousand elsewhere; I would rather be a doorkeeper in the house of my God than dwell in the tents of the wicked. For the LORD God is a sun and shield; the LORD will give grace and glory; no good thing does He withhold from those who walk in integrity. O LORD of hosts, blessed is the man who trusts in You! (Psalm 84:10-12)

Teach me Your way, O LORD; I will walk in Your truth; unite my heart to fear Your name. (Psalm 86:11)

Let those who love the LORD hate evil. He preserves the souls of His saints and delivers them from the hand of the wicked. Light is sown for the righteous, and gladness for the upright in heart. (Psalm 97:10-11)

Blessed is the man who fears the LORD, who finds great delight in His commands. (Psalm 112:1)

I will give You my heart, and let my eyes delight in Your ways. (Proverbs 23:26)

Walking in the way of Your laws, O LORD, I wait for You; Your name and Your memory are the desire of my soul. (Isaiah 26:8)

My soul yearns for You in the night; my spirit within me diligently seeks You. When Your judgments come upon the earth, the inhabitants of the world learn righteousness. (Isaiah 26:9)

I do not want to be like those who draw near to You with their mouths and honor You with their lips, but whose hearts are far from You, and whose reverence for You is made up only of rules taught by men. (Isaiah 29:13)

I will seek the LORD while He may be found and call upon Him while He is near. (Isaiah 55:6)

I will call upon You and come and pray to You, and You will listen to me. I will seek You and find You when I search for You with all my heart. (Jeremiah 29:12-13)

"The LORD is my portion," says my soul, "therefore I will wait for Him." The LORD is good to those who wait for Him, to the soul who seeks Him. It is good to hope silently for the salvation of the LORD. (Lamentations 3:24-26)

Father in heaven, hallowed be Your name. Your kingdom come; Your will be done on earth as it is in heaven. (Matthew 6:9-10)

He who loves his father or mother more than You is not worthy of You; he who loves his son or daughter more than You is not worthy of You. (Matthew 10:37)

I want to walk in the steps of Jesus, who often withdrew to lonely places and prayed. (Mark 1:35; Luke 5:16)

I will not be afraid of those who kill the body and after that can do no more. But I will fear the One who, after killing, has authority to cast into hell. (Luke 12:4-5)

Whoever acknowledges You before men, the Son of Man will also acknowledge him before the angels of God. But he who disowns You before men will be denied before the angels of God. (Luke 12:8-9)

If anyone comes to You and does not hate his father and mother, his wife and children, his brothers and sisters—yes, even his own life—he cannot be Your disciple. And whoever does not carry his cross and follow You cannot be Your disciple. (Luke 14:26-27)

As the Father has loved You, You also have loved me. I must abide in Your love. If I keep Your commandments, I will abide in Your love, just as You kept Your Father's commandments and abide in His love. You have told me this so that Your joy may be in me and that my joy may be full. (John 15:9-11)

We are Your friends if we do what You command. No longer do You call us servants, because a servant does not know what his master is doing. Instead, You have called us friends, for everything that You learned from Your Father, You have made known to us. We did not choose You, but You chose us and appointed that we should go and bear fruit, and that our fruit should remain, that whatever we ask the Father in Your name, He may give to us. (John 15:14-16)

The Father Himself loves me, because I have loved You and have believed that You came forth from God. (John 16:27)

This is eternal life: that I may know You, the only true God, and Jesus Christ, whom You have sent. (John 17:3)

I do not want to be conformed to the pattern of this world but to be transformed by the renewing of my mind, that I may prove that the will of God is good and acceptable and perfect. (Romans 12:2)

A natural man does not receive the things of the Spirit, for they are foolishness to him, and he cannot understand them, because they are spiritually discerned. "For who has known the mind of the LORD that he may instruct Him?" But we have the mind of Christ. (1 Corinthians 2:14, 16)

If anyone loves God, he is known by God. (1 Corinthians 8:3)

God made known to me the mystery of His will according to His good pleasure, which He purposed in Himself, that in the stewardship of the fullness of the times, He might gather together all things in Christ, things in the heavens and things upon the earth. (Ephesians 1:9-10)

May the God of my Lord Jesus Christ, the Father of glory, give me a spirit of wisdom and of revelation in the full knowledge of Him, and may the eyes of my heart be enlightened, in order that I may know what is the hope of His calling, what are the riches of His glorious inheritance in the saints, and what is the incomparable greatness of His power toward us who believe. (Ephesians 1:17-19)

May God grant me, according to the riches of His glory, to be strengthened with power through His Spirit in my inner being, so that Christ may dwell in my heart through faith. And may I, being rooted and grounded in love, be able to comprehend with all the saints what is the width and length and height and depth of the love of Christ, and to know this love that surpasses knowledge, that I may be filled to all the fullness of God. (Ephesians 3:16-19)

Grace be with all who love our Lord Jesus Christ with an incorruptible love. (Ephesians 6:24)

May my love abound more and more in full knowledge and depth of insight, so that I may be able to approve the things that are excellent, in order to be sincere and blameless until the day of Christ — having been filled with the fruit of righteousness that comes through Jesus Christ, to the glory and praise of God. (Philippians 1:9-11)

May God fill me with the knowledge of His will through all spiritual wisdom and understanding, so that I may walk worthy of the Lord and please Him in every way, bearing fruit in every good work, and growing in the knowledge of God; strengthened with all power according to His glorious might, so that I may have great endurance and patience with joy. (Colossians 1:9-11)

May our hearts be encouraged, being joined together in love, so that we may have the riches of the full assurance of understanding. (Colossians 2:2)

May the Lord direct my heart into the love of God and into the patience of Christ. (2 Thessalonians 3:5)

As one who shares in the heavenly calling, I should fix my thoughts on Jesus, the Apostle and High Priest of my confession. (Hebrews 3:1)

Though I have not seen Jesus, I love Him; and though I do not see Him now but believe in Him, I rejoice with joy inexpressible and full of glory, for I am receiving the end of my faith, the salvation of my soul. (1 Peter 1:8-9)

May I grow in the grace and knowledge of my Lord and Savior Jesus Christ. To Him be glory both now and forever. (2 Peter 3:18)

Those who obey Christ's commandments abide in Him, and He in them. And this is how I know that He abides in me: by the Spirit whom He has given me. (1 John 3:24)

I know that I abide in Christ, and He in me, because He has given me of His Spirit. (1 John 4:13)

Praising and Thanking God

The LORD is my Banner. (Exodus 17:15)

My heart rejoices in the LORD; my horn is exalted in the LORD. My mouth boasts over my enemies, for I delight in Your salvation. (1 Samuel 2:1)

I will give thanks to the LORD, call upon His name, and make known to others what He has done. I will sing to Him, sing praises to Him, and tell of all His wonderful acts. (1 Chronicles 16:8-9)

Glory in the holy name of the LORD; let the hearts of those who seek the LORD rejoice. Seek the LORD and His strength; seek His face always. Remember the wonderful works He has done, His miracles, and the judgments He pronounced. (1 Chronicles 16:10-12)

I will praise You, O LORD, with all my heart; I will tell of all Your wonders. I will be glad and rejoice in You; I will sing praise to Your name, O Most High. (Psalm 9:1-2)

I trust in Your loyal love; my heart rejoices in Your salvation. I will sing to the LORD, for He has dealt bountifully with me. (Psalm 13:5-6)

The LORD lives! Blessed be my rock! Exalted be the God of my salvation! (Psalm 18:46)

Rejoice in the Lord, O you righteous; praise is becoming to the upright. (Psalm 33:1)

I will bless the LORD at all times; His praise will always be in my mouth. (Psalm 34:1)

I will sing of Your strength; yes, I will sing of Your mercy in the morning, for You have been my stronghold, my refuge in times of trouble. To You, O my Strength, I will sing praises, for God is my fortress, my loving God. (Psalm 59:16-17)

Because Your lovingkindness is better than life, my lips will praise You. So I will bless You as long as I live; I will lift up my hands in Your name. (Psalm 63:3-4)

The righteous shall rejoice in the LORD and trust in Him, and all the upright in heart shall glory. (Psalm 64:10)

I will praise the name of God in song and magnify Him with thanksgiving. (Psalm 69:30)

I will praise You, O Lord my God, with all my heart, and I will glorify Your name forever. For great is Your love toward me, and You have delivered my soul from the depths of the grave. (Psalm 86:12-13)

Blessed are those who have learned to acclaim You, who walk in the light of Your presence, O LORD. They rejoice in Your name all day long, and they are exalted in Your righteousness. (Psalm 89:15-16)

Bless the LORD, O my soul, and forget not all His benefits; who forgives all your iniquities and heals all your diseases; who redeems your life from the pit and crowns you with love and compassion; who satisfies your desires with good things, so that your youth is renewed like the eagle's. (Psalm 103:2-5)

I will sing to the LORD as long as I live; I will sing praise to my God while I have my being. May my meditation be pleasing to Him; I will be glad in the LORD. (Psalm 104:33-34)

My mouth will speak the praise of the LORD, and all flesh will bless His holy name for ever and ever. (Psalm 145:21)

I will praise the LORD while I live; I will sing praises to my God while I have my being. (Psalm 146:2)

I will exult in the LORD; I will rejoice in the God of my salvation. The Lord GOD is my strength; He makes my feet like the feet of a deer and enables me to go on the heights. (Habakkuk 3:18-19)

We should not get drunk on wine, for that is dissipation. Instead, we should be filled with the Spirit, speaking to one another with psalms, hymns, and spiritual songs; singing and making music in our hearts to the Lord, always giving thanks to God the Father for everything, in the name of our Lord Jesus Christ. (Ephesians 5:18-20)

I will rejoice in the Lord always. (Philippians 4:4)

I will rejoice always, pray without ceasing, and give thanks in all circumstances, for this is God's will for us in Christ Jesus. (1 Thessalonians 5:16-18)

Since I am receiving a kingdom that cannot be shaken, I will be thankful and so worship God acceptably with reverence and awe, for my God is a consuming fire. (Hebrews 12:28-29)

Through Jesus, I will continually offer to God a sacrifice of praise, that is, the fruit of lips that give thanks to His name. (Hebrews 13:15)

I will fear God and give Him glory, because the hour of His judgment has come. I will worship Him who made the heavens and the earth, the sea and the springs of water. (Revelation 14:7)

Identity and Life in Christ

I am the salt of the earth, but if the salt loses its flavor, how can it be made salty again? It is no longer good for anything, except to be thrown out and trampled underfoot by men. I am the light of the world. A city set on a hill cannot be hidden. Neither do people light a lamp and put it under a basket, but on a lampstand, and it gives light to all who are in the house. In the same way, I must let my light shine before men, that they may see my good deeds and praise my Father in heaven. (Matthew 5:13-16)

You have asked the Father, and He has given me another Comforter to be with me forever, even the Spirit of truth, whom the world cannot receive, because it neither sees Him nor knows Him. But I know Him, for He lives in me. (John 14:16-17)

Jesus is in His Father, and I am in Jesus, and He is in me. (John 14:20)

It is for my good that You returned to the Father, because You have sent the Counselor, the Holy Spirit, to me. (John 16:7)

He is a Jew who is one inwardly; and circumcision is circumcision of the heart, by the Spirit, not by the written code. Such a man's praise is not from men, but from God. (Romans 2:29)

I died to sin; how can I live in it any longer? (Romans 6:2)

All of us who were baptized into Christ Jesus were baptized into His death. I was therefore buried with Him through baptism into death, in order that just as Christ was raised from the dead through the glory of the Father, so I too may walk in newness of life. (Romans 6:3-4)

If I have been united with Christ in the likeness of His death, I will certainly also be united with Him in the likeness of His resurrection. (Romans 6:5)

I know that my old self was crucified with Christ, so that the body of sin might be done away with, that I should no longer be a slave to sin; for the one who has died has been freed from sin. (Romans 6:6-7)

If I died with Christ, I believe that I will also live with Him, knowing that Christ, having been raised from the dead, cannot die again; death no longer has dominion over Him. For the death that He died, He died to sin once for all; but the life that He lives, He lives to God. In the same way, I must consider myself to be dead to sin, but alive to God in Christ Jesus. (Romans 6:8-11)

I have become dead to the law through the body of Christ, that I might belong to another, to Him who was raised from the dead, in order that I might bear fruit to God. But now, by dying to what once bound me, I have been released from the law so that I serve in newness of the Spirit and not in oldness of the written code. (Romans 7:4, 6)

I delight in the law of God in my inner being. (Romans 7:22)

There is now no condemnation for those who are in Christ Jesus, because the law of the Spirit of life in Christ Jesus has set me free from the law of sin and death. (Romans 8:1-2)

I am not in the flesh but in the Spirit, if the Spirit of God lives in us. And if anyone does not have the Spirit of Christ, he does not belong to Christ. (Romans 8:9)

If Christ is in me, my body is dead because of sin, yet my spirit is alive because of righteousness. And if the Spirit of Him who raised Jesus from the dead is living in me, He who raised Christ from the dead will also give life to my mortal body through His Spirit, who lives in me. (Romans 8:10-11)

I did not receive a spirit of slavery again to fear, but I received the Spirit of adoption by whom I cry, "Abba, Father." The Spirit Himself testifies with my spirit that I am a child of God. (Romans 8:15-16)

None of us lives to himself alone, and none of us dies to himself alone. If we live, we live to the Lord; and if we die, we die to the Lord. So, whether we live or die, we belong to the Lord. (Romans 14:7-8)

I have been sanctified in Christ Jesus and called to be a saint, together with all those everywhere who call on the name of our Lord Jesus Christ, their Lord and ours. (1 Corinthians 1:2)

It is because of God that I am in Christ Jesus, who has become for me wisdom from God and righteousness and sanctification and redemption. (1 Corinthians 1:30)

We are the temple of God, and the Spirit of God lives in us. (1 Corinthians 3:16)

He who is joined to the Lord is one with Him in spirit. (1 Corinthians 6:17)

We were all baptized by one Spirit into one body—whether Jews or Greeks, slave or free—and we were all given the one Spirit to drink. (1 Corinthians 12:13)

He who makes me stand firm in Christ and anointed me is God, who also sealed me and gave me the Spirit in my heart as a deposit. (2 Corinthians 1:21-22)

We are an epistle from Christ, written not with ink, but with the Spirit of the living God, not on tablets of stone, but on tablets of human hearts. (2 Corinthians 3:3)

I am not competent in myself to claim anything for myself, but my competence comes from God. He has made me competent as a minister of a new covenant, not of the letter, but of the Spirit; for the letter kills, but the Spirit gives life. (2 Corinthians 3:5-6)

We all, with unveiled face beholding as in a mirror the glory of the Lord, are being transformed into the same image from glory to glory, which comes from the Lord, who is the Spirit. (2 Corinthians 3:18)

God who said, "Let light shine out of darkness" made His light shine in my heart to give me the light of the knowledge of the glory of God in the face of Christ. But I have this treasure in an earthen vessel to show that this all-surpassing power is from God and not from me. (2 Corinthians 4:6-7)

If anyone is in Christ, he is a new creation; the old things passed away; behold, they have become new. (2 Corinthians 5:17)

Christ is not weak in dealing with us but is powerful among us. For though He was crucified in weakness, yet He lives by the power of God. For we are weak in Him, yet by the power of God we will live with Him to serve others. (2 Corinthians 13:3-4)

Through the law I died to the law so that I might live for God. I have been crucified with Christ; and it is no longer I who live, but Christ lives in me; and the life which I now live in the flesh, I live by faith in the Son of God, who loved me and gave Himself for me. (Galatians 2:19-20)

We are all sons of God through faith in Christ Jesus, for all of us who were baptized into Christ have clothed ourselves with Christ. (Galatians 3:26-27)

If I belong to Christ, then I am Abraham's seed and an heir according to the promise. (Galatians 3:29)

Because I am a son, God has sent the Spirit of His Son into my heart, crying, "Abba, Father." So I am no longer a slave, but a son; and if a son, then an heir through God. (Galatians 4:6-7)

It is for freedom that Christ has set me free. I should stand firm, therefore, and not let myself be burdened again by a yoke of slavery. (Galatians 5:1)

Those who belong to Christ Jesus have crucified the flesh with its passions and desires. (Galatians 5:24)

May I never boast except in the cross of our Lord Jesus Christ, through which the world has been crucified to me, and I to the world. (Galatians 6:14)

Neither circumcision nor uncircumcision means anything; what counts is a new creation. (Galatians 6:15)

Blessed be the God and Father of our Lord Jesus Christ, who has blessed me with every spiritual blessing in the heavenly realms in Christ. (Ephesians 1:3)

I trusted in Christ when I heard the word of truth, the gospel of my salvation. Having believed, I was sealed in Him with the Holy Spirit of promise, who is a deposit guaranteeing my inheritance until the redemption of those who are God's possession, to the praise of His glory. (Ephesians 1:13-14)

God raised me up with Christ and seated me with Him in the heavenly realms in Christ Jesus, in order that in the coming ages He might show the surpassing riches of His grace in kindness toward me in Christ Jesus. (Ephesians 2:6-7)

I am God's workmanship, created in Christ Jesus for good works, which God prepared beforehand for me to do. (Ephesians 2:10)

With regard to my former way of life, I am to put off my old self, which is being corrupted by its deceitful desires, and be renewed in the spirit of my mind; and I am to put on the new self, which was created according to God in righteousness and true holiness. (Ephesians 4:22-24)

I do not want to grieve the Holy Spirit of God by whom I was sealed for the day of redemption. (Ephesians 4:30)

To me, to live is Christ and to die is gain. (Philippians 1:21)

It has been granted to me on behalf of Christ not only to believe in Him, but also to suffer for Him. (Philippians 1:29)

I am the true circumcision, who worships by the Spirit of God and glories in Christ Jesus and puts no confidence in the flesh. (Philippians 3:3)

Whatever was gain to me I now consider loss for the sake of Christ. What is more, I consider all things loss compared to the surpassing greatness of knowing Christ Jesus, my Lord, for whose sake I have suffered the loss of all things and consider them rubbish, that I may gain Christ and be found in Him, not having a righteousness of my own that comes from the law, but that which is through faith in Christ — the righteousness that comes from God on the basis of faith. (Philippians 3:7-9)

I want to know Christ and the power of His resurrection and the fellowship of His sufferings, being conformed to His death, that I may attain to the resurrection from the dead. (Philippians 3:10-11)

I have been made complete in Christ, who is the head over all rule and authority. (Colossians 2:10)

In Christ I was circumcised with a circumcision made without hands, in the removal of the body of the flesh by the circumcision of Christ, having been buried with Him in baptism and raised with Him through faith in the working of God, who raised Him from the dead. (Colossians 2:11-12)

Since I died with Christ to the basic principles of this world, I should not submit to its regulations as though I still belonged to it. (Colossians 2:20)

Since I have been raised with Christ, I should seek the things above, where Christ is seated at the right hand of God. I will set my mind on the things above, not on the things on the earth, for I died, and my life is now hidden with Christ in God. When Christ who is my life appears, then I also will appear with Him in glory. (Colossians 3:1-4)

I have put off the old self with its practices and have put on the new self, who is being renewed in full knowledge according to the image of its Creator. (Colossians 3:9-10)

I have been chosen according to the foreknowledge of God the Father, in sanctification of the Spirit, for obedience to Jesus Christ and sprinkling of His blood; grace and peace is mine in abundance. (1 Peter 1:2)

How great is the love the Father has lavished on me, that I should be called a child of God—and I am! Therefore the world does not know me, because it did not know Him. (1 John 3:1)

I am from God and am an overcomer, because He who is in me is greater than he who is in the world. (1 John 4:4)

God has given me eternal life, and this life is in His Son. He who has the Son has life; he who does not have the Son of God does not have life. Since I believe in the name of the Son of God, I know that I have eternal life. (1 John 5:11-13)

Faith, Trust, and Dependence

When Israel saw the great power the LORD displayed against the Egyptians, the people feared the LORD and put their trust in Him and in Moses His servant. (Exodus 14:31)

Hezekiah trusted in the LORD, the God of Israel, so that there was no one like him among all the kings of Judah, either before him or after him. He held fast to the LORD and did not depart from following Him, but kept His commandments. (2 Kings 18:5-6)

I will not depend on human strength, but on the LORD, my God, for help and deliverance. (2 Chronicles 16:7-8, 12)

In the morning, O LORD, You will hear my voice; in the morning I will set my prayers before You, and I will look to You. (Psalm 5:3)

Some trust in chariots and some in horses, but I will remember the name of the LORD, my God. (Psalm 20:7)

The LORD is my light and my salvation; whom shall I fear? The LORD is the strength of my life; of whom shall I be afraid? (Psalm 27:1)

The LORD is my strength and my shield; my heart trusts in Him, and I am helped. My heart greatly rejoices, and I will give thanks to Him in song. (Psalm 28:7)

I have tasted and seen that the LORD is good; blessed is the man who takes refuge in Him! (Psalm 34:8)

I will trust in the LORD and do good; I will dwell in the land and feed on His faithfulness. I will delight myself in the LORD, and He will give me the desires of my heart. I will commit my way to the LORD and trust in Him, and He will bring it to pass. I will rest in the LORD and wait patiently for Him; I will not fret because of him who prospers in his way, with the man who practices evil schemes. (Psalm 37:3-5, 7)

Lord, all my longings are before You, and my sighing is not hidden from You. (Psalm 38:9)

Blessed is the man who makes the LORD his trust, who does not look to the proud or to those who turn aside to lies. (Psalm 40:4)

I will cast my burden on the LORD, and He will sustain me; He will never allow the righteous to be shaken. (Psalm 55:22)

When I am afraid, I will trust in You. In God, whose word I praise, in God I have put my trust. I will not fear; what can mortal man do to me? (Psalm 56:3-4)

You preserve my life, and I am devoted to You. You are my God; You will save Your servant who trusts in You. (Psalm 86:2)

He who dwells in the shelter of the Most High will rest in the shadow of the Almighty. I will say of the LORD, "He is my refuge and my fortress, my God, in whom I trust." (Psalm 91:1-2)

The LORD is my stronghold, and my God is a rock of refuge to me. (Psalm 94:22)

I will seek the LORD and His strength; I will seek His face continually. I will remember the wonders He has done, His miracles, and the judgments of His mouth. (Psalm 105:4-5)

I lift up my eyes to You, to You who dwell in heaven. As the eyes of servants look to the hand of their master, as the eyes of a maid look to the hand of her mistress, so my eyes look to the LORD, my God, until He shows me His mercy. (Psalm 123:1-2)

Though I walk in the midst of trouble, You will revive me; You will stretch out Your hand against the anger of my foes, and Your right hand will save me. The LORD will perfect His work in me; Your mercy, O LORD, endures forever; You will not abandon the works of Your hands. (Psalm 138:7-8)

My eyes are upon You, O GOD, the Lord; in You I take refuge; You will not leave my soul destitute. (Psalm 141:8)

I cry out to You, O LORD, and say, "You are my refuge, my portion in the land of the living." (Psalm 142:5)

You are my lovingkindness and my fortress, my high tower and my deliverer, my shield, in whom I take refuge. (Psalm 144:2)

I will trust in the LORD with all my heart and lean not on my own understanding; in all my ways I will acknowledge Him, and He will make my paths straight. I will not be wise in my own eyes, but I will fear the LORD and depart from evil. (Proverbs 3:5-7)

Every word of God is tested; He is a shield to those who take refuge in Him. (Proverbs 30:5)

You will keep in perfect peace him whose mind is stayed on You, because he trusts in You. (Isaiah 26:3)

Because the Lord GOD helps me, I will not be disgraced. Therefore I have set my face like flint, and I know I will not be put to shame. He who vindicates me is near; who will contend with me? Surely the Lord GOD will help me; who is he that will condemn me? (Isaiah 50:7-9)

O LORD, the hope of Israel, all who forsake You will be put to shame. Those who depart from You will be written in the dust because they have forsaken the LORD, the fountain of living water. (Jeremiah 17:13)

The righteous will live by his faith. (Habakkuk 2:4)

"Not by might nor by power, but by My Spirit," says the LORD of hosts. (Zechariah 4:6)

Man shall not live on bread alone but on every word that comes from the mouth of God. (Matthew 4:4)

I look to You for my daily bread, to forgive me my debts as I also have forgiven my debtors, and to lead me not into temptation, but to deliver me from the evil one. For Yours is the kingdom and the power and the glory forever. (Matthew 6:11-13)

When I ask, it will be given to me; when I seek, I will find; when I knock, the door will be opened to me. For everyone who asks receives; he who seeks finds; and to him who knocks, the door will be opened. (Matthew 7:7-8; Luke 11:9-10)

Lord Jesus, You have said that unless I am converted and become like a little child, I will never enter the kingdom of heaven. Therefore, whoever humbles himself like a child is the greatest in the kingdom of heaven. (Matthew 18:3-4)

You did not want the little children to be hindered from coming to You, for of such is the kingdom of heaven. (Matthew 19:14)

All things are possible to him who believes. (Mark 9:23)

Whoever does not receive the Kingdom of God like a little child will never enter it. (Mark 10:15; Luke 18:17)

You have said, "Whatever you ask for in prayer, believe that you have received it, and it will be yours." (Mark 11:24)

I will believe Your words, which will come true at their proper time. (Luke 1:20)

I am the Lord's servant; may Your will be done in me according to Your word. (Luke 1:38)

He who believes in God's Son is not condemned, but he who does not believe is condemned already, because he has not believed in the name of the only begotten Son of God. (John 3:18)

The hour is coming and now is, when true worshipers will worship the Father in spirit and truth, for the Father is seeking such to worship Him. God is spirit, and those who worship Him must worship in spirit and truth. (John 4:23-24)

What I must do to work the works of God is to believe in Him whom He has sent. (John 6:28-29)

The Bread of God is He who comes down from heaven and gives life to the world. You are the Bread of life. He who comes to You will never hunger, and he who believes in You will never thirst. (John 6:33, 35)

He who believes in the Son of God has everlasting life. (John 6:47)

You are the Living Bread that came down from heaven. If anyone eats of this bread, he will live forever. This bread is Your flesh, which You have given for the life of the world. (John 6:51)

Unless I eat the flesh of the Son of Man and drink His blood, I have no life in me. Whoever eats Your flesh and drinks Your blood has eternal life, and You will raise him up at the last day. For Your flesh is true food, and Your blood is true drink. Whoever eats Your flesh and drinks Your blood abides in You, and You in him. As the living Father sent You, and You live because of the Father, so the one who feeds on You will live because of You. (John 6:53-57)

Lord Jesus, I have nowhere else to go; You have the words of eternal life. I believe and know that You are the Holy One of God. (John 6:68-69)

He who believes in You, as the Scripture has said, rivers of living water will flow from within him, because Your Spirit indwells him. (John 7:38-39)

You are the light of the world. He who follows You will not walk in the darkness but will have the light of life. (John 8:12)

I will believe the light while I have it, so that I may become a son of light. (John 12:36)

Lord Jesus, he who believes in You does not believe in You only, but in the One who sent You. And he who beholds You beholds the One who sent You. (John 12:44-45)

He who receives whomever You send receives You, and whoever receives You receives the One who sent You. (John 13:20)

I will not let my heart be troubled. I will trust in God and trust also in Christ. (John 14:1)

Peace You leave with me; Your peace You give to me. Not as the world gives, do You give to me. I will not let my heart be troubled nor let it be fearful. (John 14:27)

You are the true vine, and Your Father is the vinedresser. He cuts off every branch in You that bears no fruit, while every branch that does bear fruit He prunes, that it may bear more fruit. I will abide in You, and You will abide in me. As the branch cannot bear fruit of itself, unless it abides in the vine, neither can I, unless I abide in You. (John 15:1-2, 4)

You are the vine; I am a branch; if I abide in You, and You in me, I will bear much fruit; for apart from You, I can do nothing. (John 15:5)

If I abide in You, and Your words abide in me, I can ask whatever I wish, and it will be done for me. As I ask in Your name, I will receive, that my joy may be full. (John 15:7, 16:24)

It is in You, Lord Jesus, that I have peace. In this world I will have tribulation, but I will be of good cheer, because You have overcome the world. (John 16:33)

I believe that Jesus is the Christ, the Son of God, and by believing, I have life in His name. (John 20:31)

I want to continue in the grace of God. (Acts 13:43)

I have believed in the Lord Jesus, so that I will be saved — me and my household. (Acts 16:31)

I am not ashamed of the gospel, for it is the power of God for salvation to everyone who believes, to the Jew first, and also to the Gentile. For in it the righteousness of God is revealed from faith to faith, just as it is written: "The righteous will live by faith." (Romans 1:16-17)

Like Abraham, I will not waver through unbelief regarding the promise of God, but I want to be strengthened in my faith and give glory to God, being fully persuaded that God is able to do what He has promised. (Romans 4:20-21)

Those who live according to the flesh set their minds on the things of the flesh, but those who live according to the Spirit set their minds on the things of the Spirit. The mind of the flesh is death, but the mind of the Spirit is life and peace. (Romans 8:5-6)

If I live according to the flesh, I will die; but if by the Spirit I put to death the deeds of the body, I will live. For those who are led by the Spirit of God are sons of God. (Romans 8:13-14)

If I confess with my mouth the Lord Jesus and believe in my heart that God raised Him from the dead, I will be saved. For it is with my heart that I believe unto righteousness, and it is with my mouth that I confess unto salvation. As the Scripture says, "Whoever trusts in Him will not be put to shame." (Romans 10:9-11)

I will not think of myself more highly than I ought to think, but I will think soberly, in accordance with the measure of faith God has given me. (Romans 12:3)

It is by faith that I stand firm. (2 Corinthians 1:24)

I am always of good courage and know that as long as I am at home in the body, I am away from the Lord. For I live by faith, not by sight. I am of good courage and would prefer to be absent from the body and to be at home with the Lord. (2 Corinthians 5:6-8)

Your grace is sufficient for me, for Your power is made perfect in weakness. Therefore, I will boast all the more gladly in my weaknesses, that the power of Christ may rest upon me. Therefore, I can be content in weaknesses, in insults, in hardships, in persecutions, in difficulties, for Christ's sake. For when I am weak, then I am strong. (2 Corinthians 12:9-10)

Knowing that a man is not justified by the works of the law, but through faith in Christ Jesus, I have believed in Christ Jesus, that I may be justified through faith in Christ and not by the works of the law; for by the works of the law, no flesh will be justified. (Galatians 2:16)

Having begun in the Spirit, I will not seek to be perfected by the flesh. (Galatians 3:3)

As I walk in the Spirit, I will not fulfill the desires of the flesh. For the flesh desires what is contrary to the Spirit, and the Spirit what is contrary to the flesh; for they oppose each other, so that I may not do the things that I wish. But if I am led by the Spirit, I am not under the law. (Galatians 5:16-18)

The works of the flesh are evident, which are: immorality, impurity, sensuality, idolatry, sorcery, hatred, discord, jealousy, fits of rage, selfish ambition, dissensions, factions, envyings, drunkenness, revelries, and the like. Those who practice such things will not inherit the Kingdom of God. But the fruit of the Spirit is love, joy, peace, patience, kindness, goodness, faithfulness, gentleness, self-control; against such things there is no law. (Galatians 5:19-23)

Since I live in the Spirit, I will also walk in the Spirit. (Galatians 5:25)

In Christ Jesus, my Lord, I have boldness and confident access through faith in Him. (Ephesians 3:12)

God will supply all my needs according to His glorious riches in Christ Jesus. To my God and Father be glory for ever and ever. (Philippians 4:19-20)

Just as I received Christ Jesus the Lord, so I will walk in Him, rooted and built up in Him, and established in the faith, as I was taught, and abounding in thanksgiving. (Colossians 2:6-7)

I am not ashamed, because I know whom I have believed and am convinced that He is able to guard what I have entrusted to Him until that day. (2 Timothy 1:12)

This is a trustworthy saying: If we died with Him, we will also live with Him; if we endure, we will also reign with Him. If we deny Him, He will also deny us; if we are faithless, He will remain faithful, for He cannot deny Himself. (2 Timothy 2:11-13)

Since I have a great high priest who has passed through the heavens, Jesus, the Son of God, I will hold firmly to the faith I confess. For I do not have a high priest who is unable to sympathize with my weaknesses, but one who has been tempted in every way, just as I am, yet without sin. Therefore, I will approach the throne of grace with confidence, so that I may receive mercy and find grace to help in time of need. (Hebrews 4:14-16)

I will draw near to God with a sincere heart in full assurance of faith, having my heart sprinkled to cleanse me from an evil conscience and my body washed with pure water. (Hebrews 10:22)

Faith is the reality of things hoped for and the conviction of things not seen. (Hebrews 11:1)

Without faith it is impossible to please God, for he who comes to Him must believe that He exists, and that He is a rewarder of those who earnestly seek Him. (Hebrews 11:6)

I can say with confidence, "The LORD is my helper; I will not be afraid. What can man do to me?" (Hebrews 13:6)

Through faith I am guarded by the power of God for salvation that is ready to be revealed in the last time. (1 Peter 1:5)

Christ was chosen before the creation of the world but was revealed in these last times for our sake. Through Him I believe in God, who raised Him from the dead and glorified Him, so that my faith and hope are in God. (1 Peter 1:20-21)

Everyone who believes that Jesus is the Christ is born of God, and everyone who loves the Father loves Him who is begotten of Him. Whatever is born of God overcomes the world, and this is the victory that has overcome the world — our faith. Who is he who overcomes the world, but he who believes that Jesus is the Son of God? (1 John 5:1, 4-5)

This is the confidence I have in the Son of God, that if I ask anything according to His will, He hears me. And if I know that He hears me, whatever I ask, I know that I have the requests that I have asked from Him. (1 John 5:14-15)

Faithfulness, Commitment, and Submission

You are God Almighty; I want to walk before You and be blameless. (Genesis 17:1)

Like Abraham, I want to fear God and not withhold anything from Him. (Genesis 22:12, 16)

By God's grace, I will not despise my birthright for the things of this world. (Genesis 25:33-34)

I shall have no other gods before You. (Exodus 20:3)

I shall not make for myself an idol in any form. (Exodus 20:4)

I shall not take the name of the LORD, my God, in vain, for the LORD will not hold anyone guiltless who misuses His name. (Exodus 20:7)

I shall not revile God or curse the ruler of my people. (Exodus 22:28)

I shall dedicate the best of the firstfruits of God's provision to the Lord my God. (Exodus 23:19)

You are the LORD, my God; I will consecrate myself and be holy, because You are holy. You are the LORD who brought Your people up out of Egypt to be their God; therefore I will be holy, because You are holy. (Leviticus 11:44-45)

I shall not swear falsely by Your name and so profane the name of my God; You are the LORD. (Leviticus 19:12)

I shall consecrate myself and be holy, because You are the LORD, my God. I shall keep Your statutes and practice them; You are the LORD who sanctifies me. (Leviticus 20:7-8)

I shall be holy to You, for You the LORD are holy, and You have set me apart to be Your own. (Leviticus 20:26)

I will not let Your word depart from my mouth, but I will meditate on it day and night, so that I may be careful to do according to all that is written in it; for then I will make my way prosperous, and I will act wisely. (Joshua 1:8)

As for me and my household, we will serve the LORD. (Joshua 24:15)

Far be it from me that I should forsake the LORD to serve other gods. (Joshua 24:16)

I will not turn aside from following the LORD, but I will serve the LORD with all my heart. (1 Samuel 12:20)

I will fear the LORD and serve Him in truth with all my heart, for I consider what great things He has done for me. (1 Samuel 12:24)

I will not turn my heart away from the LORD, the God of Israel, but I will keep what the LORD has commanded. (1 Kings 11:9-10)

I will not forget the covenant You have made with me, nor will I worship other gods. But I will fear the LORD, my God; it is He who will deliver me from the hand of all my enemies. (2 Kings 17:38-39)

I want to remove the places of idolatry from my life, and like Asa, I want my heart to be fully committed to God all my days. (2 Chronicles 15:17)

Like Jehoshaphat, I want my heart to take delight in the ways of the Lord and to remove the places of idolatry from my life. (2 Chronicles 17:6)

I shall act in the fear of the LORD, faithfully and with a loyal heart. (2 Chronicles 19:9)

Naked I came from my mother's womb, and naked I will depart. The LORD gives, and the LORD takes away; blessed be the name of the LORD. (Job 1:21)

Though He slay me, yet will I hope in God. (Job 13:15)

I will not forget the God of my salvation; I will remember the rock of my refuge. (Isaiah 17:10)

By Your grace I will not forsake You, the fountain of living waters, to dig my own cisterns, broken cisterns that can hold no water. (Jeremiah 2:13)

I will return to my God, maintain mercy and justice, and wait on my God continually. (Hosea 12:6)

I shall worship the LORD, my God, and serve Him only. (Matthew 4:10)

He who does not take his cross and follow after You is not worthy of You. He who finds his life will lose it, and he who loses his life for Your sake will find it. (Matthew 10:38-39)

The kingdom of heaven is like treasure hidden in a field, which a man found and hid; and from his joy, he went and sold all he had and bought that field. Again, the kingdom of heaven is like a merchant looking for fine pearls; and finding one pearl of great value, he went away and sold all that he had and bought it. (Matthew 13:44-46)

If anyone wishes to come after You, he must deny himself and take up his cross and follow You. For whoever wants to save his life will lose it, but whoever loses his life for Your sake and the gospel's will find it. For what is a man profited if he gains the whole world, yet forfeits his soul? Or what will a man give in exchange for his soul? (Matthew 16:24-26; Mark 8:34-37; Luke 9:23-25)

Many who are first will be last, and the last first. (Matthew 19:30; Mark 10:31)

Whoever wishes to become great among others must become their servant, and whoever wishes to be first among them must be their slave. (Matthew 20:26-27; Mark 10:43-44)

Who is the faithful and wise servant, whom the master has put in charge of his household to give them their food at the proper time? Blessed is that servant whom his master finds so doing when he comes. (Matthew 24:45-46)

By Your grace, I want to hear the words, "Well done, good and faithful servant; you have been faithful with a few things; I will put you in charge of many things. Enter into the joy of your lord." (Matthew 25:21)

If anyone wants to be first, he must be the last of all and the servant of all. (Mark 9:35)

Whoever receives a little child in Your name receives You, and whoever receives You receives Him who sent You. For he who is least among us all is the one who is great. (Luke 9:48)

From everyone who has been given much, much will be required, and from the one who has been entrusted with much, much more will be asked. (Luke 12:48)

Whoever does not count the cost and renounce all his possessions cannot be Your disciple. (Luke 14:28, 33)

Whoever seeks to keep his life will lose it, and whoever loses his life will preserve it. (Luke 17:33)

The greatest among us should be like the youngest, and the one who rules like the one who serves. For who is greater, the one who is at the table or the one who serves? Is it not the one who is at the table? But Jesus came among us as the One who serves. (Luke 22:26-27)

Christ must increase; I must decrease. (John 3:30)

Like Jesus, my food is to do the will of Him who sent me and to accomplish His work. (John 4:34)

Unless a grain of wheat falls to the ground and dies, it remains alone. But if it dies, it bears much fruit. The one who loves his life will lose it, and the one who hates his life in this world will keep it for eternal life. (John 12:24-25)

If anyone serves You, he must follow You; and where You are, Your servant also will be. If anyone serves You, the Father will honor him. (John 12:26)

I am not of the world, even as Jesus is not of the world. (John 17:16)

I want the name of the Lord Jesus to be magnified in my life. (Acts 19:17)

I do not consider my life dear to me, if only I may finish my course and the ministry which I received from the Lord Jesus, to testify to the gospel of the grace of God. (Acts 20:24)

I am committed to God and to the word of His grace, which is able to build me up and give me an inheritance among all those who are sanctified. (Acts 20:32)

I will not let sin reign in my mortal body that I should obey its lusts. Nor will I present the members of my body to sin, as instruments of wickedness, but I will present myself to God as one who is alive from the dead and my members as instruments of righteousness to God. (Romans 6:12-13)

In view of God's mercy, I present my body as a living sacrifice, holy and pleasing to God, which is my reasonable worship. (Romans 12:1)

As a servant of Christ and a steward of His possessions, it is required that I be found faithful. (1 Corinthians 4:1-2)

My body is a temple of the Holy Spirit, who is in me, whom I have from God, and I am not my own. For I was bought at a price; therefore I will glorify God in my body. (1 Corinthians 6:19-20)

I will be strong in the Lord and in His mighty power. I will put on the full armor of God, so that I will be able to stand against the schemes of the devil. (Ephesians 6:10-11)

My struggle is not against flesh and blood, but against the rulers, against the authorities, against the world rulers of this darkness, against the spiritual forces of evil in the heavenly realms. Therefore, I will put on the full armor of God, so that I may be able to resist in the day of evil and, having done all, to stand. (Ephesians 6:12-13)

I will stand firm, having girded my waist with truth, having put on the breastplate of righteousness, and having shod my feet with the readiness of the gospel of peace; above all, taking up the shield of faith with which I will be able to quench all the fiery darts of the evil one. I will take the helmet of salvation and the sword of the Spirit, which is the word of God. With all prayer and petition, I will pray always in the Spirit, and to this end I will be watchful with all perseverance and petition for all the saints. (Ephesians 6:14-18)

As an obedient child, I will not conform myself to the former lusts I had when I lived in ignorance, but as He who called me is holy, so I will be holy in all my conduct, because it is written: "You shall be holy, for I am holy." (1 Peter 1:14-16)

Responsiveness and Obedience

Like Noah, I want to do everything just as God commands me. (Genesis 6:22)

I want to follow Abraham's example of willingness to offer all that I have to You, holding nothing back and trusting in Your character and in Your promises. (Genesis 22:2-11)

I want to listen carefully to the voice of the LORD, my God, and do what is right in His sight; I want to pay attention to His commandments and keep all His statutes. (Exodus 15:26)

Like Moses, I wish to do according to all that the LORD commands me. (Exodus 39:42; 40:16)

By Your grace, I want to observe Your judgments and keep Your statutes, to walk in them; You are the LORD, my God. I will keep Your statutes and Your judgments, by which a man may live if he does them; You are the LORD. (Leviticus 18:4-5)

I will observe all Your statutes and all Your judgments and follow them; You are the LORD. (Leviticus 19:37)

I will keep Your statutes and Your commandments. I will be careful to do as the LORD, my God, has commanded me; I will not turn aside to the right or to the left. (Deuteronomy 4:40; 5:32)

I will keep the commandments of the LORD, my God, to walk in His ways and to fear Him. I will follow the LORD, my God, and fear Him; I will keep His commandments, hear His voice, serve Him, and hold fast to Him. (Deuteronomy 8:6; 13:4)

The word is very near me; it is in my mouth and in my heart, so that I may obey it. (Deuteronomy 30:14)

You will honor those who honor You, but those who despise You will be disdained. (1 Samuel 2:30)

Has the LORD as much delight in burnt offerings and sacrifices as in obeying the voice of the LORD? To obey is better than sacrifice, and to heed is better than the fat of rams. For rebellion is like the sin of divination, and stubbornness is as iniquity and idolatry. (1 Samuel 15:22-23)

Like Josiah, I want to do what is right in the sight of the LORD and walk in all the ways of David, not turning aside to the right or to the left. (2 Kings 22:1-2)

Like Asa, I want to do what is good and right in the sight of the LORD, my God. (2 Chronicles 14:2)

I do not want to transgress the commandments of the LORD, for I cannot prosper in disobedience. I will not forsake the LORD. (2 Chronicles 24:20)

In my distress I will seek the favor of the LORD, my God, and humble myself greatly before the God of my fathers, for I know that the LORD is God. (2 Chronicles 33:12-13)

Like Josiah, I want a tender and responsive heart, so that I will humble myself before God when I hear His word. (2 Chronicles 34:27)

I will serve the LORD with fear and rejoice with trembling. (Psalm 2:11)

Blessed are those whose ways are blameless, who walk in the law of the LORD. Blessed are those who keep His testimonies and seek Him with all their heart. (Psalm 119:1-2)

I will incline my ear and come to You; I will hear You, that my soul may live. (Isaiah 55:3)

Everyone who hears Your words and does them is like a wise man who built his house on the rock. (Matthew 7:24)

I do not want to be like those rocky places on whom seed was thrown, who hear the word and at once receive it with joy, but since they have no root, last only a short time; when affliction or persecution comes because of the word, they quickly fall away. Nor do I want to be like those among the thorns on whom seed was sown, who hear the word, but the worries of this world, the deceitfulness of riches and pleasures, and the desires for other things come in and choke the word, making it immature and unfruitful. Instead, I want to be like the good soil on whom seed was sown, who with a noble and good heart hear the word, understand and accept it, and with perseverance, bear fruit, yielding thirty, sixty, or a hundred times what was sown. (Matthew 13:20-23; Mark 4:16-20; Luke 8:13-15)

I want to be righteous before God, walking blamelessly in all the commandments and ordinances of the Lord. (Luke 1:6)

I desire not only to call You Lord but to do what You say. By Your grace, I will come to You, hear Your words, and put them into practice. Then I will be like a man building a house, who dug down deep and laid the foundation on rock, and when a flood came, the torrent struck that house but could not shake it, because it was well built. (Luke 6:46-48)

When I have done all the things which are commanded me, I should realize that I am an unworthy servant; I have only done what I ought to have done. (Luke 17:10)

I am willing to do God's will. (John 7:17)

I must do the work of Him who sent me while it is day; night is coming, when no one can work. (John 9:4)

Since I love You, I will obey Your commandments. (John 14:15)

He who has Your commandments and obeys them, he is the one who loves You; and he who loves You will be loved by Your Father, and You will love him and manifest Yourself to him. (John 14:21)

If anyone loves You, he will keep Your word; Your Father will love him, and You and Your Father will come to him and make Your home with him. (John 14:23)

By this is Your Father glorified, that I bear much fruit, showing myself to be Your disciple. (John 15:8)

Just as I presented the members of my body as slaves to impurity and to ever-increasing lawlessness, so I now present my members as slaves to righteousness, leading to holiness. (Romans 6:19)

I want to be a doer of the word and not merely a hearer who deceives himself. For if anyone is a hearer of the word and not a doer, he is like a man who looks at his natural face in a mirror, and after looking at himself, goes away, and immediately forgets what kind of person he was. But the one who looks intently into the perfect law of freedom and continues in it and is not a forgetful hearer but a doer of the work; this one will be blessed in what he does. (James 1:22-25)

Hope and Reward

You are my shield, my very great reward. (Genesis 15:1)

If a man dies, will he live again? All the days of my hard service I will wait for my renewal to come. (Job 14:14)

I know that my Redeemer lives and that in the end He will stand upon the earth. And after my skin has been destroyed, yet in my flesh I will see God; whom I myself will see and behold with my own eyes and not another. How my heart yearns within me! (Job 19:25-27)

As for me, I will see Your face in righteousness; when I awake, I will be satisfied with Your likeness. (Psalm 17:15)

No one who waits for You will be ashamed, but those who are treacherous without cause will be ashamed. Show me Your ways, O LORD, teach me Your paths; lead me in Your truth and teach me, for You are the God of my salvation, and my hope is in You all day long. (Psalm 25:3-5)

I would have lost heart unless I had believed that I would see the goodness of the LORD in the land of the living. I will hope in the LORD and be of good courage, and He will strengthen my heart; yes, I will hope in the LORD. (Psalm 27:13-14)

I will sing praises to the LORD and give thanks at the remembrance of His holy name. For His anger lasts only a moment, but His favor is for a lifetime; weeping may endure for a night, but joy comes in the morning. (Psalm 30:4-5)

My soul waits in hope for the LORD; He is my help and my shield. My heart rejoices in Him, because I trust in His holy name. (Psalm 33:20-21)

Why are you downcast, O my soul? Why are you disturbed within me? Hope in God, for I will yet praise Him for the help of His presence. O my God, my soul is downcast within me; therefore I will remember You. Why are you downcast, O my soul? Why are you disturbed within me? Hope in God, for I will yet praise Him, the help of my countenance and my God. (Psalm 42:5-6, 11)

You are my hope, O Lord GOD; You are my trust from my youth. As for me, I will always have hope; I will praise You more and more. (Psalm 71:5, 14)

You are my hiding place and my shield; I have put my hope in Your word. (Psalm 119:114)

I wait for the LORD; my soul waits, and in His word I put my hope. I hope in the LORD, for with Him is unfailing love and abundant redemption. (Psalm 130:5, 7)

The LORD takes pleasure in those who fear Him, who put their hope in His unfailing love. (Psalm 147:11)

"I know the plans I have for you," declares the LORD, "plans to prosper you and not to harm you, plans to give you a future and a hope." (Jeremiah 29:11)

I will watch in hope for the LORD; I will wait for the God of my salvation; my God will hear me. (Micah 7:7)

Blessed are those who are persecuted for the sake of righteousness, for theirs is the kingdom of heaven. Blessed are you when people insult you, persecute you, and falsely say all kinds of evil against you because of Me. Rejoice and be glad, because great is your reward in heaven, for in the same way they persecuted the prophets who were before you. (Matthew 5:10-12)

Everyone who has left houses or brothers or sisters or father or mother or children or fields for Your sake will receive a hundred times as much and will inherit eternal life. (Matthew 19:29)

There is no one who has left house or brothers or sisters or mother or father or children or fields for Your sake and the gospel's, who will not receive a hundred times as much in this present age—houses, brothers, sisters, mothers, children and fields, along with persecutions—and in the age to come, eternal life. (Mark 10:29-30)

I have hope in God, that there will be a resurrection of both the righteous and the wicked. In view of this, I strive always to keep my conscience blameless before God and men. (Acts 24:15-16)

I rejoice in my tribulations, knowing that tribulation produces perseverance; and perseverance, character; and character, hope. And hope does not disappoint, because the love of God has been poured out into my heart through the Holy Spirit who was given to me. (Romans 5:3-5)

Since I am a child of God, I am an heir of God and a joint heir with Christ, if indeed I share in His sufferings in order that I may also share in His glory. For I consider that the sufferings of this present time are not worth comparing with the glory that will be revealed to me. (Romans 8:17-18)

Having the firstfruits of the Spirit, I groan inwardly as I wait eagerly for my adoption, the redemption of my body. For in hope I have been saved, but hope that is seen is not hope; for who hopes for what he sees? But if I hope for what we do not yet see, I eagerly wait for it with perseverance. (Romans 8:23-25)

Whatever things were written in the past were written for our learning, so that through endurance and the encouragement of the Scriptures we might have hope. (Romans 15:4)

The God of hope will fill me with all joy and peace as I trust in Him, so that I may overflow with hope by the power of the Holy Spirit. (Romans 15:13)

Eye has not seen, ear has not heard, nor have entered the heart of man the things that God has prepared for those who love Him. (1 Corinthians 2:9)

I will judge nothing before the time, until the Lord comes, who will bring to light what is hidden in darkness and will expose the motives of men's hearts; and then each one's praise will come from God. (1 Corinthians 4:5)

God both raised the Lord and will also raise me up through His power. (1 Corinthians 6:14)

Now I see dimly, as in a mirror, but then I shall see face to face. Now I know in part, but then I shall know fully, even as I am fully known. (1 Corinthians 13:12)

Since God has made me adequate as a minister of the new covenant, as I have received mercy, I do not lose heart. (2 Corinthians 3:6, 4:1)

I know that He who raised the Lord Jesus will also raise me with Jesus and present us in His presence. (2 Corinthians 4:14)

I do not lose heart; even though my outward man is perishing, yet my inner man is being renewed day by day. For this light affliction which is momentary is working for me a far more exceeding and eternal weight of glory, while I do not look at the things which are seen but at the things which are unseen. For the things which are seen are temporary, but the things which are unseen are eternal. (2 Corinthians 4:16-18)

I know that if my earthly house, or tent, is destroyed, I have a building from God, a house not made with hands, eternal in the heavens. For in this house I groan, longing to be clothed with my heavenly dwelling, because when I am clothed, I will not be found naked. For while I am in this tent, I groan, being burdened, because I do not want to be un-clothed but to be clothed, so that what is mortal may be swallowed up by life. Now it is God who has made me for this very purpose and has given me the Spirit as a guarantee. (2 Corinthians 5:1-5)

I make it my ambition to please the Lord, whether I am at home in the body or away from it. For we must all appear before the judgment seat of Christ, that each one may receive what is due for the things done while in the body, whether good or bad. (2 Corinthians 5:9-10)

Through the Spirit, by faith, I eagerly await the righteousness for which I hope. (Galatians 5:5)

I have not been made perfect, but I press on to lay hold of that for which Christ Jesus also laid hold of me. I do not consider myself yet to have attained it, but one thing I do: forgetting what is behind and stretching forward to what is ahead, I press on toward the goal to win the prize of the upward call of God in Christ Jesus. (Philippians 3:12-14)

My citizenship is in heaven, from which I also eagerly await a Savior, the Lord Jesus Christ, who will transform my lowly body and conform it to His glorious body, according to the exertion of His ability to subject all things to Himself. (Philippians 3:20, 21)

My faith in Christ Jesus and love for all the saints spring from the hope that is stored up for me in heaven, of which I have heard in the word of truth, the gospel. (Colossians 1:4-5)

I desire that the God of peace Himself will sanctify me completely, and that my whole spirit, soul, and body will be preserved blameless at the coming of my Lord Jesus Christ. He who calls me is faithful, who also will do it. (1 Thessalonians 5:23-24)

I have been called by God my Savior, and Christ Jesus is my hope. (1 Timothy 1:1)

I have set my hope on the living God, who is the Savior of all men, especially of those who believe. (1 Timothy 4:10)

Those who are rich in this present world should not be arrogant or set their hope on the uncertainty of riches but on God, who richly pro-vides us with everything for our enjoyment. They should do good, be rich in good works, and be generous and willing to share. In this way they will lay up treasure for themselves as a firm foundation for the future, so that they may lay hold of true life. (1 Timothy 6:17-19)

The Lord will deliver me from every evil work and will bring me safely to His heavenly kingdom. To Him be glory forever and ever. (2 Timothy 4:18)

My hope in God is an anchor of my soul, both sure and steadfast, and it enters the inner sanctuary behind the veil, where Jesus the forerunner has entered on my behalf, having become a high priest forever, according to the order of Melchizedek. (Hebrews 6:19-20)

I will hold fast the confession of my hope, for He who promised is faithful. (Hebrews 10:23)

Like Abraham, I am looking for a city which has foundations, whose architect and builder is God. (Hebrews 11:10)

By God's grace I want to live to the end in faith, knowing that I will not receive the promises on earth, but seeing them and welcoming them from a distance, I confess that I am a stranger and a pilgrim on the earth. Instead, I long for a better country, a heavenly one. In this way, God will not be ashamed to be called my God, for He has prepared a city for me. Like Moses, I esteem reproach for the sake of Christ as of greater value than the treasures of this world, because I am looking to the reward. (Hebrews 11:13, 16, 26)

Here I do not have an enduring city, but I am seeking the city that is to come. (Hebrews 13:14)

Blessed be the God and Father of my Lord Jesus Christ, who according to His great mercy has given me new birth into a living hope through the resurrection of Jesus Christ from the dead and into an inheritance that is incorruptible and undefiled and unfading, reserved in heaven for me. (1 Peter 1:3-4)

Now I am a child of God, and what I shall be has not yet been revealed. I know that when He is revealed, I shall be like Him, for I shall see Him as He is. And everyone who has this hope in Him purifies himself, just as He is pure. (1 John 3:2-3)

God is able to keep me from falling and to present me before His glorious presence faultless and with great joy. (Jude 24)

SEVEN

THE CHARACTER I WANT
TO CULTIVATE

Godliness and Reverence

L ike Noah, I want to be a righteous man, blameless among the people of my time, and one who walks with God. (Genesis 6:9)

I desire to be righteous before You in my generation. (Genesis 7:1)

I will be careful not to forget the LORD, my God, by failing to observe His commandments, His ordinances, and His statutes. (Deuteronomy 8:11)

The LORD rewards every man for his righteousness and faithfulness. (1 Samuel 26:23)

The God of Israel spoke, the rock of Israel said to me: "He who rules over men in righteousness, who rules in the fear of God, is like the light of morning when the sun rises, a morning without clouds, like the tender grass springing out of the earth through the sunshine after rain." (2 Samuel 23:3-4)

Like Hezekiah, I want to do what is good and right and true before the LORD, my God, by seeking Him with all my heart. (2 Chronicles 31:20-21)

Like Josiah, I desire to do what is right in the sight of the LORD, walking in the ways of David and not turning aside to the right or to the left. (2 Chronicles 34:1-2)

Like Job, I want to be blameless and upright, fearing God and shunning evil. (Job 1:1)

You know the way that I take; when You have tested me, I shall come forth as gold. My feet have held fast to Your steps; I have kept to Your way without turning aside. (Job 23:10-11)

Men fear You, for You do not regard any who are wise of heart. (Job 37:24)

The LORD knows the way of the righteous, but the way of the wicked will perish. (Psalm 1:6)

I know that the LORD has set apart the godly for Himself; the LORD hears when I call to Him. (Psalm 4:3)

LORD, who may dwell in Your tabernacle? Who may live on Your holy mountain? It is he who walks uprightly and works righteousness and speaks the truth in his heart; he does not slander with his tongue nor does evil to his neighbor nor takes up a reproach against his friend; he despises the reprobate but honors those who fear the LORD. He keeps his oath even when it hurts, lends his money without interest, and does not accept a bribe against the innocent. He who does these things will never be shaken. (Psalm 15:1-5)

Who may ascend the hill of the LORD? Who may stand in His holy place? It is he who has clean hands and a pure heart, who has not lifted up his soul to an idol or sworn by what is false. (Psalm 24:3-4)

Come, my children, listen to me; I will teach you the fear of the LORD. Who is the man who desires life and loves many days that he may see good? Keep your tongue from evil and your lips from speaking guile. Depart from evil and do good; seek peace and pursue it. The eyes of the LORD are on the righteous, and His ears are attentive to their cry. (Psalm 34:11-15)

The mouth of the righteous speaks wisdom, and his tongue speaks what is just. The law of his God is in his heart; his steps do not slide. (Psalm 37:30-31)

I will not be like the man who did not make God his strength but trusted in the abundance of his wealth and strengthened himself in his evil desires. (Psalm 52:7)

I will be careful to lead a blameless life. I will walk in the integrity of my heart in the midst of my house. I will set no wicked thing before my eyes. I hate the work of those who fall away; it will not cling to me. A perverse heart shall depart from me; I will not know evil. Whoever slanders his neighbor in secret, I will put to silence; I will not endure him who has haughty eyes and a proud heart. My eyes will be on the faithful in the land, that they may dwell with me; he whose walk is blameless will minister to me. No one who practices deceit will dwell in my house; no one who speaks falsely will stand in my presence. (Psalm 101:2-7)

It is better to take refuge in the LORD than to trust in man. (Psalm 118:8)

I will praise You with uprightness of heart as I learn Your righteous judgments. (Psalm 119:7)

I have sought You with my whole heart; do not let me stray from Your commands. (Psalm 119:10)

Direct my footsteps according to Your word, and let no iniquity have dominion over me. (Psalm 119:133)

Trouble and anguish have come upon me, but Your commands are my delight. (Psalm 119:143)

I rejoice at Your word as one who finds great spoil. I hate and abhor falsehood, but I love Your law. Great peace have they who love Your law, and nothing causes them to stumble. O LORD, I hope for Your salvation, and I follow Your commands. My soul keeps Your testimonies, for I love them greatly. I keep Your precepts and Your testimonies, for all my ways are known to You. (Psalm 119:162-163, 165-168)

Unless the LORD builds the house, its builders labor in vain. Unless the LORD guards the city, the watchmen stay awake in vain. (Psalm 127:1)

Blessed is everyone who fears the LORD, who walks in His ways. (Psalm 128:1)

Surely the righteous will give thanks to Your name; the upright will dwell in Your presence. (Psalm 140:13)

I will honor the LORD with my wealth and with the firstfruits of all my increase. (Proverbs 3:9)

The path of the righteous is like the first gleam of dawn, shining ever brighter until the full light of day. But the way of the wicked is like darkness; they do not know what makes them stumble. (Proverbs 4:18-19)

I will let my eyes look straight ahead, and fix my gaze straight before me. I will ponder the path of my feet so that all my ways will be established. I will not turn to the right or to the left but keep my foot from evil. (Proverbs 4:25-27)

The ways of a man are before the eyes of the LORD, and He examines all his paths. (Proverbs 5:21)

The prospect of the righteous is joyful, but the hopes of the wicked will perish. (Proverbs 10:28)

Riches do not profit in the day of wrath, but righteousness delivers from death. (Proverbs 11:4)

The righteousness of the blameless makes a straight way for them, but the wicked will fall by their own wickedness. (Proverbs 11:5)

He who trusts in his riches will fall, but the righteous will flourish like a green leaf. (Proverbs 11:28)

In the way of righteousness there is life, and in that pathway there is no death. (Proverbs 12:28)

Righteousness exalts a nation, but sin is a disgrace to any people. (Proverbs 14:34)

The LORD is far from the wicked, but He hears the prayer of the righteous. (Proverbs 15:29)

All a man's ways are pure in his own eyes, but the LORD weighs the motives. (Proverbs 16:2)

I will commit my works to the LORD, and my plans will be established. (Proverbs 16:3)

The name of the LORD is a strong tower; the righteous run to it and are safe. (Proverbs 18:10)

Blessed is the man who always fears God, but he who hardens his heart falls into trouble. (Proverbs 28:14)

The fear of man brings a snare, but he who trusts in the LORD is set on high. (Proverbs 29:25)

I will fear God and keep His commandments, for this applies to every person. (Ecclesiastes 12:13)

I will stop trusting in man, whose breath is in his nostrils. For in what should he be esteemed? (Isaiah 2:22)

Who among us fears the LORD and obeys the word of His Servant? Let him who walks in darkness and has no light trust in the name of the LORD and rely upon his God. (Isaiah 50:10)

As one who knows righteousness, who has Your law in my heart, I will not fear the reproach of men or be terrified by their revilings. (Isaiah 51:7)

A person's wickedness will punish him; his backsliding will reprove him. I know, therefore, and see that it is evil and bitter to forsake the LORD, my God, and have no fear of Him. (Jeremiah 2:19)

Cursed is the one who trusts in man, who depends on flesh for his strength, and whose heart turns away from the LORD. But blessed is the man who trusts in the LORD, whose confidence is in Him. (Jeremiah 17:5, 7)

I want to let justice roll down like a river and righteousness like an ever-flowing stream. (Amos 5:24)

You have shown me what is good, and what does the LORD require of me but to act justly and to love mercy and to walk humbly with my God? (Micah 6:8)

Blessed are those who hunger and thirst for righteousness, for they shall be satisfied. (Matthew 5:6)

I will take heed not to practice my righteousness before men to be seen by them. Otherwise, I will have no reward from my Father in heaven. (Matthew 6:1)

A disciple is not above his teacher, nor a servant above his master. It is enough for the disciple to be like his teacher, and the servant like his master. (Matthew 10:24-25)

I will not fear those who kill the body but cannot kill the soul, but rather, I will fear the One who is able to destroy both soul and body in hell. (Matthew 10:28)

I want to be more concerned about the things of God than the things of men. (Mark 8:33)

I do not want to justify myself in the eyes of men; God knows our hearts, and what is highly esteemed among men is detestable in the sight of God. (Luke 16:15)

I do not want to love praise from men more than praise from God. (John 12:43)

Like Barnabas, I want to be a good man, full of the Holy Spirit and of faith. (Acts 11:24)

I will not be lacking in zeal, but I will keep fervent in spirit, serving the Lord. (Romans 12:11)

The hour has come for me to wake up from sleep, for my salvation is nearer now than when I first believed. The night is nearly over; the day is almost here. Therefore I will cast off the works of darkness and put on the armor of light. (Romans 13:11-12)

The Kingdom of God is not a matter of eating and drinking, but of righteousness and peace and joy in the Holy Spirit. (Romans 14:17)

Whatever is not from faith is sin. (Romans 14:23)

I must not test the Lord or grumble as some of the Israelites did. (1 Corinthians 10:9-10)

Whatever I do, I should do all to the glory of God. (1 Corinthians 10:31)

I want my conscience to testify that I have conducted myself in the world in the holiness and sincerity that are from God, not in fleshly wisdom but in the grace of God, especially in my relations with others. (2 Corinthians 1:12)

Since I have God's promises, I will cleanse myself from all pollution of body and spirit, perfecting holiness in the fear of God. (2 Corinthians 7:1)

I am not trying to win the approval of men, but of God. If I were still trying to please men, I would not be a servant of Christ. (Galatians 1:10)

God is not mocked, for whatever a man sows, this he will also reap. The one who sows to please his flesh will reap corruption; the one who sows to please the Spirit will of the Spirit reap eternal life. (Galatians 6:7-8)

I was once darkness, but now I am light in the Lord. I will walk as a child of light (for the fruit of the light consists in all goodness and righteousness and truth), learning what is pleasing to the Lord. (Ephesians 5:8-10)

I will conduct myself in a manner worthy of the gospel of Christ, standing firm in one spirit with other believers, with one mind striving together for the faith of the gospel. (Philippians 1:27)

I will work out my salvation with fear and trembling, for it is God who works in me to will and to act according to His good purpose. (Philippians 2:12-13)

I will not seek my own interests, but those of Christ Jesus. (Philippians 2:21)

Whatever I do, whether in word or in deed, I will do all in the name of the Lord Jesus, giving thanks to God the Father through Him. (Colossians 3:17)

Since I have been approved by God to be entrusted with the gospel, I speak not as pleasing men, but God, who tests my heart. I will not seek glory from men. (1 Thessalonians 2:4, 6)

As I have been instructed how I ought to walk and to please God, I want to follow Paul's exhortation in the Lord Jesus to do this more and more. (1 Thessalonians 4:1)

Physical exercise profits a little, but godliness is profitable for all things, since it holds promise for both the present life and the life to come. (1 Timothy 4:8)

I want to be an example for other believers in speech, in behavior, in love, in faith, and in purity. (1 Timothy 4:12)

I will be strong in the grace that is in Christ Jesus. (2 Timothy 2:1)

I will flee youthful lusts and pursue righteousness, faith, love, and peace, with those who call on the Lord out of a pure heart. (2 Timothy 2:22)

As one who has believed in God, I want to be careful to devote myself to doing what is good. These things are good and profitable for everyone. (Titus 3:8)

I will pursue peace with all men and sanctification, without which no one will see the Lord. (Hebrews 12:14)

To him who knows the good he ought to do and does not do it, to him it is sin. (James 4:17)

Since I call on the Father who judges each man's work impartially, I should conduct myself in fear during the time of my sojourn on earth. (1 Peter 1:17)

I should live as a free man without using my freedom as a cloak for evil, but as a servant of God. (1 Peter 2:16)

Whoever would love life and see good days must keep his tongue from evil and his lips from speaking guile. He must turn from evil and do good; he must seek peace and pursue it. For the eyes of the LORD are on the righteous, and His ears attend to their prayer, but the face of the LORD is against those who do evil. (1 Peter 3:10-12)

I will be diligent to add to my faith virtue; and to virtue, knowledge; and to knowledge, self-control; and to self-control, perseverance; and to perseverance, godliness; and to godliness, brotherly kindness; and to brotherly kindness, love. For if these qualities are mine in increasing measure, they will keep me from being barren and unfruitful in the full knowledge of our Lord Jesus Christ. (2 Peter 1:5-8)

If we say that we have fellowship with Christ and yet walk in the darkness, we lie and do not practice the truth. But if we walk in the light, as He is in the light, we have fellowship with one another, and the blood of Jesus, His Son, purifies us from all sin. (1 John 1:6-7)

My desire is to continue to walk in the truth and to take pleasure when others do the same. (3 John 3-4)

I will not imitate what is evil but what is good. The one who does good is of God; the one who does evil has not seen God. (3 John 11)

Love and Compassion

I will not let love and truth leave me; I will bind them around my neck and write them on the tablet of my heart. (Proverbs 3:3)

A righteous man has regard for the needs of his animal, but the mercies of the wicked are cruel. (Proverbs 12:10)

Through love and truth, iniquity is atoned for; and by the fear of the LORD, one turns aside from evil. When a man's ways are pleasing to the LORD, he makes even his enemies live at peace with him. (Proverbs 16:6-7)

What is desired in a man is unfailing love. (Proverbs 19:22)

He who pursues righteousness and love finds life, righteousness, and honor. (Proverbs 21:21)

You desire mercy, not sacrifice, and the knowledge of God more than burnt offerings. (Hosea 6:6)

I will sow righteousness, reap the fruit of unfailing love, and break up my fallow ground; for it is time to seek the LORD, until He comes and rains righteousness on me. (Hosea 10:12)

Blessed are the merciful, for they shall obtain mercy. (Matthew 5:7)

If I speak in the tongues of men and of angels, but have not love, I am only a resounding gong or a clanging cymbal. And if I have the gift of prophecy and understand all mysteries and all knowledge, and if I have all faith so as to remove mountains, but have not love, I am nothing. And if I give all my possessions to the poor, and if I deliver my body to be burned, but have not love, it profits me nothing. (1 Corinthians 13:1-3)

Love is patient, love is kind, it does not envy; love does not boast, it is not arrogant, it does not behave rudely; it does not seek its own, it is not provoked, it keeps no record of wrongs; it does not rejoice in unrighteousness but rejoices with the truth; it bears all things, believes all things, hopes all things, endures all things. Love never fails. (1 Corinthians 13:4-8)

I want everything I do to be done in love. (1 Corinthians 16:14)

I want to abound in faith, in speech, in knowledge, in all diligence, in love, and in the grace of giving. (2 Corinthians 8:7)

I will be an imitator of God as a beloved child, and I will walk in love, just as Christ loved me and gave Himself up for me as a fragrant offering and sacrifice to God. (Ephesians 5:1-2)

As one who has been chosen of God, holy and beloved, I will put on a heart of compassion, kindness, humility, gentleness, and patience, bearing with others and forgiving others even as the Lord forgave me; and above all these things, I will put on love, which is the bond of perfection. (Colossians 3:12-14)

The goal of our instruction is love, which comes from a pure heart and a good conscience and a sincere faith. (1 Timothy 1:5)

I will keep the pattern of sound teaching that I have heard, in faith and love which are in Christ Jesus. (2 Timothy 1:13)

I want to abound in love and faith toward the Lord Jesus and to all the saints. (Philemon 5)

I will not love with words or tongue, but in deed and in truth. By this I will know that I am of the truth and will assure my heart before Him; for if my heart condemns me, God is greater than my heart, and knows all things. If my heart does not condemn me, I have confidence before God and receive from Him whatever I ask, because I keep His commandments and do the things that are pleasing in His sight. (1 John 3:18-22)

This is love: that I walk in obedience to God's commandments. And this is the commandment: that as I have heard from the beginning, I should walk in love. (2 John 6)

Wisdom, Discernment, and Understanding

I ask for a wise and understanding heart to discern between good and evil. (1 Kings 3:9, 12)

The fear of the Lord, that is wisdom, and to depart from evil is understanding. (Job 28:28)

LORD, make me to know my end and what is the measure of my days; let me know how fleeting is my life. (Psalm 39:4)

A man who has honor, yet without understanding, is like the beasts that perish. (Psalm 49:20)

Surely you desire truth in the inner parts, and in the hidden part You make me know wisdom. (Psalm 51:6)

Teach me to number my days, that I may gain a heart of wisdom. (Psalm 90:12)

Whoever is wise will consider the lovingkindness of the LORD. (Psalm 107:43)

The fear of the LORD is the beginning of wisdom; all who practice His commandments have a good understanding. His praise endures forever. (Psalm 111:10)

The entrance of Your words gives light; it gives understanding to the simple. (Psalm 119:130)

The fear of the LORD is the beginning of knowledge, but fools despise wisdom and discipline. (Proverbs 1:7)

The waywardness of the simple will kill them, and the complacency of fools will destroy them; but whoever listens to wisdom will live securely and be at ease from the fear of evil. (Proverbs 1:32-33)

I will receive the words of wisdom and treasure her commands within me, turning my ear to wisdom and applying my heart to understanding. If I cry for discernment and lift up my voice for understanding, if I seek her as silver and search for her as for hidden treasures, then I will understand the fear of the LORD and find the knowledge of God. (Proverbs 2:1-5)

The LORD gives wisdom; from His mouth come knowledge and understanding. He stores up sound wisdom for the upright; He is a shield to those who walk in integrity, guarding the paths of justice and protecting the way of His saints. Then I will understand righteousness and justice and honesty — every good path. For wisdom will enter my heart, and knowledge will be pleasant to my soul. Discretion will protect me, and understanding will guard me. (Proverbs 2:6-11)

Blessed is the man who finds wisdom, and the man who gains understanding, for its profit is greater than that of silver, and its gain than fine gold. She is more precious than jewels, and nothing I desire can compare with her. Long life is in her right hand; in her left hand are riches and honor. Her ways are pleasant ways, and all her paths are peace. She is a tree of life to those who embrace her, and happy are those who hold her fast. (Proverbs 3:13-18)

I will preserve sound wisdom and discretion, not letting them out of my sight; they will be life to my soul. (Proverbs 3:21-22)

Wisdom is foremost; therefore I will get wisdom, and though it costs all I have, I will get understanding. I will esteem her, and she will exalt me; I will embrace her, and she will honor me. (Proverbs 4:7-8)

I will guard my heart with all diligence, for out of it flow the issues of life. (Proverbs 4:23)

Wisdom is better than jewels, and all desirable things cannot be compared with her. Wisdom dwells together with prudence and finds knowledge and discretion. (Proverbs 8:11-12)

Blessed is the man who listens to wisdom, watching daily at her gates, waiting at her doorposts. For whoever finds wisdom finds life and obtains favor from the LORD. But he who sins against her injures his own soul; all who hate her love death. (Proverbs 8:34-36)

The fear of the LORD is the beginning of wisdom, and the knowledge of the Holy One is understanding. (Proverbs 9:10)

Doing evil is like sport to a fool; so is wisdom to a man of understanding. (Proverbs 10:23)

The fruit of the righteous is a tree of life, and he who wins souls is wise. (Proverbs 11:30)

The teaching of the wise is a fountain of life to turn one away from the snares of death. (Proverbs 13:14)

There is a way that seems right to a man, but its end is the way of death. (Proverbs 14:12)

The fear of the LORD is a fountain of life to turn one away from the snares of death. (Proverbs 14:27)

He who gets wisdom loves his own soul; he who keeps understanding will find good. (Proverbs 19:8)

There is no wisdom or understanding or counsel that can succeed against the LORD. (Proverbs 21:30)

He who trusts in his own heart is a fool, but he who walks in wisdom will be delivered. (Proverbs 28:26)

Wisdom excels folly as light excels darkness. (Ecclesiastes 2:13)

There is a time for everything and a season for every activity under heaven. (Ecclesiastes 3:1)

I will not say, "Why were the former days better than these?" For it is not wise to ask such questions. (Ecclesiastes 7:10)

There is a proper time and procedure for every matter. (Ecclesiastes 8:6)

The words of the wise are like goads and like nails driven by the masters who collect them; they are given by one Shepherd. (Ecclesiastes 12:11)

Woe to those who call evil good and good evil, who put darkness for light and light for darkness, who put bitter for sweet and sweet for bitter. (Isaiah 5:20)

To the law and to the testimony! If men do not speak according to Your word, they have no light of dawn. (Isaiah 8:20)

You are the stability of our times, a wealth of salvation, wisdom, and knowledge; the fear of the LORD is the key to this treasure. (Isaiah 33:6)

Whoever is wise understands these things; whoever is discerning knows them. The ways of the LORD are right; the righteous will walk in them, but transgressors will stumble in them. (Hosea 14:9)

Like the Bereans, I want the nobility of mind to receive the word with great eagerness and to examine the Scriptures daily. (Acts 17:11)

In my obedience, I want to be wise about what is good and innocent about what is evil. (Romans 16:19)

I will not be unequally yoked together with unbelievers. For what does righteousness share with wickedness? Or what fellowship does light have with darkness? (2 Corinthians 6:14)

Though I walk in the flesh, I do not war according to the flesh. The weapons of my warfare are not fleshly, but divinely powerful to overthrow strongholds, casting down arguments and every pretension that sets itself up against the knowledge of God, and taking every thought captive to the obedience of Christ. (2 Corinthians 10:3-5)

I will watch carefully how I walk, not as the unwise but as wise, making the most of every opportunity, because the days are evil. I will not be foolish, but understand what the will of the Lord is. (Ephesians 5:15-17)

Whatever is true, whatever is noble, whatever is right, whatever is pure, whatever is lovely, whatever is of good report — if anything is excellent or praiseworthy — I will think about such things. The things I have learned and received and heard and seen in those who walk with Christ I will practice, and the God of peace will be with me. (Philippians 4:8-9)

I will see to it that no one takes me captive through philosophy and empty deceit, according to the tradition of men, according to the basic principles of this world, and not according to Christ. (Colossians 2:8)

I will examine all things, hold fast to the good, and abstain from every form of evil. (1 Thessalonians 5:21-22)

Anyone who partakes only of milk is not accustomed to the word of righteousness, for he is an infant. But solid food is for the mature, who because of use have their senses trained to distinguish good from evil. Therefore I will leave the elementary teachings about Christ and go on to maturity. (Hebrews 5:13-6:1)

If I lack wisdom, I should ask of God, who gives generously to all without reproach, and it will be given to me. (James 1:5)

Whoever is wise and understanding will show it by his good conduct and works done in the humility that comes from wisdom. If I harbor bitter envy and selfish ambition in my heart, I should not boast about it and lie against the truth. This wisdom does not come down from above, but is earthly, natural, demonic. For where there is envy and selfish ambition, there is disorder and every evil practice. (James 3:13-16)

The wisdom that comes from above is first pure, then peaceable, gentle, submissive, full of mercy and good fruits, without partiality and hypocrisy. And the fruit of righteousness is sown in peace by those who make peace. (James 3:17-18)

We have the prophetic word made more certain, to which I will do well to pay attention, as to a light shining in a dark place, until the day dawns, and the morning star rises in my heart. (2 Peter 1:19)

Moral Integrity and Honesty

I shall not murder. (Exodus 20:13)

I shall not commit adultery. (Exodus 20:14)

I shall not steal. (Exodus 20:15)

I will not follow the crowd in doing wrong. (Exodus 23:2)

I will not accept a bribe, for a bribe blinds those who see and perverts the words of the righteous. (Exodus 23:8)

I will not steal, nor deal falsely, nor deceive others. (Leviticus 19:11)

I will not be dishonest in judgment, in measurement of weight or quantity. I will be honest and just in my business affairs. (Leviticus 19:35-36)

I will not show partiality in judgment; I will hear both small and great alike. I will not be afraid of any man, for judgment belongs to God. (Deuteronomy 1:17)

I will not pervert justice or show partiality. I will not accept a bribe, for a bribe blinds the eyes of the wise and perverts the words of the righteous. (Deuteronomy 16:19)

I will have accurate and honest standards in my business practices. (Deuteronomy 25:15)

I know, my God, that you test the heart and are pleased with integrity. (1 Chronicles 29:17)

I will let the fear of the LORD be upon me, and I will be careful in what I do, for with the LORD, my God, there is no injustice or partiality or bribery. (2 Chronicles 19:7)

I want to be a faithful person who fears God. (Nehemiah 7:2)

I will be careful that no one entices me by riches; I will not let a large bribe turn me aside. (Job 36:18)

May those who hope in You not be ashamed because of me, O Lord GOD of hosts; may those who seek You not be dishonored because of me, O God of Israel. (Psalm 69:6)

Blessed are they who maintain justice, who do righteousness at all times. (Psalm 106:3)

I will not enter the path of the wicked or walk in the way of evil men. (Proverbs 4:14)

There are six things the LORD hates, seven that are detestable to Him: haughty eyes, a lying tongue, hands that shed innocent blood, a heart that devises wicked plans, feet that run swiftly to evil, a false witness who breathes lies, and one who causes strife among brothers. (Proverbs 6:16-19)

The fear of the LORD is to hate evil; wisdom hates pride and arrogance and the evil way and the perverse mouth. (Proverbs 8:13)

He who walks in integrity walks securely, but he who perverts his way will be found out. (Proverbs 10:9)

Dishonest scales are an abomination to the LORD, but an accurate weight is His delight. (Proverbs 11:1)

The integrity of the upright guides them, but the unfaithful are destroyed by their duplicity. (Proverbs 11:3)

The thoughts of the righteous are just, but the advice of the wicked is deceitful. (Proverbs 12:5)

Wealth gained by dishonesty will dwindle, but he who gathers by labor will increase. (Proverbs 13:11)

Poverty and shame will come to him who refuses instruction, but whoever heeds correction will be honored. (Proverbs 13:18)

He who walks in uprightness fears the LORD, but he who is devious in his ways despises Him. (Proverbs 14:2)

He who justifies the wicked, and he who condemns the just; both of them are detestable to the LORD. (Proverbs 17:15)

A good name is more desirable than great riches; favor is better than silver or gold. (Proverbs 22:1)

Extortion turns a wise man into a fool, and a bribe corrupts the heart. (Ecclesiastes 7:7)

When the sentence for an evil deed is not executed speedily, the heart of the sons of men is fully set in them to do evil. (Ecclesiastes 8:11)

Everyone who looks at a woman to lust for her has already committed adultery with her in his heart. (Matthew 5:28)

He who is faithful with very little is also faithful with much, and whoever is dishonest with very little will also be dishonest with much. If one is not faithful in handling worldly wealth, who will trust him with true riches? And if one is not faithful with someone else's property, who will give him property of his own? (Luke 16:10-12)

I will walk properly as in the daytime, not in revelings and drunkenness, not in promiscuity and debauchery, not in strife and jealousy. Rather, I will put on the Lord Jesus Christ and make no provision to gratify the lusts of the flesh. (Romans 13:13-14)

I will keep the feast of Christ, my Passover, not with old leaven, or with the leaven of malice and wickedness, but with the unleavened of sincerity and truth. (1 Corinthians 5:7-8)

I will flee from sexual immorality. All other sins a man commits are outside his body, but the immoral person sins against his own body. (1 Corinthians 6:18)

I will not set my heart on evil things, or be an idolater, or commit sexual immorality. (1 Corinthians 10:6-8)

I do not want even a hint of immorality, or any impurity, or greed, in my life, as is proper for a saint. Nor will I give myself to obscenity, foolish talk, or coarse joking, which are not fitting, but rather to giving of thanks. (Ephesians 5:3-4)

I will have nothing to do with the fruitless deeds of darkness, but rather I will expose them. (Ephesians 5:11)

I will consider the members of my earthly body as dead to immorality, impurity, passion, evil desires, and greed, which is idolatry. Because of these, the wrath of God is coming, and in them I once walked when I lived in them. (Colossians 3:5-7)

This is the will of God, my sanctification, that I abstain from immorality and learn to possess my own vessel in sanctification and honor. For God did not call me to be impure, but to live a holy life. (1 Thessalonians 4:3-4, 7)

I desire to have a clear conscience and to live honorably in all things. (Hebrews 13:18)

I will not say when I am tempted, "I am being tempted by God"; for God cannot be tempted by evil, nor does He tempt anyone. But each one is tempted when he is drawn away and enticed by his own lust. Then, after lust has conceived, it gives birth to sin; and sin, when it is full-grown, gives birth to death. (James 1:13-15)

I will put away all filthiness and the overflow of wickedness, and in meekness I will accept the word planted in me, which is able to save my soul. (James 1:21)

I have been born again, not of perishable seed, but of imperishable, through the living and abiding word of God. Therefore, I will put away all malice and all guile and hypocrisy and envy and all slander. (1 Peter 1:23; 2:1)

As an alien and a stranger in the world, I will abstain from fleshly lusts, which war against my soul. (1 Peter 2:11)

Truthfulness and Prudence

I shall not bear false witness against my neighbor. (Exodus 20:16)

I will not spread false reports, nor will I help a wicked man by being a malicious witness. (Exodus 23:1)

I will not go about spreading slander among people, nor will I do anything that endangers the life of my neighbor. (Leviticus 19:16)

I will put away perversity from my mouth and keep corrupt talk far from my lips. (Proverbs 4:24)

The mouth of the righteous is a fountain of life, but violence covers the mouth of the wicked. (Proverbs 10:11)

In a multitude of words, transgression does not cease, but he who restrains his lips is wise. (Proverbs 10:19)

A talebearer reveals secrets, but he who is trustworthy conceals a matter. (Proverbs 11:13)

A man will be satisfied with good from the fruit of his mouth, and the deeds of a man's hands will return to him. (Proverbs 12:14)

He who speaks truth reveals what is right; but a false witness, deceit. (Proverbs 12:17)

Reckless words pierce like a sword, but the tongue of the wise brings healing. (Proverbs 12:18)

Lying lips are hateful to the LORD, but He delights in those who deal faithfully. (Proverbs 12:22)

A rod of pride is in the mouth of a fool, but the lips of the wise will preserve them. (Proverbs 14:3)

A simple man believes everything, but a prudent man considers his steps. (Proverbs 14:15)

A gentle answer turns away wrath, but a harsh word stirs up anger. The tongue of the wise uses knowledge rightly, but the mouth of the fool pours out folly. (Proverbs 15:1-2)

The tongue that brings healing is a tree of life, but perverseness in it crushes the spirit. (Proverbs 15:4)

A man finds joy in giving an apt reply—and how good is a timely word! (Proverbs 15:23)

A man lacking in judgment strikes hands in pledge and puts up security for his neighbor. (Proverbs 17:18)

A fool has no delight in understanding, but only in airing his own opinions. (Proverbs 18:2)

The words of a gossip are like choice morsels; they go down into a the innermost parts of the body. (Proverbs 18:8)

He who answers a matter before he hears; that is his folly and his shame. (Proverbs 18:13)

The tongue has the power of death and life, and those who love it will eat its fruit. (Proverbs 18:21)

What is desirable in a man is his kindness, and it is better to be a poor man than a liar. (Proverbs 19:22)

A prudent man sees evil and hides himself, but the simple keep going and suffer for it. (Proverbs 22:3; 27:12)

Better is open rebuke than love that is concealed. (Proverbs 27:5)

Faithful are the wounds of a friend, but the kisses of an enemy are deceitful. (Proverbs 27:6)

These are the things I shall do: speak the truth to others, judge with truth and justice for peace, not plot evil against my neighbor, and not love a false oath; for all these things the LORD hates. (Zechariah 8:16-17)

I will not let any corrupt word come out of my mouth but only what is helpful for building others up according to their needs, that it may impart grace to those who hear. (Ephesians 4:29)

I will put away all of these things: anger, wrath, malice, slander, and abusive language from my mouth. (Colossians 3:8)

Everyone should be quick to hear, slow to speak, and slow to anger, for the anger of man does not produce the righteousness of God. (James 1:19-20)

Likewise the tongue is a small part of the body, but it makes great boasts. Consider what a great forest is set on fire by a small spark. The tongue also is a fire, a world of evil, that is set among the parts of the body, that corrupts the whole body, and sets the whole course of our life on fire and is set on fire by hell. (James 3:5-6)

All kinds of animals, birds, reptiles, and creatures of the sea are being tamed and have been tamed by man, but no man can tame the tongue. It is a restless evil, full of deadly poison. With the tongue we praise our Lord and Father, and with it we curse men, who have been made in the likeness of God; out of the same mouth come blessing and cursing, and this should not be. (James 3:7-10)

Humility

When I am blessed with abundance, I will beware lest my heart becomes proud, and I forget the LORD, my God, who provided all good things, thinking that it was my power and the strength of my hand that brought this wealth. (Deuteronomy 8:11-14, 17)

When pride comes, then comes dishonor, but with humility comes wisdom. (Proverbs 11:2)

The fear of the LORD is the instruction for wisdom, and humility comes before honor. (Proverbs 15:33)

Pride goes before destruction, and a haughty spirit before a fall. (Proverbs 16:18)

It is better to be of a humble spirit with the lowly than to divide the spoil with the proud. (Proverbs 16:19)

Before his downfall the heart of a man is haughty, but humility comes before honor. (Proverbs 18:12)

Haughty eyes and a proud heart, the lamp of the wicked, are sin. (Proverbs 21:4)

Humility and the fear of the LORD bring wealth and honor and life. (Proverbs 22:4)

I will not boast about tomorrow, for I do not know what a day may bring forth. (Proverbs 27:1)

I will let another praise me and not my own mouth; a stranger, and not my own lips. (Proverbs 27:2)

A man's pride brings him low, but the humble of spirit will gain honor. (Proverbs 29:23)

The proud looks of man will be humbled, and the loftiness of men brought low; the LORD alone will be exalted. (Isaiah 2:11)

Woe to those who are wise in their own eyes and clever in their own sight! (Isaiah 5:21)

This is the one You esteem: he who is humble and contrite of spirit, and who trembles at Your word. (Isaiah 66:2)

Thus says the LORD: "Let not the wise man boast of his wisdom, and let not the strong man boast of his strength, and let not the rich man boast of his riches; but let him who boasts boast about this: that he understands and knows Me, that I am the LORD, who exercises lovingkindness, justice, and righteousness on earth; for in these I delight," declares the LORD. (Jeremiah 9:23-24)

Should I seek great things for myself? I will seek them not. (Jeremiah 45:5)

You have called the humble of the earth who have upheld Your justice to seek the LORD, to seek righteousness, and to seek humility. (Zephaniah 2:3)

Blessed are the poor in spirit, for theirs is the kingdom of heaven. Blessed are those who mourn, for they will be comforted. Blessed are the meek, for they will inherit the earth. (Matthew 5:3-5)

Whoever exalts himself will be humbled, and whoever humbles himself will be exalted. (Matthew 23:12; Luke 14:11; 18:14)

I will not trust in myself or in my own righteousness, nor will I view others with contempt. (Luke 18:9)

I will be of the same mind with others; I will not be haughty in mind or wise in my own estimation, but I will associate with the humble. (Romans 12:16)

Let him who boasts, boast in the LORD. (1 Corinthians 1:31)

Who makes me different from anyone else? And what do I have that I did not receive? And if I did receive it, why should I boast as though I had not received it? (1 Corinthians 4:7)

Let him who thinks he stands take heed lest he fall. (1 Corinthians 10:12)

I do not dare to classify or compare myself with other people, for it is unwise to measure or compare myself with others. I will not boast beyond proper limits but within the sphere of the gospel of Christ. "Let him who boasts boast in the LORD." For it is not the one who commends himself who is approved, but the one whom the Lord commends. (2 Corinthians 10:12-14, 17-18)

If anyone thinks he is something when he is nothing, he deceives himself. (Galatians 6:3)

I want to walk in a way that is worthy of the calling with which I was called, with all humility and meekness and patience. (Ephesians 4:1-2)

I should let my gentleness be evident to all men; the Lord is near. (Philippians 4:5)

The brother in humble circumstances should glory in his high position, and the one who is rich should glory in his humiliation, because he will pass away like a flower of the field. (James 1:9-10)

I will submit myself to God and resist the devil, and he will flee from me. I will humble myself before the Lord, and He will exalt me. (James 4:7, 10)

I should not say, "Today or tomorrow I will go to this or that city, spend a year there, carry on business, and make a profit." For I do not even know what my life will be tomorrow. I am a vapor that appears for a little while and then vanishes away. Instead, I ought to say, "If the Lord wills, I will live and do this or that." Otherwise, I boast in my arrogance, and all such boasting is evil. (James 4:13-16)

I will humble myself under the mighty hand of God, that He may exalt me in due time, casting all my anxiety upon Him, because He cares for me. (1 Peter 5:6-7)

Teachability

Before I was afflicted, I went astray, but now I keep Your word. It was good for me to be afflicted, so that I might learn Your statutes. (Psalm 119:67, 71)

Your commandment is a lamp; Your teaching is a light, and Your reproofs of discipline are the way to life. (Proverbs 6:23)

Instruct a wise man, and he will be wiser still; teach a righteous man, and he will increase in learning. (Proverbs 9:9)

The wise in heart accept commands, but a chattering fool will be thrown down. (Proverbs 10:8)

He who heeds instruction is on the path of life, but he who refuses correction goes astray. (Proverbs 10:17)

Whoever loves instruction loves knowledge, but he who hates correction is stupid. (Proverbs 12:1)

The way of a fool is right in his own eyes, but a wise man listens to counsel. (Proverbs 12:15)

Pride breeds nothing but strife, but wisdom is found in those who take advice. (Proverbs 13:10)

He who listens to a life-giving rebuke will be at home among the wise. He who refuses instruction despises himself, but he who heeds correction gains understanding. (Proverbs 15:31-32)

He who heeds the word prospers, and blessed is he who trusts in the LORD. (Proverbs 16:20)

A rebuke goes deeper into a wise man than a hundred lashes into a fool. (Proverbs 17:10)

The heart of the prudent acquires knowledge, and the ear of the wise seeks knowledge. (Proverbs 18:15)

It is not good for a person to be without knowledge, and he who hastens with his feet sins. (Proverbs 19:2)

Listen to counsel and accept instruction, that you may be wise in your latter days. (Proverbs 19:20)

All Scripture is God-breathed and is useful for teaching, for reproof, for correction, for training in righteousness, that the man of God may be thoroughly equipped for every good work. (2 Timothy 3:16-17)

I will not forget the exhortation that addresses me as a son: "My son, do not despise the Lord's discipline, nor lose heart when you are rebuked by Him, for whom the LORD loves He disciplines, and He chastises every son whom He receives." (Hebrews 12:5-6)

I will endure discipline, for God is treating me as a son. For what son is not disciplined by his father? If I am without discipline, of which all have become partakers, then I am an illegitimate child and not a true son. Moreover, we have all had human fathers who disciplined us, and we respected them; how much more should I be subjected to the Father of spirits and live? (Hebrews 12:7-9)

Our fathers disciplined us for a little while as they thought best, but God disciplines us for our good, that we may share in His holiness. No discipline seems pleasant at the time, but painful; later on, however, it produces the peaceable fruit of righteousness for those who have been trained by it. (Hebrews 12:10-11)

Contentment, Single-mindedness, and Peace

I shall not covet my neighbor's house, my neighbor's wife, his manservant or maidservant, his ox or donkey, or anything that belongs to my neighbor. (Exodus 20:17)

This is the day the LORD has made; I will rejoice and be glad in it. (Psalm 118:24)

A heart at peace gives life to the body, but envy is rottenness to the bones. (Proverbs 14:30)

Better a little with the fear of the LORD than great wealth with turmoil. (Proverbs 15:16)

Better is a little with righteousness than great income with injustice. (Proverbs 16:8)

Better is a dry crust with quietness than a house full of feasting with strife. (Proverbs 17:1)

I will not wear myself out to get rich; I will have the understanding to cease. I will not set my desire on what flies away, for wealth surely sprouts wings and flies into the heavens like an eagle. (Proverbs 23:4-5)

Everyone who eats and drinks and sees good in all his labor—it is the gift of God. (Ecclesiastes 3:13)

He who loves money will not be satisfied with money; nor he who loves abundance, with its increase. (Ecclesiastes 5:10)

Blessed are the pure in heart, for they shall see God. Blessed are the peacemakers, for they shall be called sons of God. (Matthew 5:8-9)

I will not lay up for myself treasures on earth, where moth and rust destroy and where thieves break in and steal. But I will lay up for myself treasures in heaven, where moth and rust do not destroy and where thieves do not break in and steal. For where my treasure is, there my heart will be also. (Matthew 6:19-21; Luke 12:34)

No one can serve two masters; for either he will hate the one and love the other, or he will be devoted to the one and despise the other. I cannot serve God and wealth. (Matthew 6:24; Luke 16:13)

I will not worry about my life, what I will eat or what I will drink; or about my body, what I will wear. Life is more than food, and the body more than clothes. The birds of the air do not sow or reap or gather into barns, and yet my heavenly Father feeds them. Am I not much more valuable than they? Who by worrying can add a single hour to his life? And why do I worry about clothes? I will consider how the lilies of the field grow; they neither labor nor spin, yet not even Solomon in all his splendor was dressed like one of these. But if God so clothes the grass of the field, which is here today and tomorrow is thrown into the fire, will He not much more clothe me? So I will not worry, saying, "What shall I eat?" or "What shall I drink?" or "What shall I wear?" For the pagans run after all these things, and my heavenly Father knows that I need them. But I will seek first His kingdom and His righteousness, and all these things will be added to me. (Matthew 6:25-33; Luke 12:22-31)

I will not worry about tomorrow, for tomorrow will worry about itself. Each day has enough trouble of its own. (Matthew 6:34)

I do not want to be worried and troubled about many things; only one thing is needed. Like Mary, I want to choose the good part, which will not be taken away from me. (Luke 10:41, 42)

I will beware and be on my guard against all covetousness, for my life does not consist in the abundance of my possessions. (Luke 12:15)

I do not want to lay up treasure for myself without being rich toward God. (Luke 12:21)

I will covet no one's money or possessions. (Acts 20:33)

I will be anxious for nothing, but in everything by prayer and petition with thanksgiving, I will let my requests be known to God. And the peace of God, which transcends all understanding, will guard my heart and my mind in Christ Jesus. (Philippians 4:6-7)

I want to learn to be content in whatever circumstances I am. Whether I am abased or in abundance, whether I am filled or hungry, I want to learn the secret of being content in any and every situation. I can do all things through Him who strengthens me. (Philippians 4:11-13)

I will let the peace of Christ rule in my heart, to which I was called as a member of one body, and I will be thankful. (Colossians 3:15)

Godliness with contentment is great gain. For I brought nothing into the world, and I can take nothing out of it. But if I have food and clothing, with these I will be content. (1 Timothy 6:6-8)

Those who want to get rich fall into temptation and a snare and into many foolish and harmful desires that plunge men into ruin and destruction. For the love of money is a root of all kinds of evil, and some by longing for it have wandered from the faith and pierced themselves with many sorrows. But I will flee from these things, and pursue righteousness, godliness, faith, love, patience, and gentleness. (1 Timothy 6:9-11)

I will keep my life free from the love of money and be content with what I have, for You have said, "I will never leave you, nor will I forsake you." (Hebrews 13:5)

I want to be a person of faith, who does not doubt the promise of God, and not a double-minded man, who is unstable in all his ways. (James 1:6, 8)

I know that friendship with the world is enmity toward God. Anyone who wants to be a friend of the world makes himself an enemy of God. (James 4:4)

I will not love the world or the things in the world. If anyone loves the world, the love of the Father is not in him. For all that is in the world—the lust of the flesh, the lust of the eyes, and the pride of life—is not of the Father but of the world. And the world and its lusts are passing away, but the one who does the will of God abides forever. (1 John 2:15-17)

Discipline and Self-control

Like Ezra, I want to set my heart to study the word of the LORD, and to do it, and to teach it to others. (Ezra 7:10)

Blessed is the man who does not walk in the counsel of the wicked or stand in the way of sinners or sit in the seat of scorners. But his delight is in the law of the LORD, and in His law he meditates day and night. And he shall be like a tree planted by streams of water, which yields its fruit in its season and whose leaf does not wither; and whatever he does will prosper. (Psalm 1:1-3)

How can a young man keep his way pure? By keeping it according to Your word. (Psalm 119:9)

I have hidden Your word in my heart that I might not sin against You. (Psalm 119:11)

The LORD is my portion; I have promised to keep Your words. I considered my ways and turned my steps to Your testimonies. (Psalm 119:57, 59)

I have kept my feet from every evil path that I might keep Your word. I gain understanding from Your precepts; therefore I hate every false way. (Psalm 119:101, 104)

Your word is a lamp to my feet and a light to my path. I have inclined my heart to perform Your statutes to the very end. (Psalm 119:105, 112)

A fool shows his annoyance at once, but a prudent man overlooks an insult. (Proverbs 12:16)

A wise man fears and departs from evil, but a fool is arrogant and bold. A quick-tempered man acts foolishly, and a man of evil plots is hated. (Proverbs 14:16-17)

A hot-tempered man stirs up dissension, but he who is slow to anger calms a quarrel. (Proverbs 15:18)

He who is slow to anger is better than the mighty, and he who rules his spirit than he who takes a city. (Proverbs 16:32)

Laziness casts one into a deep sleep, and an idle person will be hungry. (Proverbs 19:15)

A man of great wrath must pay the penalty; if you rescue him, you will have to do it again. (Proverbs 19:19)

I will not be quickly provoked in my spirit, for anger rests in the bosom of fools. (Ecclesiastes 7:9)

I will watch and pray so that I will not fall into temptation; the spirit is willing, but the flesh is weak. (Matthew 26:41)

In my anger I will not sin; I will not let the sun go down while I am still angry, and I will not give the devil a foothold. (Ephesians 4:26-27)

I will devote myself to prayer, being watchful in it with thanksgiving. (Colossians 4:2)

I will make it my ambition to lead a quiet life, to mind my own business, and to work with my own hands, so that I may walk properly toward those who are outside and may lack nothing. (1 Thessalonians 4:11-12)

We are all sons of the light and sons of the day. We do not belong to the night or to the darkness. So then, let us not be like others who are asleep, but let us be alert and self-controlled. (1 Thessalonians 5:5-6)

Since I belong to the day, I will be self-controlled, putting on the breastplate of faith and love, and the hope of salvation as a helmet. (1 Thessalonians 5:8)

I should rejoice always and pray without ceasing; in everything I will give thanks, for this is the will of God for me in Christ Jesus. (1 Thessalonians 5:16-18)

I want to be above reproach, temperate, sensible, respectable, hospitable, able to teach, not given to drunkenness, not violent but gentle, not quarrelsome, not a lover of money, one who manages his own family well, and who keeps his children under control with proper respect. And I want a good reputation with outsiders, so that I will not fall into disgrace and the snare of the devil. (1 Timothy 3:2-4, 7)

I want to be worthy of respect, not double-tongued, not addicted to wine, not fond of dishonest gain, but holding the mystery of the faith with a clear conscience. (1 Timothy 3:8-9)

I will not neglect my spiritual gifts. (1 Timothy 4:14)

God has not given me a spirit of timidity, but a spirit of power, of love, and of self-control. (2 Timothy 1:7)

I will be diligent to present myself approved to God, a workman who does not need to be ashamed and who correctly handles the word of truth. (2 Timothy 2:15)

I want to be above reproach, blameless as a steward of God, not self-willed, not quick-tempered, not given to wine, not violent, not fond of dishonest gain, but hospitable, a lover of what is good, sensible, just, holy, and self-controlled. (Titus 1:6-8)

The grace of God has appeared, bringing salvation to all men, teaching us to deny ungodliness and worldly passions and to live sensibly, righteously, and godly in the present age. (Titus 2:11-12)

I will prepare my mind for action and be self-controlled, setting my hope fully on the grace to be brought to me at the revelation of Jesus Christ. (1 Peter 1:13)

The end of all things is near; therefore I will be clear minded and self-controlled for prayer. (1 Peter 4:7)

I will be self-controlled and alert; my adversary the devil prowls around like a roaring lion looking for someone to devour. But I will resist him, standing firm in the faith, knowing that my brothers throughout the world are undergoing the same kind of sufferings. (1 Peter 5:8-9)

Courage and Perseverance

I will be strong and courageous, being careful to obey Your word; I will not turn from it to the right or to the left, that I may act wisely wherever I go. (Joshua 1:7)

I will be strong and courageous; I will not be afraid or discouraged, for the LORD, my God, will be with me wherever I go. (Joshua 1:9)

I will be strong and courageous, and act. I will not be afraid or discouraged, for the LORD God is with me. He will not fail me or forsake me. (1 Chronicles 28:20)

I will be strong and courageous; I will not be afraid or discouraged because of my adversaries, for there is a greater power with me than with them, for the LORD, my God, is with me to help me. (2 Chronicles 32:7-8)

I will not be afraid of my adversaries, but I will remember the Lord, who is great and awesome. (Nehemiah 4:14)

I will take courage and not be afraid, for the Lord Jesus is with me. (Mark 6:50)

I will rejoice in hope, persevere in affliction, and continue steadfastly in prayer. (Romans 12:12)

Thanks be to God, who gives us the victory through our Lord Jesus Christ. Therefore I will be steadfast, immovable, abounding in the work of the Lord, knowing that my labor in the Lord is not in vain. (1 Corinthians 15:57-58)

I will be on my guard, stand firm in the faith, act with courage, and be strong. (1 Corinthians 16:13)

I am hard pressed on every side, but not crushed; perplexed, but not in despair; persecuted, but not forsaken; struck down, but not destroyed; always carrying about in my body the death of Jesus, so that the life of Jesus may also be revealed in my body. For we who live are always being delivered over to death for Jesus' sake, so that His life may be revealed in our mortal body. (2 Corinthians 4:8-11)

God's servants have commended themselves in every way: in great endurance, in afflictions, in needs, in distresses, in beatings, in imprisonments, in tumults, in labors, in sleeplessness, in hunger, in purity, in knowledge, in patience, in kindness, in the Holy Spirit, in sincere love, in the word of truth, in the power of God—through the weapons of righteousness in the right hand and in the left, through glory and dishonor, through bad report and good report—as deceivers, and yet true; as unknown, and yet well known; as dying, and yet living; as beaten, and yet not killed; as sorrowful, yet always rejoicing; as poor, yet making many rich; as having nothing, and yet possessing everything. (2 Corinthians 6:4-10)

I will not become weary in doing good, for at the proper time I will reap a harvest if I do not give up. (Galatians 6:9)

I want the Lord to establish my heart as blameless and holy before our God and Father at the coming of our Lord Jesus with all His saints. (1 Thessalonians 3:13)

May our Lord Jesus Christ Himself and God, our Father, who has loved us and has given us eternal consolation and good hope by grace, comfort our hearts and strengthen us in every good work and word. (2 Thessalonians 2:16-17)

I do not want to grow weary in doing what is right. (2 Thessalonians 3:13)

I will fight the good fight of faith and lay hold of the eternal life to which I was called when I made the good confession in the presence of many witnesses. In the sight of God, who gives life to all things, and of Christ Jesus, who testified the good confession before Pontius Pilate, I want to keep this command without spot or blame until the appearing of our Lord Jesus Christ. (1 Timothy 6:12-14)

I will be self-controlled in all things, endure hardship, do the work of an evangelist, and fulfill my ministry. (2 Timothy 4:5)

I will fight the good fight, finish the race, and keep the faith, so that there will be laid up for me the crown of righteousness, which the Lord, the righteous Judge, will award to me on that day; and not only to me, but also to all who have longed for His appearing. (2 Timothy 4:7-8)

I desire to be diligent to realize the full assurance of hope to the end. I do not want to become sluggish but to imitate those who through faith and patience inherit the promises. (Hebrews 6:11-12)

Since I have a great cloud of witnesses surrounding me, I want to lay aside every impediment and the sin that so easily entangles and run with endurance the race that is set before me, fixing my eyes on Jesus, the author and perfecter of my faith, who for the joy set before Him endured the cross, despising the shame, and sat down at the right hand of the throne of God. I will consider Him who endured such hostility from sinners, so that I will not grow weary and lose heart. (Hebrews 12:1-3)

Consider it pure joy, my brothers, whenever you face trials of many kinds, because you know that the testing of your faith develops perseverance. Perseverance must finish its work, so that you may be mature and complete, not lacking anything. (James 1:2-4)

Blessed is the man who perseveres under trial, because when he has stood the test, he will receive the crown of life that God has promised to those who love him. (James 1:12)

I greatly rejoice in my salvation, though now for a little while, if necessary, I have been grieved by various trials, so that the proving of my faith, being much more precious than gold that perishes, even though refined by fire, may be found to result in praise, glory, and honor at the revelation of Jesus Christ. (1 Peter 1:6-7)

Who is going to harm you if you are eager to do good? But even if you should suffer for what is right, you are blessed. "Do not fear what they fear; do not be frightened." (1 Peter 3:13, 14)

So then, those who suffer according to God's will should commit themselves to their faithful Creator and continue to do good. (1 Peter 4:19)

Since everything will be destroyed in this way, what kind of people ought you to be? You ought to live holy and godly lives as you look forward to the day of God and speed its coming. But in keeping with His promise, we are looking forward to a new heaven and a new earth, the home of righteousness. So then, dear friends, since you are looking forward to this, make every effort to be found spotless, blameless, and at peace with Him. (2 Peter 3:11-14)

And now, dear children, continue in Him, so that when He appears we may be confident and unashamed before Him at His coming. (1 John 2:28)

But you, dear friends, build yourselves up in your most holy faith and pray in the Holy Spirit. Keep yourselves in God's love as you wait for the mercy of our Lord Jesus Christ to bring you to eternal life. (Jude 20, 21)

EIGHT

MY RELATIONSHIP
TO OTHERS

Love and Acceptance

I will not hate my brother in my heart. (Leviticus 19:17)

I will not take vengeance or bear a grudge against others, but I will love my neighbor as myself. (Leviticus 19:18)

Hatred stirs up strife, but love covers all transgressions. (Proverbs 10:12)

Better a meal of vegetables where there is love than a fattened calf with hatred. (Proverbs 15:17)

He who covers a transgression seeks love, but he who repeats a matter separates close friends. (Proverbs 17:9)

A friend loves at all times, and a brother is born for adversity. (Proverbs 17:17)

I will love my enemies and pray for those who persecute me. (Matthew 5:44)

If I forgive men for their transgressions, my heavenly Father will also forgive me. (Matthew 6:14)

I will not judge, so that I will not be judged. For in the same way I judge others, I will be judged; and with the measure I use, it will be measured to me. (Matthew 7:1-2)

Whatever I want others to do to me, I will also do to them, for this is the law and the prophets. (Matthew 7:12)

Peter came to Jesus and asked, "Lord, how often shall my brother sin against me, and I forgive him? Up to seven times?" Jesus said to him, "I tell you, not seven times, but up to seventy times seven." (Matthew 18:21-22)

"You shall love the LORD, your God, with all your heart and with all your soul and with all your mind." This is the first and great commandment. And the second is like it: "You shall love your neighbor as yourself." All the law and the prophets hang on these two commandments. (Matthew 22:37-40)

The foremost commandment is this: "Hear, O Israel! the LORD, our God, the LORD is one, and you shall love the LORD, your God, with all your heart and with all your soul and with all your mind and with all your strength." The second is this: "You shall love your neighbor as yourself." There is no commandment greater than these. To love God with all the heart and with all the understanding and with all the strength, and to love one's neighbor as himself are more important than all burnt offerings and sacrifices. (Mark 12:29-31, 33)

I will love my enemies, do good to those who hate me, bless those who curse me, and pray for those who mistreat me. Just as I want others to do to me, I will do to them in the same way. (Luke 6:27-28, 31)

I will love my enemies, do good to them, and lend to them, expecting nothing in return. Then my reward will be great, and I will be a child of the Most High; for He is kind to the ungrateful and evil. I will be merciful just as my Father is merciful. (Luke 6:35-36)

If I do not judge, I will not be judged; if I do not condemn, I will not be condemned; if I forgive, I will be forgiven. (Luke 6:37)

You have given us a new commandment to love one another even as You have loved us, so we must love one another. By this all men will know that we are Your disciples, if we have love for one another. (John 13:34)

This is Your commandment: that we love one another, as You have loved us. (John 15:12)

My love must be sincere. I will hate what is evil and cling to what is good. (Romans 12:9)

We must be devoted to one another in brotherly love, honoring one another above ourselves. (Romans 12:10)

I will bless those who persecute me; I will bless and not curse. (Romans 12:14)

I will rejoice with those who rejoice and weep with those who weep. (Romans 12:15)

I will owe nothing to anyone except to love them, for he who loves his neighbor has fulfilled the law. For the commandments, "You shall not commit adultery," "You shall not murder," "You shall not steal," "You shall not covet," and if there is any other commandment, it is summed up in this saying: "You shall love your neighbor as yourself."

Love does no harm to a neighbor; therefore love is the fulfillment of the law. (Romans 13:8-10)

I will accept him whose faith is weak without passing judgment on his opinions. Who am I to judge another's servant? To his own master he stands or falls, and he will stand, for the Lord is able to make him stand. (Romans 14:1, 4)

I will not judge my brother or regard him with contempt. Instead of judging him, I will resolve not to put a stumbling block or obstacle in my brother's way. (Romans 14:10, 13)

I will accept others just as Christ accepted me to the glory of God. (Romans 15:7)

Knowledge puffs up, but love builds up. (1 Corinthians 8:1)

I was called to freedom, but I will not use my freedom to indulge the flesh, but through love I will serve others. For the whole law is summed up in this word: "You shall love your neighbor as yourself." (Galatians 5:13-14)

I will put away all bitterness and anger and wrath and shouting and slander, along with all malice. And I will be kind and compassionate to others, forgiving them just as God in Christ also forgave me. (Ephesians 4:31-32)

I will bear with others and forgive whatever complaints I have against them; I will forgive just as the Lord forgave me. (Colossians 3:13)

May the Lord make me increase and abound in my love for believers and for unbelievers. (1 Thessalonians 3:12)

Concerning brotherly love, we have been taught by God to love each other, and the Lord urges us to increase more and more. (1 Thessalonians 4:9-10)

We must let brotherly love continue. (Hebrews 13:1)

I will not slander other believers. Anyone who slanders his brother or judges his brother slanders the law and judges the law. When I judge the law, I am not a doer of the law, but a judge. There is only one Lawgiver and Judge, the One who is able to save and to destroy. Who am I to judge my neighbor? (James 4:11-12)

In obedience to the truth I will purify my soul for a sincere love of the brethren, and I will love others fervently from the heart. (1 Peter 1:22)

Above all, I will have a fervent love for others, because love covers a multitude of sins. (1 Peter 4:8)

The one who loves his brother abides in the light, and there is no cause for stumbling in him. But the one who hates his brother is in the darkness and walks in the darkness and does not know where he is going, because the darkness has blinded his eyes. (1 John 2:10-11)

This is the message we heard from the beginning, that we should love one another. We know that we have passed out of death into life, because we love the brethren. The one who does not love abides in death. By this we know love, that Christ laid down His life for us, and we ought to lay down our lives for the brethren. (1 John 3:11, 14, 16)

This is God's commandment: that we believe in the name of His Son, Jesus Christ, and love one another as He commanded us. (1 John 3:23)

We should love one another, for love is from God, and everyone who loves has been born of God and knows God. Whoever does not love does not know God, for God is love. (1 John 4:7-8)

In this is love, not that we loved God, but that He loved us and sent His Son to be the propitiation for our sins. Since God so loved us, we also ought to love one another. No one has ever seen God; but if we love one another, God abides in us, and His love is perfected in us. (1 John 4:10-12)

We love, because God first loved us. If anyone says, "I love God," and hates his brother, he is a liar; for the one who does not love his brother whom he has seen, cannot love God whom he has not seen. And we have this commandment from Him: that the one who loves God must also love his brother. (1 John 4:19-21)

Giving and Serving

I will give generously to others without a grudging heart. (Deuteronomy 15:10)

I will not withhold good from those to whom it is due, when it is in my power to act. (Proverbs 3:27)

A generous man will prosper, and he who waters will himself be refreshed. (Proverbs 11:25)

He who oppresses the poor reproaches their Maker, but whoever is kind to the needy honors Him. (Proverbs 14:31)

He who is kind to the poor lends to the LORD, and He will reward him for what he has done. (Proverbs 19:17)

He who is generous will be blessed, for he shares his food with the poor. (Proverbs 22:9)

I will learn to do good, seek justice, remove the oppressor, defend the orphan, and plead for the widow. (Isaiah 1:17)

Is this not the fast You have chosen: to loose the bonds of wickedness, to undo the cords of the yoke, and to let the oppressed go free and break every yoke? Is it not to share our food with the hungry and to provide the poor wanderer with shelter; when we see the naked, to clothe him, and not to turn away from our own flesh? Then our light will break forth like the dawn, and our healing will quickly appear, and our righteousness will go before us; the glory of the LORD will be our rear guard. Then we will call, and the LORD will answer; we will cry, and He will say, "Here I am." If we put away the yoke from our midst, the pointing of the finger and malicious talk, and if we extend our souls to the hungry and satisfy the afflicted soul, then our light will rise in the darkness, and our gloom will become like the noonday. (Isaiah 58:6-10)

When Christ comes to reign as king on His glorious throne, He will say to the sheep on His right hand, "Come, you who are blessed of My Father, inherit the kingdom prepared for you from the foundation of the world. For I was hungry, and you gave Me something to eat; I was thirsty, and you gave Me something to drink; I was a stranger, and you invited Me in; I was naked, and you clothed Me; I was sick, and you visited Me; I was in prison, and you came to Me." Then the righteous will answer Him, "Lord, when did we see You hungry and feed You, or thirsty and give You something to drink? And when did we see You a stranger and invite You in, or naked and clothe You? And when did we see You sick or in prison and come to You?" And the King will answer and say to them, "I tell you the truth, inasmuch as you did it to one of the least of these brothers of Mine, you did it to Me." (Matthew 25:31, 34-40)

Whoever gives another a cup of water to drink because of his name as a follower of Christ will by no means lose his reward. (Mark 9:41)

When I give, it will be given to me; good measure, pressed down, shaken together, running over, they will pour into my lap. For with the measure I use, it will be measured back to me. (Luke 6:38)

When I give a reception, if I invite the poor, the crippled, the lame, and the blind, I will be blessed, because they cannot repay me; for I will be repaid at the resurrection of the righteous. (Luke 14:13-14)

I must help the weak and remember the words of the Lord Jesus, that He said, "It is more blessed to give than to receive." (Acts 20:35)

I will contribute to the needs of the saints and practice hospitality. (Romans 12:13)

He who sows sparingly will also reap sparingly, and he who sows bountifully will also reap bountifully. Each one should give as he has decided in his heart, not reluctantly or under compulsion; for God loves a cheerful giver. And God is able to make all grace abound to us, so that always having all sufficiency in everything, we may abound in every good work. As it is written: "He has scattered abroad His gifts to the poor; His righteousness endures forever." Now He who supplies seed to the sower and bread for food will also supply and increase our seed and will increase the fruits of our righteousness. (2 Corinthians 9:6-10)

Because of our ministry of supplying the needs of the saints, they will glorify God for the obedience that accompanies our confession of the gospel of Christ, and for the liberality of sharing with them and with everyone else. (2 Corinthians 9:13)

I will not forget to show hospitality to strangers, for by so doing some have entertained angels without knowing it. (Hebrews 13:2)

I will remember those in prison, as though bound with them, and those who are mistreated, since I myself am also in the body. (Hebrews 13:3)

I will not forget to do good and to share with others, for with such sacrifices God is well pleased. (Hebrews 13:16)

This is pure and undefiled religion before our God and Father: to visit orphans and widows in their affliction and to keep oneself unspotted from the world. (James 1:27)

I will be hospitable to others without grumbling. (1 Peter 4:9)

As each one has received a gift, he should use it to serve others, as a good steward of the manifold grace of God. (1 Peter 4:10)

General Affirmations

I will not defraud my neighbor or rob him. (Leviticus 19:13)
I will do no injustice in judgment nor show partiality to the poor or favoritism to the great, but I will judge my neighbor fairly. (Leviticus 19:15)

I will not hate my brother in my heart, but I will reprove my neighbor frankly and not incur sin because of him. (Leviticus 19:17)

I will not mistreat my neighbor, but I will fear my God; for You are the LORD, my God. (Leviticus 25:17)

I will trust in You enough to honor You as holy in the sight of others. (Numbers 20:12)

Far be it from me that I should sin against the LORD by ceasing to pray for others. (1 Samuel 12:23)

I will not plan evil against my neighbor, since he lives trustfully by me. (Proverbs 3:29)

I will not strive with a man without cause, if he has done me no harm. (Proverbs 3:30)

An anxious heart weighs a man down, but a good word makes him glad. (Proverbs 12:25)

A righteous man guides his friends, but the way of the wicked leads them astray. (Proverbs 12:26)

I will stay away from a foolish man, for I will not find knowledge on his lips. (Proverbs 14:7)

Starting a quarrel is like breaching a dam, so I will stop a quarrel before it breaks out. (Proverbs 17:14)

I will not make friends with a hot-tempered man or associate with one easily angered, lest I learn his ways and set a snare for my soul. (Proverbs 22:24-25)

As iron sharpens iron, so one man sharpens another. (Proverbs 27:17)

The sons of this world are more shrewd in dealing with their own kind than are the sons of light. I would be wise to use worldly wealth to make friends for myself, so that when it is gone, they may welcome me into the eternal dwellings. (Luke 16:8-9)

I will not repay anyone evil for evil, but I will seek to do what is right in the sight of all men. (Romans 12:17)

If it is possible, as far as it depends on me, I will live at peace with all men. (Romans 12:18)

I will not take revenge but leave room for the wrath of God, for it is written: "Vengeance is Mine; I will repay," says the Lord. I will not be overcome by evil, but overcome evil with good. (Romans 12:19, 21)

I will submit myself to the governing authorities. For there is no authority except from God, and the authorities that exist have been established by God. Consequently, he who resists authority has opposed the ordinance of God, and those who do so will bring judgment on themselves. (Romans 13:1-2)

I will give to all what they are due: taxes to whom taxes are due, custom to whom custom, respect to whom respect, honor to whom honor. (Romans 13:7)

We who are strong ought to bear the weaknesses of those who are not strong and not to please ourselves. Each of us should please his neighbor for his good, to build him up. (Romans 15:1-2)

No one should seek his own good, but the good of others. (1 Corinthians 10:24)

God comforts us in all our afflictions, so that we can comfort those in any affliction with the comfort we ourselves have received from God. (2 Corinthians 1:4)

I will not give cause for offense in anything, so that my ministry will not be discredited. (2 Corinthians 6:3)

I will not become conceited, provoking others and envying others. (Galatians 5:26)

I will obey those who are in authority over me with fear and trembling and with sincerity of heart, as to Christ; not with external service as a pleaser of men, but as a slave of Christ, doing the will of God from my heart. With good will I will serve as to the Lord and not to men, knowing that I will receive back from the Lord whatever good I do. (Ephesians 6:5-8)

I will treat subordinates with respect, not threatening them, knowing that both their Master and mine is in heaven, and there is no partiality with Him. (Ephesians 6:9)

I will do nothing out of selfish ambition or vain conceit, but in humility, I will esteem others as more important than myself. I will look not only to my own interests but also to the interests of others. (Philippians 2:3-4)

I will do all things without complaining or arguing, so that I may become blameless and pure, a child of God without fault in the midst of a crooked and perverse generation, among whom I shine as a light in the world, holding fast the word of life. (Philippians 2:14-16)

I will obey those who are in authority over me in all things, not with external service as a pleaser of men, but with sincerity of heart, fearing the Lord. Whatever I do, I will work at it with all my heart, as to the Lord and not to men, knowing that I will receive the reward of the inheritance from the Lord. It is the Lord Christ I am serving. (Colossians 3:22-24)

I will provide my subordinates with what is just and fair, knowing that I also have a Master in heaven. (Colossians 4:1)

What is my hope or joy or crown of rejoicing in the presence of the Lord Jesus at His coming? My glory and joy is the people in whose lives I have been privileged to have a ministry. (1 Thessalonians 2:19-20)

I will not repay evil for evil to anyone, but I will pursue what is good for others. (1 Thessalonians 5:15)

If anyone does not provide for his own and especially for his family, he has denied the faith and is worse than an unbeliever. (1 Timothy 5:8)

I will avoid foolish and ignorant disputes, knowing that they produce quarrels. The Lord's servant must not quarrel but be gentle toward all, able to teach, and patient. (2 Timothy 2:23-24)

I will hold firmly to the faithful word as I have been taught, so that I can exhort others by sound doctrine and refute those who oppose it. (Titus 1:9)

I will remind others to be subject to rulers and authorities, to be obedient, to be ready for every good work, to slander no one, to be peaceable and gentle, and to show true humility toward all men. (Titus 3.1-2)

In my faith in our glorious Lord Jesus Christ, I will not show partiality to some people above others. (James 2:1)

I will submit myself for the Lord's sake to every human authority, whether to a king as being supreme, or to governors as sent by him to punish evildoers and to praise those who do right; for it is the will of God that by doing good I may silence the ignorance of foolish men. (1 Peter 2:13-15)

I will honor all people, love the brotherhood of believers, fear God, and honor the king. (I Peter 2:17)

I will not return evil for evil or insult for insult, but blessing instead, because to this I was called, that I may inherit a blessing. (1 Peter 3:9)

Young men should be submissive to those who are older, and all of us should clothe ourselves with humility toward one another, for "God opposes the proud but gives grace to the humble." (1 Peter 5:5)

Husband or Wife

The LORD God said, "It is not good for the man to be alone; I will make a helper suitable for him." And the LORD God made a woman from the rib He had taken out of the man, and He brought her to the man. And the man said, "This is now bone of my bones and flesh of my flesh; she shall be called 'Woman,' because she was taken out of man." For this reason a man shall leave his father and mother, and shall cleave to his wife, and they shall become one flesh. (Genesis 2:18, 22-24)

A virtuous wife is the crown of her husband, but she who causes shame is like decay in his bones. (Proverbs 12:4)

Houses and wealth are inherited from fathers, but a prudent wife is from the LORD. (Proverbs 19:14)

Who can find a virtuous wife? She is worth far more than jewels. (Proverbs 31:10)

Charm is deceptive, and beauty is fleeting; but a woman who fears the LORD, she shall be praised. (Proverbs 31:30)

Love is as strong as death, and jealousy is as cruel as the grave; its flames are flames of fire, a flame of the LORD. Many waters cannot quench love, nor can rivers overflow it. If a man were to give all the wealth of his house for love, it would be utterly scorned. (Song of Solomon 8:6, 7)

Since she is a companion and a wife by covenant, a husband should not deal treacherously against the wife of his youth. The LORD God of hosts seeks a godly offspring and hates divorce; therefore we must take heed to our spirit and not deal treacherously. (Malachi 2:14-16)

From the beginning of creation God "made them male and female. For this reason a man shall leave his father and mother and shall cleave to his wife, and the two shall become one flesh." So they are no longer two, but one flesh. Therefore what God has joined together, let man not separate. (Matthew 19:4-6; Mark 10:6-9)

The husband should fulfill his marital duty to his wife, and likewise the wife to her husband. The wife's body does not belong to her alone, but also to her husband. In the same way, the husband's body does not belong to him alone, but also to his wife. (1 Corinthians 7:3-4)

Wives should submit to their own husbands as to the Lord. For the husband is the head of the wife, as Christ also is the head of the Church; and He is the Savior of the body. But as the Church is subject to Christ, so also wives should be to their husbands in everything. (Ephesians 5:22-24)

Husbands should love their wives, just as Christ also loved the Church and gave Himself up for her that He might sanctify and cleanse her by the washing with water through the word, that He might present her to Himself as a glorious Church, without spot or wrinkle or any other blemish, but holy and blameless. So husbands ought to love their own wives as their own bodies. He who loves his own wife loves himself; for no one ever hated his own flesh, but nourishes and cherishes it, just as Christ also does the Church, for we are members of His body. (Ephesians 5:25-30)

Each husband must love his own wife as he loves himself, and each wife must respect her husband. (Ephesians 5:33)

Wives should submit to their husbands, as is fitting in the Lord. (Colossians 3:18)

Husbands should love their wives and not be bitter toward them. (Colossians 3:19)

Marriage should be honored by all, and the marriage bed should be undefiled; for God will judge fornicators and adulterers. (Hebrews 13:4)

Wives should be submissive to their own husbands, so that even if any of them disobey the word, they may be won without a word by the behavior of their wives, when they see their purity and reverence. (1 Peter 3:1-2)

Husbands should be considerate as they live with their wives and treat them with respect as the weaker vessel and as co-heirs of the grace of life. (1 Peter 3:7)

Children

Like Abraham, I should direct my children and my household after me to keep the way of the LORD by doing what is right and just. (Genesis 18:19)

I will honor my father and my mother. (Exodus 20:12)

I will learn to fear You all the days I live on the earth and teach Your words to my children. (Deuteronomy 4:10)

Your commandments will be upon my heart, and I will teach them diligently to my children and talk about them when I sit in my house and when I walk along the way and when I lie down and when I rise up. (Deuteronomy 6:6-7)

I will lay up Your words in my heart and in my soul and teach them to my children, talking about them when I sit in my house and when I walk along the way and when I lie down and when I rise up. (Deuteronomy 11:18-19)

A wise son heeds his father's instruction, but a scoffer does not listen to rebuke. (Proverbs 13:1)

He who spares his rod hates his son, but he who loves him is careful to discipline him. (Proverbs 13:24)

A fool despises his father's discipline, but whoever heeds correction is prudent. (Proverbs 15:5)

I will discipline my child while there is hope and not be a willing party to his death. (Proverbs 19:18)

I will train up each child according to his way; even when he is old he will not depart from it. (Proverbs 22:6)

Foolishness is bound up in the heart of a child, but the rod of discipline will drive it far from him. (Proverbs 22:15)

I will not withhold discipline from a child; if I strike him with the rod, he will not die. (Proverbs 23:13)

The father of the righteous will greatly rejoice, and he who begets a wise son will be glad in him. May my father and mother be glad; may she who gave me birth rejoice. (Proverbs 23:24-25)

The rod and reproof impart wisdom, but a child left to himself brings shame to his mother. (Proverbs 29:15)

Correct your son, and he will give you rest; he will bring delight to your soul. (Proverbs 29:17)

Children should obey their parents in the Lord, for this is right. "Honor your father and mother" — which is the first commandment with a promise — "that it may go well with you, and that you may live long on the earth." (Ephesians 6:1-3)

Fathers should not provoke their children to wrath but bring them up in the discipline and instruction of the Lord. (Ephesians 6:4)

Children should obey their parents in everything, for this is well-pleasing to the Lord. (Colossians 3:20)

Fathers should not provoke their children, or they will become discouraged. (Colossians 3:21)

Believers

How good and pleasant it is when brothers live together in unity! (Psalm 133:1)

The Lord Jesus prayed these words for the unity of all who would believe in Him: "[I ask] that all of them may be one, Father, just as You are in Me and I am in You, that they also may be in Us, that the world may believe that You sent Me. And the glory which You gave Me I have given to them, that they may be one, just as We are one: I in them, and You in Me, that they may be perfected in one, that the world may know that You have sent Me and have loved them, even as You have loved Me." (John 17:21-23)

I want to speak words of encouragement to other believers. (Acts 20:2)

We must take heed to ourselves and to all the flock of which the Holy Spirit has made us overseers to shepherd the Church of God, which He purchased with His own blood. (Acts 20:28)

Just as we have many members in one body, but all the members do not have the same function, so we who are many are one body in Christ and individually members of one another. And we have different gifts, according to the grace given to us. (Romans 12:4-6)

I will pursue the things that lead to peace and to mutual edification. (Romans 14:19)

May the God who gives endurance and encouragement grant us to be of the same mind toward one another according to Christ Jesus, so that with one accord and one mouth we may glorify the God and Father of our Lord Jesus Christ. (Romans 15:5-6)

Since we were called into fellowship with the Lord Jesus Christ, all of us should agree with one another, so that there may be no divisions among us, and that we may be perfectly joined together in the same mind and in the same judgment. (1 Corinthians 1:9-10)

I will be careful not to let my liberty in Christ become a stumbling block to the weak. (1 Corinthians 8:9)

There are different kinds of gifts, but the same Spirit. And there are different kinds of service, but the same Lord. And there are different kinds of working, but the same God works all of them in all people. But to each one the manifestation of the Spirit is given for the common good. (1 Corinthians 12:4-7)

Just as the body is one but has many members, and all the members of the body, being many, are one body; so also is Christ. (1 Corinthians 12:12)

There should be no division in the body, but its members should have the same concern for each other. If one member suffers, all the members suffer with it; if one member is honored, all the members rejoice with it. Now we are the body of Christ, and each one of us is a member of it. (1 Corinthians 12:25-27)

There is neither Jew nor Greek, there is neither slave nor free, there is neither male nor female, for we are all one in Christ Jesus. (Galatians 3:28)

If someone is caught in a trespass, we who are spiritual should restore him in a spirit of gentleness, considering ourselves, lest we also be tempted. (Galatians 6:1)

We should bear one another's burdens and so fulfill the law of Christ. (Galatians 6:2)

As we have opportunity, we should do good to all people, especially to those who belong to the family of faith. (Galatians 6:10)

In Christ Jesus, God's whole building is joined together and growing into a holy temple in the Lord, in whom we also are being built together into a dwelling of God in the Spirit. (Ephesians 2:21-22)

We should bear with one another in love and make every effort to keep the unity of the Spirit in the bond of peace. (Ephesians 4:2-3)

Grace has been given to each one of us according to the measure of the gift of Christ. And He gave some to be apostles, some to be prophets, some to be evangelists, and some to be pastors and teachers, for the equipping of the saints for the work of ministry, for the building up of the body of Christ. (Ephesians 4:7, 11-12)

We must all attain to unity of the faith and of the knowledge of the Son of God to a mature man, to the measure of the stature of the fullness of Christ, so that we will no longer be infants, blown and carried around by every wind of doctrine, by the cunning and craftiness of men in their deceitful scheming; but speaking the truth in love, we must grow up in all things into Him who is the Head, that is, Christ. (Ephesians 4:13-15)

From Christ the whole body is being joined and held together by every supporting ligament, according to the effective working of each individual part, and this causes the growth of the body for the edifying of itself in love. (Ephesians 4:16)

Each of us must put off falsehood and speak truthfully to his neighbor, for we are members of one another. (Ephesians 4:25)

We should submit to one another out of reverence for Christ. (Ephesians 5:21)

If we have any encouragement from being united with Christ, if any comfort from His love, if any fellowship of the Spirit, if any affection and compassion, we should also be like-minded, having the same love, being one in spirit and one in purpose. (Philippians 2:1-2)

We should let the word of Christ dwell in us richly as we teach and admonish one another with all wisdom and as we sing psalms, hymns, and spiritual songs with gratitude in our hearts to God. (Colossians 3:16)

We should always thank God for other believers, mentioning them in our prayers. (1 Thessalonians 1:2)

We should encourage one another and build each other up in Christ Jesus. (1 Thessalonians 5:11)

We should ask for one another's prayers. (1 Thessalonians 5:25)

We ought always to thank God for other believers and pray that their faith would grow more and more, and that the love each of them has toward one another would increase. (2 Thessalonians 1:3)

We should always pray for other believers, that our God may count them worthy of His calling and may fulfill every desire for goodness and every work of faith with power. (2 Thessalonians 1:11)

We should ask that the name of our Lord Jesus may be glorified in others, and they in Him, according to the grace of our God and the Lord Jesus Christ. (2 Thessalonians 1:12)

We must encourage one another daily, as long as it is still called "Today," lest any of us be hardened by the deceitfulness of sin. (Hebrews 3:13)

God is not unjust to be forgetful of our work and the love we have shown toward His name in having ministered and continuing to minister to the saints. (Hebrews 6:10)

We should consider how to stir up one another toward love and good works. (Hebrews 10:24)

We must not forsake our meeting together, as some are in the habit of doing, but encourage one another, and all the more as we see the day approaching. (Hebrews 10:25)

I will remember those who led me, who spoke the word of God to me. I will consider the outcome of their way of life and imitate their faith. (Hebrews 13:7)

I will obey those who lead me and submit to them, for they keep watch over my soul as those who must give an account. I will obey them, so that they may do this with joy and not with grief, for this would be unprofitable for me. (Hebrews 13:17)

We should all be of one mind and be sympathetic, loving as brothers, compassionate, and humble. (1 Peter 3:8)

Unbelievers

How beautiful on the mountains are the feet of those who bring good news, who proclaim peace, who bring good tidings, who proclaim salvation. (Isaiah 52:7)

As I follow You, You will make me a fisher of men. (Matthew 4:19; Mark 1:17)

The harvest is plentiful, but the workers are few. Therefore, I will pray that the Lord of the harvest will send out workers into His harvest. (Matthew 9:37-38; Luke 10:2)

Whoever acknowledges You before men, You will also acknowledge him before Your Father in heaven. But whoever denies You before men, You will also deny him before Your Father in heaven. (Matthew 10:32-33)

You have called us to go and make disciples of all nations, baptizing them in the name of the Father and of the Son and of the Holy Spirit, teaching them to observe everything You have commanded us. And surely You are with us always, even to the end of the age. (Matthew 28:19-20)

You have called me to go and proclaim the Kingdom of God. (Luke 9:60)

Concerning the lost, Jesus said, "What man among you, if he has a hundred sheep and loses one of them, does not leave the ninety-nine in the open country and go after the one that is lost until he finds it? And when he finds it, he lays it on his shoulders, rejoicing. And when he comes into his house, he calls his friends and neighbors together and says to them, 'Rejoice with me, for I have found my sheep which was lost!' I tell you that in the same way there will be more joy in heaven over one sinner who repents than over ninety-nine righteous persons who need no repentance. There is joy in the presence of the angels of God over one sinner who repents." (Luke 15:4-7, 10)

Do you not say, "Four months more and then comes the harvest"? Behold, I say to you, lift up your eyes and look at the fields, for they are white for harvest. Even now the reaper draws his wages, and gathers fruit for eternal life, that he who sows and he who reaps may rejoice together. (John 4:35-36)

As the Father sent the Son into the world, He also has sent us into the world. And He has prayed for those who will believe in Him through our message. (John 17:18, 20)

Jesus said, "As the Father has sent Me, I also send you." (John 20:21)

We are the fragrance of Christ to God among those who are being saved and among those who are perishing; to the one an aroma from death to death; to the other, an aroma from life to life. And who is sufficient for these things? (2 Corinthians 2:15-16)

All things are for our sakes, so that the grace that is reaching more and more people may cause thanksgiving to abound to the glory of God. (2 Corinthians 4:15)

Knowing the fear of the Lord, I seek to persuade men. (2 Corinthians 5:11)

From now on I will regard no one only according to the flesh. (2 Corinthians 5:16)

All things are from God, who reconciled us to Himself through Christ and gave us the ministry of reconciliation: namely, that God was reconciling the world to Himself in Christ, not counting their trespasses against them. And He has committed to us the message of reconciliation. Therefore, we are ambassadors for Christ, as though God were appealing through us, as we implore others on Christ's behalf, to be reconciled to God. (2 Corinthians 5:18-20)

I pray that words may be given to me, that I may open my mouth boldly to make known the mystery of the gospel. (Ephesians 6:19)

I pray that God may open to me a door for the word, so that I may speak the mystery of Christ and proclaim it clearly, as I ought to speak. (Colossians 4:3-4)

I should walk in wisdom toward outsiders, making the most of every opportunity. My speech should always be with grace, seasoned with salt, so that I may know how to answer each person. (Colossians 4:5-6)

I should offer petitions, prayers, intercessions, and thanksgivings on behalf of all men, for kings and all those who are in authority, that we may live peaceful and quiet lives in all godliness and reverence. This is good and acceptable in the sight of God our Savior, who desires all men to be saved and to come to a knowledge of the truth. (1 Timothy 2:1-4)

I will not be ashamed to testify about our Lord, but I will join with others in suffering for the gospel according to the power of God. (2 Timothy 1:8)

I pray that the sharing of my faith may become effective through the knowledge of every good thing which is in me for Christ. (Philemon 6)

I will sanctify Christ as Lord in my heart, always being ready to make a defense to everyone who asks me to give the reason for the hope that is in me, but with gentleness and respect. (1 Peter 3:15)

I will have mercy on those who are doubting. (Jude 22)

PART THREE

PERSONAL AFFIRMATIONS PAGES

Use these pages to write in the affirmations that are particularly meaningful to you as you use the Evening and Topical Affirmations Guides

Use these pages to write in the affirmations that are particularly meaningful to you as you use the Evening and Topical Affirmations Guides

Use these pages to write in the affirmations that are particularly meaningful to you as you use the Evening and Topical Affirmations Guides

Use these pages to write in the affirmations that are particularly meaningful to you as you use the Evening and Topical Affirmations Guides

Use these pages to write in the affirmations that are particularly meaningful to you as you use the Evening and Topical Affirmations Guides

Use these pages to write in the affirmations that are particularly meaningful to you as you use the Evening and Topical Affirmations Guides

Use these pages to write in the affirmations that are particularly meaningful to you as you use the Evening and Topical Affirmations Guides

Use these pages to write in the affirmations that are particularly meaningful to you as you use the Evening and Topical Affirmations Guides

Use these pages to write in the affirmations that are particularly meaningful to you as you use the Evening and Topical Affirmations Guides

Use these pages to write in the affirmations that are particularly meaningful to you as you use the Evening and Topical Affirmations Guides

ABOUT THE AUTHOR

D r. Kenneth D. Boa has been the Director of Research and Writing for Search Ministries in Lutherville, Maryland, since 1982. He also serves as part-time consultant and teacher for Effective Communication and Development, Inc., of Ossining, New York.

Dr. Boa received the Ph.D. degree from New York University in 1985 and has done Post-doctoral studies at the University of Oxford, England. In addition, he has earned a Th.M. degree from Dallas Theological Seminary.

His professional experience includes many years of teaching and writing. And for several years he was associated with Walk Thru the Bible Ministries of Atlanta, Georgia.

As an author Dr. Boa has published fourteen books and several journal articles. He is the editor and co-author of the introductions to the individual books of *The Open Bible*.

He lives with his wife, Karen, and daughter, Heather, in Marietta, Georgia.

The typeface for the text of this book is *Goudy Old Style*. Its creator, Frederic W. Goudy, was commissioned by American Type Founders Company to design a new Roman type face. Completed in 1915 and named Goudy Old Style, it was an instant bestseller. However, its designer had sold the design outright to the foundry, so when it became evident that additional versions would be needed to complete the family, the work was done by the foundry's own designer, Morris Benton. From the original design came seven additional weights and variants, all of which sold in great quantity. However, Goudy himself received no additional compensation for them. He later recounted a visit to the foundry with a group of printers, during which the guide stopped at one of the busy casting machines and stated, "Here's where Goudy goes down to posterity, while American Type Founders Company goes down to prosperity."

Substantive Editing:
Michael S. Hyatt

Copy Editing:
Russell A. Sorensen

Cover Design:
Kent Puckett Associates, Atlanta, Georgia

Page Composition:
Xerox Ventura Publisher
Printware 720 IQ Laser Printer

Printing and Binding:
Maple-Vail Book Manufacturing Group,
York, Pennsylvania

Dust Jacket Printing:
Weber Graphics, Chicago, Illinois